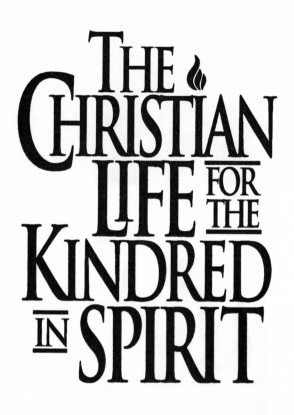

THE CHRISTIAN LIFE FOR THE KINDRED IN SPIRIT

THE CHRISTIAN LIFE FOR THE KINDRED IN SPIRIT

FOREWORD BY CHARLES R. SWINDOLL

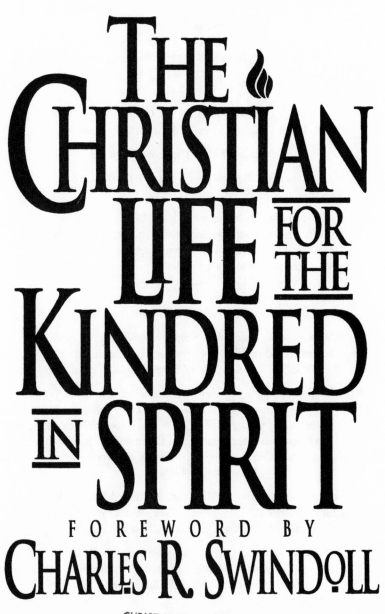

VISION™
HOUSE
PUBLISHING, INC.
Gresham, Oregon 97230

THE CHRISTIAN LIFE FOR THE
KINDRED IN SPIRIT
© 1994 by Vision House Publishing, Inc.

Edited by Dr. Chip MacGregor
Cover Design by Multnomah Graphics/Printing

Printed in the United States of America

International Standard Book Number: 1-885305-06-0

94 95 96 97 98 99 00 01 02 — 10 9 8 7 6 5 4 3 2 1

This book is dedicated to
the editors of KINDRED SPIRIT,
A Dallas Seminary publication.

James C. Killion	1977-1980
Jack Van Vessen	1981-1983
C. Mike Fluent	1983-1985
Kenneth Durham	1985-1990
Michael D. Edwards	1990-

CONTENTS

Foreword. 9

A. ENJOYING GOD

1. WOULD I LIKE YOUR GOD?. 15
2. NAME ABOVE ALL NAMES 20
3. HOLY, HOLY, HOLY 25
4. HE LOVES YOU THROUGH IT ALL 31
5. GOD'S AMAZING GRACE 38
6. GOD'S GREAT SALVATION 43
7. GOD'S UNEXPECTED GIFT. 47
8. HE IS ALIVE 50

B. EXPERIENCING GOD'S WORD

1. YOUR BIBLE CAN HELP YOU GROW. 59
2. WHY I TRUST THE BIBLE. 64
3. READING GOD'S WORD 69
4. DISCOVERING GOD'S WORD 74
5. MEDITATING ON GOD'S WORD. 78
6. SPENDING TIME IN GOD'S WORD 82
7. WISDOM FROM GOD'S WORD 87
8. PRACTICING GOD'S WORD 92

C. EQUIPPING FOR THE CHRISTIAN LIFE

1. IS THE HOLY SPIRIT TRANSFORMING YOU?. 101
2. ARE YOU OUT OF BALANCE? 109
3. DIVINE ALTERNATIVES! 115
4. AND TWO AT PARBAR. 120
5. WHAT ARE YOU DOING? 124
6. CHOSEN FOR A PURPOSE 129
6. A WISE INVESTMENT. 135
8. THE TEMPTATION TRAP 141
9. THE PERFECT MOUTH 146
10. THOU SHALT NOT! 153
11. SAVORING YOUR AGE 160
12. GOD'S WAITING ROOM 166
13. WHERE IS GOD WHEN BAD THINGS HAPPEN?. 174
14. HOPING FOR THE BEST 180
15. WHEN THE EXCITEMENT FADES 185

D. EXPRESSING PRAISE AND PRAYER

1. ENCOUNTERING HIS HOLINESS 195
2. DELIGHTING HIS HEART 200
3. WELCOME IN HIS PRESENCE 205
4. CELEBRATING HIS BIRTH 212
5. COMMUNICATING WITH GOD 218
6. TALKING TO GOD AT THE TABLE 224
7. DISCOVERING THE IMPORTANCE OF PRAYER 227
8. PRAYING FROM THE HEART 232
9. OUR MODEL FOR PRAYER 239
10. WHEN GOD DOESN'T ANSWER 245

E. ESTEEMING GOD'S PEOPLE

1. WHAT MARKS YOUR FRIENDSHIPS? 253
2. YOU CAN COUNT ON ME 257
3. WE'RE IN THIS TOGETHER 264
4. SERVING EACH OTHER 270
5. PRACTICING HOSPITALITY 277
6. WORDS THAT HEAL 281
7. COMFORTING IN A CRISIS 286
8. RESTORING THE WOUNDED 292
9. YOU'VE BEEN CHOSEN TO CLAP AND CHEER 297

Contributors 303
Permissions and Credits 307

foreword

૪૪

Let's face it: Most of us could use a little help when it comes to living the Christian life. As the countdown of this millennium ticks off, it is all the more imperative that we Christians practice what we preach!

This book is for people who want a fresh look at the character and grace of God. It is also for those who need biblical counsel on such practical subjects as hospitality, patience, balance, fruitbearing and stewardship. While gaining a new appreciation for God and His Word, you will acquire help for the grit of reality and the grinding demands of life. This needed blend is laced throughout its pages.

For years the greater Dallas Theological Seminary family and friends have enjoyed the good news contained in this volume. For the most part these writings were first written and published over a span of several years for KINDRED SPIRIT, a seminary publication. Included are selections by former seminary presidents—Lewis Sperry Chafer, John F. Walvoord, and Donald K. Campbell, along with three of mine. Distinguished faculty contributions have come from men like Howard G. Hendricks, Lanier Burns, and Mark Bailey. Outstanding graduates who now lead significant world-wide ministries—such as Joseph Stowell III, president of Moody Bible Institute; Anthony Evans, president of The Urban Alternative; and Bruce Wilkinson, president of Walk Thru the Bible—have contributed chapters. Leaders of women's ministries, including Dorothy Martin, author and Bible study leader; noted author Carole Mayhall; and Maxine Toussaint, a women's conference and retreat speaker, have contributed significant articles. Pastors Ross Rainey, Ronald Jones, and James Borror are among several who write from their experience of "feeding the flock." Additional contributors who have excelled in the secular world, such as Peggy Wehmeyer a reporter for ABC, Jim Killion of Killion McCabe, and Waylon Ward of the Christian counseling field, are among those who have given a unique biblical perspective in their articles.

Included are more than forty authors, all addressing in their own way and from their own experience some aspect of the Christian life. This unique group of authors—coming from the fields of education, theology, psychology, church ministry, broadcasting, writing, advertising and homemaking—have all contributed to make this volume a veritable kaleidoscope of practical expertise! The elements that mark the contributors are their love for our Lord, excellence in their fields, and maturity in the Christian life.

When a book has one author, it is often more cohesive and unified. By the same token, it has the limitations and restrictions of a single author's knowledge and experience.

We are indebted to Dr. Chip McGregor for his skill in honing this volume into a whole from "specialists" from many walks of life. He selected a broad range of works from qualified authors to create this anthology.

I know many of the contributors to this volume personally —they are my friends. In fact, I have profited from the teachings, writings and friendship of most.

On the one hand, the book is on doctrine—biblical doctrine. The need for scriptural knowledge today is obvious. All too often Christians want to live for the Lord but lack the facts—lots of pizzazz and enthusiasm, but a bit in the fog when it comes to what the Bible teaches. The content of THE CHRISTIAN LIFE FOR THE KINDRED IN SPIRIT is not pablum—it is porterhouse! This is not fast-food—it is a full course meal. Maximum benefit will be achieved if you do not try to bite off too much in one sitting. "Food" of this caliber must be chewed slowly and digested well—savoring the flavor for a healthy spiritual diet.

Let me urge you to take your time... read each section thoughtfully... carefully... giving your mind the "windows" to assimilate each thought being communicated. In fact, I plan to use this volume myself to be reminded again of some of the timeless insights and principles that make this Christian life so attainable, practical, and satisfying.

CHARLES R. SWINDOLL
President, Dallas Theological Seminary

Enjoying God

As the deer pants for streams of water,
so my soul pants for you, O God.
My soul thirsts for God, for the living God.
(PSALM 42: 1-2)

Have you ever experienced that sort of longing for God? Have you ever felt so spiritually parched that you desired to drink deeply from the well of the Lord Almighty? Like the Sons of Korah in Psalm 42, do you find yourself wanting more of God? I don't mean do you want more information about Him, but do you want more of Him? If that is your desire, I think you'll find these next few pages a satisfying experience. These are thoughts about standing in the presence of the Father. Here you will find rich, deep experiences that will help you enjoy God afresh. So bring your cup, and enjoy a deep, refreshing draught of our Lord.

Would I Like Your God?

If you could give me an accurate picture of the God you worship, would I like Him? If you described your God for me, could I love Him? Each of us has a "God-image"—a picture of God—in our minds. Some of us have a good God-image; others have a very distorted God image. Different people have different pictures of God.

One lady came to me for help and began our relationship by describing her God-image. She said, "I don't want to talk about God, because God to me is like an eight-foot cobra sitting on the floor waiting to strike me dead." Others say they like Jesus but not God. They can talk about Jesus, even pray to Him, but not God. Still others cannot picture God being like a father. Some have even said, "I hope He is not like my father!"

THE IMAGE OF GOD

The evidence would seem to indicate that behind every theological problem—and to some extent behind every psychological problem—there is a wrong view of God. At the root of most of these problems lies a distorted God-image. The tragedy is that history and experience reveal that worshippers tend to become like the god they worship! You may see this illustrated in many of the cults in today's culture.

In idolatry, the worshipper creates a picture or an image of his god to which he can relate. Idolatry, at its root, consists of having thoughts and ideas and concepts of God which are utterly unworthy of the God of Scripture. Idolatry is a libel against the character of God and it begins with a wrong God-image. History demonstrates that a distorted image of God has often been a powerful tool in the hands of a sick person.

WHAT IS YOUR GOD LIKE?

What is your God like? Have you taken time to examine your God-image? It is a fair question because if many of us re really honest, we might say that we don't like our God ery much. Whom do you picture in your mind when you pray or worship or read the Scriptures? In whom do you put your trust when your world seems to crumble? For many it is only in a crisis that we see what kind of God-image we really have. Or maybe it is a time of some mystical spiritual encounter that we see what our God is like—the one we talk to and picture in our minds when we worship, pray, and read the Scriptures.

Our God-image is made up of the ideas, thoughts, and feelings we have about God, fabricated through the years by an assortment of experiences. While the experiences themselves have been forgotten long ago, they still influence our thinking and feelings about God. Our basic attitude toward life, including our hopes, expectations, and understanding of life, is affected by the way we picture God. Our interpretation of the events in our lives can likewise be dominated by the way we see God.

One woman felt that her husband's death was God punishing her. Another felt that since she could never bear children, God does not approve of her. Still another thought God must be angry at him because he has no one to marry. Each of these individuals is interpreting a life situation in light of a distorted God-image. They all see God as being like themselves or their parents. Therefore, they interpret the events of their lives as evidence of God's wrath, injustice, insensitivity, or punishment. Their self-images are distorted because they are building them on the foundation of a distorted view of God. If a person thinks rightly about God it can help solve the other problems in his theological structure, and will serve as a solid basis for his personal emotional growth.

IS GOD LIKE YOUR PARENTS?

Our basic God-image is formed very early in life in our relational experiences with parents. Children tend to see God as being like their parents since, to the small infant, mom and dad are God-like in their power and control. As a child we come to believe that God feels about us the same way our parents do.

An experience with my young daughter clearly illustrates this early formation of a God-image. On several occasions when I would pray with her at night, she would bow her head, close her eyes, and fold her hands in her normal prayer posture. Then she would begin, "Daddy, I pray that…" Usually she would catch herself and start giggling because she realized that she was calling God in heaven, "Daddy." I didn't laugh because I was overwhelmed with the responsibility I had to portray God accurately for her.

On another occasion I remember my son, Tim, who was then eight years old, calling me at the office. He had a heavy burden about a bicycle that needed fixing. We talked about it and when he finished he said, "Amen," and hung up the phone. It seems humorous now, but again, it was a humbling experience for me to see the responsibility I have as a father.

In the same way, every person's God-image is to some degree shaped by his parents. Our emotional experiences with our parents affect our view of God because we conclude that God is like our parents, that He feels about us the same way our parents do.

Often a person's God-image is a hindrance to his emotional and spiritual growth. Clearly, we must come to see God as He is in the Scriptures. The question is, how do we transform our image of God? How do we take the distorted view of God that may have developed in our childhood and transform it into an accurate image of God? In Luke 15, Jesus encountered a God-image problem. His example as He dealt with the Pharisees is very instructive for us as we attempt to arrive at a Scriptural view of God.

Jesus regularly associated with the people of His day who were commonly known as "sinners." They were ordinary ple: tax collectors, common laborers, prostitutes—people ло were lost (Luke 19: 10). The Pharisees pictured God as a noly God who could have nothing to do with sinners. Because of His holiness, God must hate not only sin but sinners as well. Therefore, they reasoned, since Jesus associated with sinners, He must not be from God. This was the essence of the problem. The Pharisees were interpreting events in light of their image of God and were criticizing Jesus for His behavior.

Jesus challenged their God-image, but not with a theological argument. He could have no doubt destroyed them in a brilliant debate, but instead He chose to use three parables in which He painted a picture of God that was wholly different from the Pharisees' God-image.

JESUS' PICTURE OF GOD

The first parable is that of the determined shepherd (Luke 15:3-7). It is the story of a shepherd who has a hundred sheep and loses one. He searches for that one lost sheep "until he finds it." When he finds the sheep he lays it across his shoulders and carries it home. When he arrives home rejoicing he calls his friends to celebrate with him for he has found that which was lost.

Gently, but pointedly, Jesus tells the Pharisees that God is like that determined shepherd. He does not reject a person who is lost, but seeks him out, brings him to Himself, and rejoices over that person's repentance. God is interested in every person, even the "sinners."

In His second parable Jesus describes a woman who has lost one of her ten wedding coins (Luke 15:8-10). She searches her house carefully. She lights a lamp, rolls up the reed mats, and sweeps the dirt floor. She searches until she finds it, and then she calls her friends together and they celebrate because her diligent search has paid off. Jesus is clearly pointing out to the Pharisees that God is more like a diligent woman who rejoices over that which was lost than He is like their distorted picture of Him.

The third parable concerns the loving father who had lost two sons (Luke 15:11-32). The younger son demands his inheritance, so the loving father gives him his portion (v. 12). The boy goes to a far country and quickly loses his wealth. A famine occurs in that country, so he hires himself out to work feeding pigs. He becomes so hungry that he wants to fill his stomach with the pigs' food. What a horrible picture for Jesus to paint for the Pharisees! A Jewish boy, breaking Jewish law, wanting to eat the food of an unclean animal. What could be worse?

In the parable Jesus says that the boy comes to his senses and goes home. While he is still a long way off, the father sees him and runs to him, embraces him, and kisses him. The father does not care that the boy still has the grime and smell of pigs on his body. He loves his son and warmly receives him back. When the boy begins to make an issue of his worthiness to be a son, the father interrupts with a demonstration of his true worth. He dresses him as a son and an heir because the father makes the son worthy by receiving him unto himself. What a beautiful picture of a father's love for an unlovely child! What a beautiful picture of God the Father!

The older brother returns home in the midst of this celebration, but does not go in to see what is happening. He calls a servant to find out. When he hears that his brother has returned, he refuses to go inside. When the loving father comes to him, the older son bursts forth his rage and jealousy demonstrating his selfishness and lack of relationship with the father. The father listens, receives all of his child's anger, and explains that he had to rejoice because the older son's brother has come home. Jesus ends the parable without giving his listeners a decision from the older son. Did he go in or did he continue to refuse and reject his brother and his father?

The younger son in this parable represents the lost sinners, the ones Jesus came to seek and to save. The father is a picture of a loving heavenly Father who hates sin but loves the sinner.

He is so different from the Pharisees' image! The older brother represents the Pharisees who have been in the father's house but not in a relationship with the father. Jesus subtly drives the point home to his hostile audience. You claim to know God, He says, yet you demonstrate by your attitudes that you do not really know Him. God is not like your image of Him!

Jesus refused to debate with the Pharisees. Rather, in this startling chapter He took human feelings and relationships and used very human experiences to tell us what His Father is like. In so doing He provided us with a completely authentic image of God, one which He Himself mirrored perfectly during His own life and ministry among us (John 14:9).

Would I like your God? If he is like the One Jesus shows me, I'm sure I would.

—Waylon O. Ward

Name Above All Names

Have you ever noticed the significance of names in the Bible? While some names have little connection to their places in history ("Annas"—"to be gracious" and "Judas"—"praised") other names are directly related to the destinies of major biblical personalities ("David" —"beloved"; "Jesus"—"Salvation"; and "Peter"—"rock").

Moreover, the names given to Jesus Christ have significance far beyond the ordinary. His names are expressions of His being and character, and sometimes are object lessons that help us grasp a difficult aspect of His person. A careful study of His names can bring depth to our relationship with Him, joy to our fellowship, and power to our walk. Such are the names found in Isaiah 9:6, a prophecy of the coming Messiah who will ultimately rule the world.

I believe the four names found in that passage can speak to us in our times of greatest need, when we need wisdom, power, security, and assurance. The names are "Wonderful Counselor," "Mighty God," "Everlasting Father," and "Prince of Peace."

WONDERFUL COUNSELOR

The first name is sometimes broken into two separate names, but I believe they belong together. It reads literally, "wonder counselor." Perhaps our television mentality reminds us of Wonder Woman. In a way, it is a good illustration. She is a woman who does "wonders," deeds beyond our ability and anticipation. In the same way, Christ is a Counselor whose advice not only is wonderful, but also is a "wonder"— out of this world. He is able to intercede in a situation and provide the perfect solution to an "impossible" problem. He sees beyond the present, therefore He gives futuristic advice, And He not only shows the way out, He also shows the way up—to glory.

How is He a wonder counselor? The word "wonder" means "extraordinary, surpassing." A "counselor" is one who gives advice, most notably to kings! He is the kind of counselor a king alone would employ and be able to afford! And He is our personal, constant, and ready counselor! That is security.

What makes Him so different from other counselors? First, His counsel is always based on truth. He always speaks of things as they are, not as they appear, therefore He provides the right perspective. Second, His counsel is always righteous and holy. He would never resort to "situation ethics," letting the situation, not the principle, determine the action. He always advises to do what is right, not what is expedient or escapist. Third, His counsel is utterly practical. He is a "wise" counselor, skilled in the arts of living life.

When I think of Jesus as the "Wonderful Counselor" I see certain events in my mind, such as the time the rich young ruler approached Him and asked how he could gain eternal life. Jesus told him the truth, what was right, and even got down to the practicalities. He didn't hedge either. When the rich young ruler hung his head and meandered away deeply troubled, Jesus didn't stop him and say, "Look, I know that was a little rough. Here, I'll give you some other solutions." No, Jesus gave His advice and left it to the young man to act on it. Jesus doesn't provide "six easy steps to success." He is THE way alone.

I also think of the time Nicodemus sought Him for counsel. Jesus was directive and prescriptive. He was not like so many counselors today who ask multitudes of questions hoping to lead you to some deep "insight" that will lead you into joy.

Or what about Zacchaeus, the woman at the well, and the thief on the cross? All found peace and joy in the counsel and love of Jesus. Because of His counsel, Jesus drew thousands to Himself in His days on earth, and millions since.

Where, then, is His counsel? It is the Word of God. If we want to learn His counsel on any subject, we can study, memorize, and meditate on the Word. In every problem and need of life, He speaks to us through His Word so that we have the "divine line" for each critical situation.

MIGHTY GOD

Again, the words used here are important. "Mighty" comes from a word that means "strong" and can refer especially to a warrior's or king's ability to rescue, save, and give victory to his friends. The word for God is "El" which always speaks of God in His omnipotence—the King and Sovereign of the universe.

This name has great significance. Jesus is our rescuer, not only from sin and this world of evil, but also from our enemies in this world—Satan, persecutors, and those who would destroy us. Nothing can stand against Him. No one can stand up to Him. He is our refuge, fortress, strong tower, and horn of salvation.

How does Jesus live up to this name in the New Testament? One example is His rescue of Peter who, when he tried to walk on water, became afraid and began to sink. Jesus never mocks us or abandons us in our mistakes. He rescues us and then instructs us.

EVERLASTING FATHER

This third name poses a problem. How can Jesus be called "Father" when the Father is the first Person of the Trinity? Isn't this "modalism" (an early heresy in which God was said to appear in three forms—the Father, Son, and Spirit—who were all the same person) which denies the doctrine of the Trinity?

Actually, the term does not focus on Jesus' person, but rather on His character. Isaiah was speaking of Jesus' fatherliness, the way He treats His children. When he spoke of the "everlasting" Father, he was highlighting Jesus' loyalty. Just as a true father would never desert his child in this life, so Jesus will never desert His children for all eternity.

We see Jesus living out this name in several instances, notably when He told His disciples to let the little children come to Him. As the Everlasting Father, Jesus is approachable. No one was ever repulsed by Jesus except those who rejected Him. Jesus welcomes with kindness, understanding, and acceptance all who come to Him.

PRINCE OF PEACE

The last name is undoubtedly the most well known: Prince of Peace. The expression connects two common Hebrew words, SAR-SHALOM. Undoubtedly, you recognize the famous Hebrew greeting and good-bye word, shalom, which can mean "peace." The other word means "chieftain" or "leader" or even "prince" or "king." But it is the union of the two words that is most intriguing. What is a "prince of peace"?

The picture is of a ruler or chief who seeks peace, not war. For example, Adolph Hitler was a prince of war. He sought war. He pressed for war. And if he didn't get it, he destroyed any pacifist in his path. With him, it was either fight or be trampled.

A "prince of peace" is altogether different. He seeks peace. He wants to make peace. His agenda is peace from start to finish. But it is not peace "at any price." It is peace "at the right price." We know that the Prince of Peace made peace for us with God by dying in our places. He paid the price of peace with His own blood.

Thus, as Prince of Peace, Jesus can give us peace with God, peace with ourselves, and peace with one another. That is His ultimate goal. The way He does it is by redeeming us. He brings us out of the domain of darkness and into the kingdom of light. He makes us new creatures. He cleanses, fills, and guides us so that His children cooperate, agree, and live in unity. That is real peace.

But how can these names help you function more effectively as a Christian? First, meditate on them. Instead of picturing Jesus as an artist might, picture Him as Wonderful Counselor, Mighty God, Everlasting Father, and Prince of Peace. Remind yourself that this One is with you wherever you are.

Second, seek Him in these roles. Solicit His counsel in the moment of need. Await His mighty deliverance in a time of trial. Draw close to Him as to a father.

Third, examine yourself and find out where you are failing to let Him relate to you in these ways. Do you act on His counsel? Do you let Him protect you? Is your peace founded on Him or something else?

Finally, worship Him because of who He is. Too often we thank Him for what He's done, pray to Him to help us, and listen to His words, commenting on their eloquence and wisdom. But do we love Him for Himself? May we continually recognize that He is indeed a Wonderful Counselor, The Mighty God, Everlasting Father, and Prince of Peace.

—Mark R. Littleton

Holy, Holy, Holy

There is a simple yet profound word which occurs 900 times in the Bible. You see it first in Genesis, as we are told how God created heaven and earth. You see it last in the closing chapter of Revelation, where we are told about God's creation of a new heaven and a new earth. Except for a few grand old hymns of the faith, you do not see this word much today. Yet it remains a very important word, one which describes the uniqueness of our God, and the quality we are to pursue as His children.

This awesome little word is holy. We get our words saint, sanctify, and sanctification from the same root words. All these terms carry the idea of being set apart. And as you well know, if you are holy today, you are definitely set apart!

THE HOLINESS OF GOD

The holiness of God is an overpowering concept. It goes beyond our ability to measure or comprehend the extent of its richness. We are not holy, we are not above the imperfections of this world, and we are not ethically and morally pure. On the contrary, we are tainted people; and sometimes we are worse than that.

Perhaps this awesome and foreign nature of holiness is why we read or hear so little about it. To even write of it is a foreboding challenge. Yet the more you read the Bible and what it says about holiness, the more you must conclude that this is an important issue. To ignore it or deny it is to do great violence to the foundation of our beliefs. Because if our God is anything at all, He is holy.

You see, just as all the colors of the spectrum come together to form the pure white light which illuminates our world, so all the attributes of God come together in His holiness. And if our God is active at all in this world, then His holiness must be of real importance to you and me. If that is true, then what the Bible says about God's holiness has profound implications for how we relate to Him. And the Scriptures suggest that God's holiness tells us three very important things about Him.

GOD IS SEPARATE

First, the Bible teaches that God is separate from and above His creation. Remember when Moses saw that burning bush in the wilderness? The message was powerful: "Do not come any closer," God said. "Take off your sandals, for the place where you are standing is holy ground" (Exod. 3:5). The soil was not holy, nor was the bush—but God was there and His presence separated that soil and that bush from all the other elements like it in the wilderness of Horeb.

From what Moses said years later, we can tell that the lesson was not lost on him:

> Who among the gods is like you, O Lord?
> Who is like you—majestic in holiness,
> awesome in glory, working wonders?
> (Exod. 15:11).

Isaiah, perhaps the greatest of all the prophets, records an even stronger message from God:

> "To whom will you compare me?
> Or who is my equal?" says the Holy One.
> "Lift your eyes and look to the heavens:
> Who created all these?"
> (Isa. 40:25-26a).

Perhaps it is a bit easier to understand this separateness if we think of a brilliant orchestra conductor. He chooses the music, arranges it, and conducts the orchestra—but he is not a member of the orchestra. He is separate from the players, though he knows and interacts with them as their leader. [Be careful not to push this analogy too far. The conductor may direct the music, but he allows the players to decide on their own what they want for lunch; they even make mistakes playing for the conductor—though he wishes they would not!]

But if the holiness of God stops there—with His separateness—then His holiness is merely a signal of our utter inferiority, and an explanation of why we so often keep the topic buried! But, gladly, that is not the case: there are two other sides to this prism.

GOD IS RELATED

Second, the Bible teaches that God is related to His creation. This aspect demonstrates His unique position as One morally and ethically superior to all created beings. The prophet Hosea, who lived as trying a life as anyone has, was given a clear picture of God's unique position:

"For I am God, and not man—
the Holy One among you." (Hos. 11:9)

The idea expressed in Hosea can also be described with our orchestra conductor. It is as though the great conductor now steps down from his podium, picks up a violin, and takes a seat. And because of his great and extraordinary skill, it is obvious that he is not just any violin player, he is the first chair—the best. He is flawless in his ability to play the violin ... and for that matter, any other instrument he should choose to pick up. In this case, the conductor is a player like the others, yet he is in a class which far exceeds anyone else in the orchestra. To get a fuller picture, look at some of the most eloquent songs ever written—the Psalms—and watch as their musicians sing praises of this Great Musician (Psalm 99 is a good example).

Still, if God can only relate to us as a distant conductor or a vastly superior player, it offers us little comfort. That's why it's important for us to add the third side to our prism—the side which reflects the way God relates His holiness to us.

GOD IS PERFECT

Third, the Bible teaches that God is morally perfect. He thinks and does only the good and right things, and ultimately will not tolerate evil from anyone else (see Hab. 1:13). This means that He will always deal with us fairly, consistently, honorably. Unlike the boss who promises a bonus and never pays it, or the friend who betrays your confidence in him, God won't act that way. He guarantees that He will do the right thing for and with you. You can count on it.

Now our conductor takes on more relational qualities. He is concerned with the well-being of all his players. He is anxious to bring out the most harmonious sounds. His motives are never questionable. He wouldn't dream of photocopying copyrighted music. You can trust Him, appreciate Him, admire all that He does. There's no conductor like Him!

Why are these three aspects of God's holiness important to us? Aren't they just theological exercises ? No. In fact, these admirable characteristics lead to big problems for both God and man.

You see, this incredibly holy God exists in utter contrast—and in opposition—to sin, and to sinful people like us. That puts you and me on the spot, and God's holiness becomes a very important personal issue. We are sinners. And His holiness can only point to our guilt. That, my friend, is a cause for concern.

But once again, God does the good thing (remember that His holiness guarantees that He will treat us fairly)! God the Father decided to make His holiness—and our need for redemption and sanctification—crystal clear through His only begotten Son.

Look at what happened. First, Jesus Christ made God's holiness and our sinfulness indisputable. Second, He provided a solution to that grave dilemma.

My favorite preacher, the late Wilbur M. Smith, makes the point clear: "Jesus, living in Nazareth and ministering in Palestine, brought into the experience of mankind the very thought that God is holy and we are not holy; we are sinners. We need something to bridge that gulf between our sinfulness and the holiness of God."

Of course, that bridge is Jesus Christ Himself. His life showed us the way of holy living. His death paid the price for our sinfulness. His resurrection makes it possible for us to walk the path of righteousness. And His Comforter, the Holy Spirit, empowers us for our walk.

"This is the message we have heard from him and declare to you: God is light; in him there is no darkness at all [He is holy]. If we claim to have fellowship with him yet walk in the darkness [continue unchanged in our sinful ways], we lie and do not live by the truth. But if we walk in the light [His way revealed to us], as he is in the light, we have fellowship with one another, and the blood of Jesus. his Son, purifies us from every sin" (1 John 1:5-7).

GOD'S HOLINESS IS THE STANDARD

John's message to us is clear. God's holiness is the standard, and as believers we are expected to walk in the way He illuminates for us. This process, which we call sanctification, is not something we are expected to accomplish on our own. We are given the Scriptures as a written guide to personal holiness, and we are given the Holy Spirit as an indwelling guide on this journey into conformity with the image of God. And fortunately, our Father sees our spiritual development as a process, and lights more of the path as we grow.

Perhaps you've been a Christian for many years. Maybe, like me, you have been a believer since childhood. But you don't feel too holy. In fact, at times you feel oppressively sinful. How do you break out of that defeating cycle?

I believe you become holy by slowly yet faithfully walking in the light that He has revealed to you. It's not mystical; it's a natural growth process that you can ignore or choose to be a part of.

You see, "holy men" are not bearded, ascetic-looking old men from the Himalayas. Nor are they thin, pious-appearing monks with dour faces. They are people like you and me who are becoming more like Jesus as we walk in His light despite our unholy surroundings. When God says to His people, "Be holy because I, the Lord your God, am holy" (Lev. 19:2), He is not asking us to do the impossible.

Instead, God is asking us to begin to walk His way in little steps. He asks us not to cheat on our taxes, our wives, or our employers. He asks us to care for widows and orphans. He wants us to make the right choices, not the expedient ones. He implores us to choose to be different as He works in us to sanctify us.

Of course. we can fight Him. He's the conductor, not the puppeteer. And just like our human father, He has ways of getting our attention if we ignore Him: "Our fathers disciplined us for a little while as they thought best; but God disciplines us for our good, that we may share in his holiness" (Heb. 12:10).

"Oh," but you say, "I'm hopeless." No one is, not even you. In fact, even our unholy world has hope.

I like the summary of The New Bible Dictionary when it comes to our chances for holiness: "The Bible holds out the promise that the holiness of God will sweep the universe clean, and create new heavens and a new earth in which righteousness will dwell."

So take heart. Our great and holy God does not plan to leave us wallowing in our sin in the midst of a decaying world. Without compromising His integrity, He gave us hope both now and for eternity:

For this is what the high and lofty One says -
he who lives forever, whose name is holy:
"I live in a high and holy place,
but also with him who is
contrite and lowly in spirit,
to revive the spirit of the lowly
and to revive the heart of the contrite" (Isa. 57:15).

Holiness. It's a part of God we seem to have forgotten. And it's a way of life we have not found. But our holy God has not given up on you or me. Instead He gives us light by which to walk, and through a very human disciple, He challenges us to "… live holy and godly lives as [we] look forward to the day of God and speed its coming" (2 Pet. 3:11b-l2a).

—Jim Killion

He Loves You Through It All

The day was cloudless. The desert sun shimmered as it reflected on slanted rocks and bounced off hard-packed sand. The cacti ranged from giant saguaros, huge arms curving toward heaven, to squat, round, spiny humps clinging to earth. My husband Jack and I had been silent for many miles, each absorbed in thought as we drove home from Phoenix that April day. But as we entered a small town, I glanced at a sign and laughed, shattering the companionable silence.

The sign read:

AZTEC, NEW MEXICO
5,667 friendly people
and 6 old soreheads.

Somebody in Aztec has a delightful sense of humor.

My next thought was, "I wonder if the six old soreheads recognize who they are. Or maybe each of the 5,667 friendly people from time to time thinks he or she is one of those soreheads."

I would.

In *Lord of My Rocking Boat* I wrote about many of the things that cause us to lose our cool— pressures, pain, people. Lately I've been realizing that a primary factor in understanding and accepting those pressures, trials, and suffering, is our view of the purpose of life.

I have heard it said that "God did not give us a happy spirit to make us happy, but a Holy Spirit to make us holy." Whenever I get squeezed into believing that the purpose of life is to bring delight to me, I'm in trouble. God wants to delight me, to be sure. He desires to shower my life with His riches, His treasures, His good things. And that is exactly what He does. But if I consider those "good things" to be plenty of money, gobs of love, unconditional acceptance from other people, and untold happiness throughout my life, then I must have a reading disability.

FILLED WITH THE KNOWLEDGE OF GOD'S WILL

Paul says very clearly, "For this reason, since the day we heard about you, we have not stopped praying for you and asking God to fill you with the knowledge of His will through all spiritual wisdom and understanding. And we pray this in order that you may live a life worthy of the Lord" (Col. 1:9-10).

We as believers are to be filled with the knowledge of God's will. But how? Through all spiritual wisdom and understanding. Why? So we may live a life worthy of the Lord!

"Filled" means to be complete, satisfied, saturated, occupied to capacity.

"Knowledge" means understanding, enlightenment, discernment, comprehension, acquaintance.

We are called to be saturated with enlightenment concerning the will of God—occupied to capacity with understanding concerning His desire for our lives.

Our whole age is obsessed with negative thinking. The world lacks true understanding. Its philosophy is one without lasting purpose or hope. Actor and director Alan Alda, speaking to his daughter's graduation class, expressed this sense of relative futility:

"The door is inching a little closer toward the latch and I still haven't said it. Let me dig a little deeper. Life is absurd and meaningless—unless you bring meaning to it, unless you make something of it. It is up to us to create our own existence."

I almost cried when I finished this article. I thought, "With all his talent and intellect, is that the only hope he can give to his daughter and her graduation class?" What a contrast to Paul's ringing words of hope—"asking God to fill you with the knowledge of His will through all spiritual wisdom and understanding."

Think of it! God gives us spiritual wisdom and understanding, enabling us to have knowledge of His will. And this knowledge, when we are filled with it, makes our lives worthy of the Lord!

BEING CONFORMED TO HIS IMAGE

Some factors of His will are that we be holy, joyful, always praying, doing good, obeying God, and being filled with His Spirit. But the one factor we don't like to think about, as we bask in the light of His riches and treasures, is that His will for each of us includes suffering.

Did you say, "How's that again?" Many books these days proclaim health, wealth, and happiness as the legacy of every Christian. I am convinced that this philosophy is man's dream, not God's plan. Some people have not done their scriptural homework.

The prime purpose of this life is to know God and to be conformed to the image of His Son. When we grasp the deep, vital truth that God achieves His purposes largely through trials and temptations, then we can "welcome them as friends" (James 1:2-5, Ph.).

The story is told of a heavyset woman who went to an exercise and diet clinic. The first thing the supervisor did was draw a silhouette on a mirror in the shape she wished to become. As she stood before the mirror, she bulged out over the silhouette. The instructor told her, "Our goal is for you to fit this shape."

For many weeks the woman dieted and exercised. Each week she would stand in front of the mirror, but her volume, while decreasing, still overflowed. And so she exercised harder and dieted more rigidly. Finally one day, to everyone's delight, as she stood in front of the mirror she was conformed to the image of the silhouette.

It takes time and work to be conformed to the image of God's Son. The discipline of sorrow and suffering, the exercise of pain and trials conform us to His image.

Suffering According To God's Will

A sculptor once fashioned a magnificent lion out of solid stone. When asked how he had accomplished such a wonderful masterpiece, he replied, "It was easy. All I did was to chip away everything that didn't look like a lion." All God does is chip away everything in our lives that doesn't look like Christ.

Peter states, "Those who suffer according to God's will should commit themselves to their faithful Creator and continue to do good" (1 Pet. 4:19).

Sometimes suffering brings unanswered questions.

Two weeks before, in what the world would look upon as a tragic, meaningless accident, a woman's teenage son had skidded on ice, crashed into a wall, and been thrown out of the car directly in the path of another vehicle. The truck dragged him for a half mile before releasing his body in a snow-covered field. Tragic? Yes. Meaningless? No.

After just two weeks, several of the boy's teenage friends had received his Savior. Immeasurable grace had lifted the hearts of parents and family, bringing forth praise and thanksgiving in their hearts and on their lips. Grace to overcome many of the "why's."

Of course there was weeping. Mourning. Pain. Grief. But they know that the pain was on their side, the joy on their son's.

Still, her concerned face turned toward us and her voice trembled.

"He was so young," she said. "My one great concern is, Will he have any trophies for the Master? Or did he go to heaven empty-handed?"

A deep and probing question. Without answer, really. And yet...

I had just been reading the life story of Amy Carmichael. Time after time she spoke of small children dying, reaching out their arms to Jesus as He welcomed them home. Did they go "empty-handed'?

Jim Elliot once said, "God is not in the business of peopling heaven just with old people." He died at 29, martyred in Ecuador at the full flush of his ministry. Did he go with fewer "trophies" than if he'd lived to his three-score years and ten? Would that be fair of a just and loving Father? Two possibilities come to mind:

(1) We each have an allotted time—an assignment of a precise length. It is not the length of life but what I do with the length I have that is the pertinent factor.

(2) God is all-knowing. He knows what Jim Elliot would have done with another 40-plus years of life had it been allotted to him. In His greatness, would God not give

Jim the "trophies" he would have won for the Master so that Jim could have the privilege of laying them at his Savior's feet?

There is no Scripture that in black and white answers this question. There are certain secret things that alone belong to God (Deut. 29:29). But we can know that our God, who names all the stars in the heavens, does all things well.

TRIALS OF THE FAITH

We should take on the perspective of David, who said, "As for me, my contentment is not in wealth but in seeing you and knowing all is well between us. And when I awake in heaven, I will be fully satisfied, for I will see you face to face" (Ps. 17:15, LB).

Death for us means awakening in heaven and seeing our Lord—face to face. What comfort it is to know that death is not an end but a beginning—to know that we are not in the land of the living going to the land of the dying, but that we are in the land of the dying going to the land of the living.

When the great chemist Sir Michael Faraday was on his deathbed, some journalists questioned him as to his speculations concerning the soul and death. "Speculations!" said the dying man in astonishment. "I know nothing about speculations. I am resting on certainties."

Have you ever reflected on the difference between an ordinary trial and a "trial of your faith" (1 Pet. 1:6-7)? Such a trial takes place when you cannot see the promises of God operating at the moment. Of course, the promises of God are always operating, but sometimes it seems like God is not arriving, or else arriving late. During these times our very souls suffer.

I remember years ago when almost everything in our lives was falling apart. We were broke, friends close to us were critical of us (that is an understatement), and we felt that our ministry was a total failure. We were in the ministry because of certain promises from God, but as far as I could see they were not coming to pass. It was a "trial of my faith."

Each morning I cried to God, "Lord, I can't get through

this day without You. Help!" And God's presence filled my heart so that I could survive the day—barely. During that time, I never doubted God's existence or His presence in my life. But I did wonder if He had put us on the shelf, or if we had done something to make Him give up on us. We were seeing no answers to prayer nor were we seeing His promises to us fulfilled.

During that time, a Christian leader who did not know anything about what we were enduring began to talk about trials. He said, "When I finish going through a trial, l want to be able to look back and say, 'I never once doubted God.'"

I was sick inside. I wanted to shout at him, "Yes, I'd like to be able to say that, too! But I am doubting! Every day I am just barely making it! I am terrified when I think that perhaps God has given up on us."

God taught me some precious lessons through that time— lessons we couldn't have learned any other way. He brought me (a ministry-oriented, people-pleasing person) to the place where I prayed—and meant it, too—"Lord, if You never want me to succeed or have a ministry again in this life, it's all right. I know that the first thing you want is me, and for me to be conformed to Your image. If my never having any ministry again is the best way for You to accomplish these purposes, I am willing."

And then one day we turned the corner from that awful period. God began to fulfill His promises so fast that we couldn't keep up writing them down. It was as if He were saying, "Carole, I love you. I am a faithful God. Your questions and fears will never make Me deny My character. I will be faithful to you even when you question, I will love you when you lack love for Me. I will be true to you when you doubt."

I fell in love with my Father more deeply than ever before. God loves me when I don't even deserve it. He loves me when I am confused and doubting. He loves me.

— *Carole Mayhall*

God's Amazing Grace

Continuing education is one of the popular trends in our day. High schools, colleges, YMCA's and other community organizations are offering classes for adults whose formal schooling has ceased, but who wish to go on learning, growing, and enriching their lives. Many are taking advantage of the opportunity.

Actually every child of God is involved in a continuing educational process, though some may not realize they are still in school. Like a few students on any campus, they live in a fog, unaware that learning can be such an exciting and gratifying experience. There are other Christians who, while knowing they are in school, are not paying very close attention. A spiritual report card would leave a sick feeling in the pits of their stomachs. But thankfully there are also believers who are putting themselves into their education enthusiastically and wholeheartedly. They are learning and growing and thoroughly enjoying it.

God's school is called The School of Grace and the Apostle Paul wrote the catalog for it in Titus 2:11-15. He told us when the school expanded its operations, what its curriculum includes, what built-in incentives for learning it offers, and what provision God has made for the student's progress. So let's go back to school and grow.

THE APPEARANCE OF GRACE (V. 11)

"For the grace of God has appeared, bringing salvation to all men." Don't miss the word "for". Paul has just finished telling older men and women, younger men and women, and slaves how God wants them to live. The reason he could expect them to live that way was because God's grace has appeared. There is no more important element for godly living than an understanding and appropriation of God's grace. It provides the motive and the power to obey God's commands.

Grace is God's inclination to give good things to people who do not deserve them, who cannot earn them, and who can never do enough to pay for them. God loves to give. He has always been that way. His School of Grace has been operating from eternity past. But at one point in time, when He gave us His Son, His grace appeared as it never had before.

The word "appear" was sometimes used of light dawning on the darkness (cf. Luke 1:79; Acts 27:20). What a beautiful display of God's creative genius it is when the sun begins to appear on the horizon, splashing colorful light across the canvas of the sky! Just so, the birth of Jesus Christ, His perfect life, His unselfish ministry, His sacrificial death, and His glorious resurrection were all a beautiful display of God's grace.

Incidentally, "bringing salvation to all men" does not suggest that all will be saved, as some have tried to teach. "To all men" may be rendered "for all men." The grace that was manifested in Christ makes it possible for all mankind to be saved. His death was sufficient for the sins of the whole world. Anyone, however sordid his past, who will acknowledge his sin and place his trust in the sacrificial death of God's Son, will be freely forgiven. God's grace knows no boundary. His school is open to all who will enroll by faith.

THE INSTRUCTION OF GRACE (V. 12)

At the moment we trust Christ as Savior and thus matriculate into God's School of Grace, we begin a learning process that continues for the rest of our lives. We go on exploring the fathomless depths of grace, and by it we are instructed. In other words, the same grace that saves us also schools us in successful Christian living. "… instructing us to deny ungodliness and worldly desires and to live sensibly, righteously and godly in the present age."

That term "instructing" includes just about everything involved in training a child —instructing, advising, encouraging, exhorting, admonishing, guiding, restraining, rewarding, and correcting. God's grace trains us. As we increase in an understanding of His grace, get to know the One who loves to give, and explore the depths of what He has given, we are motivated to grow. We become more proficient and effective in living the Christian life.

The curriculum in our training program includes two basic courses, one negative and one positive. First of all, we learn to say no to ungodliness, that is, the disregard for God which characterizes the typical unbeliever's life. He ignores God most of the time and thinks everyone else should do likewise. But we resist his efforts to make us live our lives as though God did not exist.

We also say no to worldly desires, that is, desires that are centered exclusively in this life, the fulfillment of which will have no value in eternity—things like illicit sexual desires, cravings for money and material things, for pleasure, status or dominance over people. When the immensity of God's grace toward us begins to penetrate our minds, it diminishes our desire for the things tied to this world and increases our desire for Him.

The second major course in the curriculum of God's School of Grace is positive. Once we let Him bulldoze the trash away, then He can build some positive spiritual qualities into our lives. An understanding of God's grace teaches us, first of all, to live sensibly. That word involves both sound judgment and self-control, both the ability to be discreet and prudent as well as the ability to master our impulses and passions. A greater comprehension of what God has provided for us in Christ helps us do the right thing at the right time and in the proper way.

Secondly, grace teaches us to live righteously, that is, fairly, honestly, and justly toward others. We cannot know the God of all grace intimately, then turn around and cheat others, take advantage of them, belittle them, or gossip about them. When we realize how much God has done for us, we are going to reach out in love and consideration toward others.

In the third place, grace teaches us to live godly. That old attitude of disregard for God will be replaced with new love and devotion toward Him, as well as with a heightened desire to live for His praise, to give Him the adoration He deserves, and to allow Him to be part of everything we do.

All this may be tough to do. Some will even protest that it is not possible to live sensibly, righteously, and godly in this present sinful world. But Paul insists that it is. People who do it may be rare, but now we know the secret of their success. They have applied themselves enthusiastically and wholeheartedly to knowing the God who loves to give and who keeps on giving good things to people like us who don't deserve them.

THE MOTIVATION OF GRACE (V. 13)

Most of us would agree that it is easier to learn when we have something to look forward to—an "A" on our report card, promotion to the next grade, graduation day, an honor award, or a scholarship of some kind. Our secular educational system has built-in incentives, and God's School of Grace has one too. We have something to look forward to that is absolutely incomparable. "Looking for the blessed hope and the appearing of the glory of our great God and Savior, Christ Jesus."

When we are truly expecting Him to come, we keep our lives spruced up. Our expectation helps us to repudiate ungodliness and worldly lusts, and to live sensibly, righteously, and godly in the present age. It is just the motivation we need to apply ourselves in God's School of Grace.

Paul calls Christ's coming the blessed hope. A hope in the New Testament is not something we merely wish for, but something we are assured will occur in the future. And it is "blessed" because it inspires happiness and delight. Jesus Christ appeared once nearly 2,000 years ago, as Paul pointed out in verse 11. That first coming was predicted throughout the Old Testament Scriptures and those predictions were fulfilled exactly. It is likewise prophesied that He will appear a second time, and those predictions will also be perfectly fulfilled. We as Christians are to be looking for Him, not necessarily for signs of the times, but for the glorious appearance of our great God and Savior. And when we are truly looking for Him, we will keep on learning and growing in His School of Grace.

THE ENABLEMENT OF GRACE (VV. 14-15)

It is encouraging to discover that everything we need for our progress in this school has been provided. God's supply room is Calvary. Paul wants to take us back from Christ's future appearing to His past suffering. He said that the One who is coming is the One "… who gave Himself for us, that He might redeem us from every lawless deed and purify for Himself a people for His own possession, zealous for good deeds." What an evidence of His grace! He voluntarily left the glory of heaven where he was honored and exalted by angelic hosts, to be mocked and scorned by men, and ultimately to die an excruciating and humiliating death in our place. Why did He do it?

Two reasons are suggested. The first is to "… redeem us from every lawless deed." Christ paid a ransom to release us from the bondage and power of sin. His death not only paid sin's penalty and so removed its guilt, but also broke the authority of our sinful natures and so made it possible for us to overcome sin in daily living. The grace that saves us and schools us also sanctifies us. It provides the power we need to deny ungodliness and worldly desires and to live sensibly, righteously, and godly in the present age.

The second purpose for Christ's death is similar to the first. It is to "… purify for Himself a people for His own possession." Our sin not only made us guilty and held us in bondage, but it also made us spiritually dirty. Christ's death changes all that. It cleanses us and makes us fit to be His own personal possession. The word "possession" was used to describe the special spoils of battle which a victorious king set apart for himself personally. We are Christ's own special people, and we enjoy a unique relationship with Him that nobody else can have. What a privilege!

Salvation is the gift of God's grace. But when God truly saves us by grace, that same grace helps us grow into sensible, righteous, and godly people who overcome sin and who truly care about others. What kind of progress are you making in God's School of Grace? Final exams could be rapidly approaching and graduation day surprisingly near. It would be profitable for us to apply ourselves enthusiastically and whole-heartedly to learning and growing.

—Richard L. Strauss

God's Great Salvation

It is utterly out of the question that any man could ever save himself. Of course, it depends on what we mean by "being saved." If it is merely to make oneself a little better citizen in this world, perhaps with a good deal of effort one could bring that to pass. But if it is a matter of writing one's name in heaven, of forgiving one's sin forever, of imparting eternal life, or of clothing one's self in the righteousness of God, surely we must declare—if we are honest at all—that this is something we cannot do. And, we are just as ready to admit that all the people in the world put together—should they undertake to do this for us—could not approach one of these things. God alone is able to save. The whole plan and thought of saving sinners originated with God. It never originated with man. They hardly identify it when it is brought to them, and oftentimes they have no response to it at all.

SALVATION DEMONSTRATES GOD'S GREAT LOVE

With God, this proposition of saving sinners is the most intrinsic, the most enticing, and the most desirable thing. All His love is expressed in that salvation. It is the outlet of His infinite love toward the sinner. To Him that plan of saving the lost is more important than it could be to all of those that are lost put together. It's worthwhile to fix in our mind that the salvation of one's soul means more to God than it means ever to the soul. It means more to God to have us saved than it means to all the saved people put together. It is His great satisfaction in the exercise of His love in behalf of us. And because He loves us, He has devised this. He has taken away the hindrances which we could not remove. All this unworthiness, all this intense sinfulness as seen by His holy eye, is removed. He Himself did this long, long ago—before ever we were born. He prepared the situation into which we should come and provided the salvation which would be unhindered by our sins.

People are constantly saying, "Oh, I am not worthy to be a Christian. I'm not worthy." But friend, every unworthy thing that you can name, or God can name, in your life has been taken by the Son of God onto the cross and borne for you. The only other thing that hinders God's infinite love from saving you is your own will.

SALVATION COMES THROUGH BELIEVING IN JESUS

"For God so loved the world, that He gave His only begotten Son, that whosoever believeth in Him should not perish, but have everlasting life....

He that believeth on Him is not condemned....

These are written, that ye might believe that Jesus is the

Christ, the Son of God; and that believing ye might have life through His name....

Believe on the Lord Jesus Christ, and thou shalt be saved..."

These words are only a fraction of what the New Testament declares. Upwards of one hundred and fifty passages in the New Testament condition our salvation upon the one thing: believing. Nothing else. It is ruinous, tragic to add anything. Just the one thing: "believe ... and thou shalt be saved." Thirty-five passages use another word, which is of course just a synonym, and that is "faith." This great principle of turning from confidence in ourselves or anything else and looking directly to the Lord Jesus Christ—the only qualified Savior in all this universe—that principle of looking to Him is faith, or believing.

The great Apostle described his attitude when he said, "I know whom I have believed." I have believed Him, He is my savior. He has told me of His saving grace, and I believe it. It answers all the burdens and the distress of my heart and life forever. I believe on Him.

Salvation is Simply Believing

Now there are constantly those who are insisting that there must be something added to this one simple requirement of believing. "You must believe and confess," or "you must believe and repent," or "you must believe and pray," and so on. But dear friend, if that were true, if anything were to be added to the one requirement of believing, then every one of these one hundred and fifty passages are incomplete. And if that were true, when Christ told Nicodemus that "God so loved the world, that He gave His only begotten Son, that whosoever believeth in Him should not perish, but have everlasting life," Christ was only telling Nicodemus a part of the truth and left him stranded without knowing it all. And when Paul and Silas said to that Philippian jailer when he had asked

"What shall I do to be saved," "Believe on the Lord Jesus Christ and thou shalt be saved and thine house," were they giving him only a partial statement? Are they to be reprimanded for having misguided this poor man and leaving something so important out?

My dear friend, the greatest passages of the New Testament that have to do with the human responsibility in this question of being saved never confuse the issue. It is just one and only one thing. Believe. Why? Because that's the only thing that we can do. The other things add nothing at all.

Shall I have to soften God with my tears? Must I persuade Him with my pleading? Have I got to make a public display in order to prove that I am genuine in what I think? All of this is utter folly when we are dealing with God in a matter of this kind.

Look at the great elements that make up our salvation: our name is written in heaven, our eternal life is bestowed, our sins are forgiven, and we are clothed in the righteousness of God. Who is going to do this?

God said that He will do it through Jesus Christ. It's made possible on the grounds of what Christ did for us on the cross. Therefore I can't add anything. There is nothing for me to cooperate in. There's not some teamwork here in which I do my part and He does His part. I fall helplessly and hopelessly at His feet and into His hands and His arms. I simply commit myself to the saving grace of God as it is through Jesus Christ our Lord. He never refused one who came like that. Therefore once more I leave the word definitely, definitely upon you today, "Believe on the Lord Jesus Christ and thou shalt be saved."

—Lewis Sperry Chafer

God's Unexpected Gift

Only moments before she had been cleaning house, planning her upcoming wedding—going about the daily routine shared by thousands of other Jewish girls her age. She was Mary, the daughter of Eli, the promised bride of a carpenter. But then an unannounced visitor, an angel, suddenly stood before her, announcing the power of the Most High would overshadow her and that she would bear the Son of God. Then he was gone, as quickly as he had come.

As questions flooded her mind, one must have stood out: "Why me? Why would the Lord God choose a poor girl to be the mother of the promised King?" Mary knew the Scriptures. In fact, the so called magnificat, Mary's praise to God in Luke's Gospel, is saturated with references to the Old Testament. It is clear that Mary understood she was to be the mother of Messiah, and that His coming was in fulfillment of God's promises to Abraham (Luke 1:54, 55). What is not so clear is the extent to which she understood the nature of her Son's ministry. There were seeming contradictions that would have caused her, as the Scriptures tell us, to "ponder" or try to put it all together.

Why would the King of Kings be forced to enter this world in such humility? Some of her questions could have been answered by the nature of the gifts that were presented to Jesus as first, the common people of Israel come to worship Him (the shepherds), and then aristocratic Gentiles (the magi). With what did they worship Him? With gold, and frankincense, and myrrh.

THE GIFT OF MYRRH

Undoubtedly, Mary would have expected gold and frankincense as fitting gifts for her Son, the King. Myrrh, however, was an unexpected gift. While it could be seen in a positive light, as a perfume for example, it was also used in a more pragmatic, less exalted way. It could be mixed with wine and offered to dying men as a sedative, as it was offered to Christ at His crucifixion. Myrrh could also be used in the embalming process. In other words, the gift of myrrh was indeed a gift fit for kings, but it was also a gift for dying men and for corpses. During her life, Mary would see Jesus receive the gift of myrrh on five occasions; twice from Gentiles and three times from Jews.

• On the first occasion, the Magi brought myrrh from the east in honor of Jesus as King of Kings (Matt. 2:11). This event anticipated the worship Christ will receive from the Gentile nations in the future kingdom.

• The second occasion found Jesus in the home of Simon the Pharisee receiving myrrh from the loving hand of a contrite woman who approached Jesus as her great High Priest, the One who could forgive her many sins (Luke 7:36-50).

• The third offering of myrrh came from the devout Mary of Bethany as she anointed Christ for His burial prior to His death. This showed that she understood the sacrificial nature of His ministry in a way that even His closest disciples had failed to grasp.

• Just before the crucifixion, the Roman soldiers offered Christ a fourth "gift" of myrrh mixed with wine—a kind of narcotic to dull the pain—but He refused it.

• The fifth and final offering came from the hand of Nicodemus when he provided a mixture of myrrh and aloes for anointing Christ's body following His crucifixion (John 19:39).

When Mary received the magi into her home, it is unlikely she grasped the full significance of either the magi themselves or their gifts. The gift of myrrh wasn't out of place. However, it did suggest there was more to Christ's mission than simply inheriting the throne of David.

Given the extraordinary circumstances of our Lord's humble birth, particularly in light of His announced role as King, we can easily assume the smallest detail would have been held and examined by this bright young girl for years to come. It may have been in that later reflection, perhaps even after the Cross, that Mary understood the twofold nature of that unexpected gift of myrrh. Jesus would reign indeed as King, but He would suffer first. In some dark way, the myrrh anticipated His suffering as well as His honor.

The gift of myrrh, then, was the gift of the Cross first, then the crown. In the beginning, Mary may well have suffered the present-day malady of expecting the crown without the Cross. But she came to learn—as we all must—that there is no forgiveness of sins without the shedding of blood, no exaltation apart from humility. The unexpected gift is a gift for us all. For every hard-working, goal-oriented, upwardly mobile sinner on the block.

It's for us because we can't keep tidying up our lives forever. We can't keep up the pace racing from room to room, year to year, patching things up, smoothing things over, covering up our sin and hoping that God won't notice.

The business of constantly having to rationalize our sin exhausts us; our comfortable routine becomes a rut which in turn becomes a grave. We are the busy ones, the hustlers, the crown seekers. And our perpetual excuses dull our senses and drug our souls.

But God loves us enough to wake us up. His subtle grace, gentle as an afternoon breeze, swirls in through the windows of our hearts to confront us with an unexpected gift; a Savior who is Christ the Lord.

Here is One who loved us enough to take up a cross on our behalf—not a cross enameled with gold nor perfumed with frankincense, but a roughhewn burden that cost Him

His life. He died for us, and rose again so that we might live for Him. We receive the unexpected gift of Christ Himself when we trust in His finished work—when we realize there's nothing more that we can add to His sacrifice to make us acceptable to God. That's how a person becomes a Christian. But that's only the beginning of the story.

THE GIFT OF LIFE

Once you trust in Him to save you from an eternity in hell, you begin an incredible journey in the opposite direction. And He outfits you then and there for the passage. He clothes you in His righteousness and gives you the hope of an eternal inheritance as a child of the King, an inheritance to be received at the end of your pilgrimage.

Our Lord's wonderful provision of salvation by grace through faith transforms us. It generates within us the desire and the ability to deny self, take up the cross, and follow Him.

God comes to you with an unexpected gift—the gift of self-sacrificing love—the gift of Jesus Christ Himself, Savior and Lord.

—Reg Grant

He Is Alive

In the cold gray of the early morning three women wended their way through the darkened streets of Jerusalem. It was the dawn of the first day of the week, but their hearts were heavy. Their feet plodded slowly over the rough stones of the streets of Jerusalem. The day preceding the Sabbath they had seen their hope in Jesus of Nazareth crushed. They witnessed Him dying a cruel death by crucifixion. It had been their hope that He would redeem Israel and deliver them from their Roman oppressors; but now their dreams and hopes lay in the darkened tomb.

In their hands they carried spices. As their last measure of devotion they wanted to anoint the dead body of Jesus. Each of the women had her own peculiar regard for Christ. Salome was the wife of Zebedee (Matt. 27:56; Mark 15:40) and the mother of the apostles James and John. With her was Mary of Clopas, the mother of James the Less, another of the twelve disciples. Then there was Mary Magdalene, who had been delivered from a horrible life of demon possession by the power of Jesus. In another part of Jerusalem were other women having the same purpose and the same mission, likewise finding their way to the tomb in the dim light of the early morning.

But they all had a problem. The tomb was sealed by a large stone. Could they get the heavy stone away from the door of the tomb and gain access in order to use the spices they were bringing? They did not know the solution to their problem, but nevertheless they continued on their way.

THE TOMB IS EMPTY

Unknown to the women, the garden where the tomb of Jesus was situated was in great commotion. The guards who had been watching the tomb of Jesus, as requested by the Jews to be sure that no one would steal the body, suddenly were startled in the darkness of the morning by a vision of angels descending to the tomb and rolling away the stone that had sealed the tomb. They fled in terror at this evidence of the supernatural power of God (Matt. 28:2-4).

When the women arrived at the tomb, all may have been quiet again, but the stone had been rolled away, the seal had been broken (Mark 16:4; Luke 24:2; John 20:7). What did this mean? For Mary Magdalene it could mean only one thing. Someone had stolen the body of Jesus. Without waiting for further evidence, she fled the scene back to the disciples to tell them the tragic news. The other women, however, approached the tomb.

There they saw an angel sitting at the right side of the tomb, clothed in a long, white garment. "'Don't be alarmed,' he said. 'You are looking for Jesus the Nazarene, who was crucified. He has risen! He is not here. See the place where they laid him'" (Mark 16:6). Shortly afterward other women including Joanna, the wife of Chuza, the steward of Herod, also arrived at the tomb and were apparently told the same good news (Luke 24: 10).

But Mary had already reported to Peter and John that the tomb was empty and that the body was stolen. John and Peter hastened to the tomb. Upon arriving, Peter quickly entered the tomb and saw the evidence that the body was gone. The grave clothes were still in the form of a human body, and the napkin, which had been over the head, was neatly folded in a place by itself. The silent testimony that Jesus was risen from the dead did not seem to dawn upon him. He left believing that the body was gone, but not knowing that Jesus was risen from the grave.

JESUS AND MARY MAGDALENE

By this time Mary Magdalene had come back to the tomb for the second time. She was weeping. She was sure that someone had taken the body of her Lord. Then she, too, looked into the tomb and saw two angels sitting, one at the head and the other at the feet, where Jesus' body had been laid (John 20:12). They asked why she was weeping, and she told them that someone had taken away her Lord and she knew not where the body had been placed (John 20:13). She no sooner had said this than turning back she saw Jesus standing at the door of the tomb. But she did not recognize Him. Jesus addressed the same question to her. "'Woman,' he said,' why are you crying? Who is it you are looking for?'" (John 20: 15).

Mary through her tears still did not comprehend and thought she was talking to one of the gardeners. She pled with Him, "Sir, if you have carried him away, tell me where you have put him. and I will get him" (John 20: 15).

Jesus said to her simply, "Mary." She turned immediately and said unto Him. "'Rabboni!' (which means Teacher)" (John 20: 16). Through her tears she had not recognized Christ in His resurrection body, but it was the same familiar voice, the same person. In her ecstasy she literally embraced Him. Jesus said to her, "Do not hold on to me, for I have not yet returned to the Father. Go instead to my brothers and tell them." He disappeared. Mary Magdalene lost no time in running back the second time to tell the good news to the disciples, confirming what the other women had also reported.

In these dramatic moments, never to be forgotten and preserved forever in the Scriptures, is the record of Mary Magdalene seeing Christ in His resurrection body. Embedded in the scriptural narratives of the appearance of Christ to Mary is overwhelming proof that Christ had risen from the grave. Appearances to the other women, to Peter, to the disciples on the road to Emmaus, and to ten of the faithful disciples that evening all add their weight to the scriptural proof that Christ actually rose from the dead. In all, there were seventeen appearances of Christ before His Ascension into heaven. Six further appearances to Paul, Stephen, and John occurred at various times after His Ascension.

Why did Jesus appear first to Mary Magdalene? Would it not have been more fitting for Him to have appeared first to Peter or to John or to His mother, Mary? Why was this obscure woman chosen for such a high honor?

The answer is quite simple. She was the first at the tomb in the early light of that morning hour. She was the first to report that the body was missing. She was the first to return to the tomb. She was the first to seek eagerly where they had laid the body of Christ. It was only natural that she should be the first to see the Lord whom she loved more than life.

The Certainty of the Resurrection

As Christians enter into the full significance of the resurrection story, many lessons can be learned from Mary Magdalene. She needed no proof that Christ was indeed the Son of God, for in her own body, in her own spiritual experience, she had seen the marvelous transformation from demonic control to the peace and rest of faith that she had found in Jesus Christ. No confirming evidence was necessary that He was indeed the Son of God.

What was important to her was that Jesus Christ had been delivered from death and from the tomb, that He was now released to enter into His glorious estate. Her sad heart was now glad. Her hope was now all the more real that some day after He had ascended to the Father she, too, would ascend at the coming of Christ for His own.

Years have passed since that cold, gray morn in Jerusalem. For many centuries students of the doctrine of the Resurrection of Christ have pondered the abundant historical evidence that Jesus indeed rose from the grave. They had examined the empty tomb as the witness to the Resurrection of Christ. They have traced the evidence that the disciples were willing to die rather than renounce their faith in the Christ who died and rose again. The disciples experienced a dramatic change from the hopelessness of death to the triumph of resurrection. The Gospel which they proclaimed bears witness of that transformation.

The power of the Spirit of God repeatedly manifests itself in the book of Acts. It all stemmed from that resurrection power that raised Christ from the dead. Even the day of Pentecost, with its record of the descent of the Holy Spirit to indwell the church, was based upon the certainty of the Resurrection. On that glad day, three thousand Jews, having examined the empty tomb and listened to the evidence, took their stand for faith in this risen Lord.

The young church developed and grew. It worshipped in a special way on the first day of the week in recognition of the fact that this was the day on which Christ had risen. The power of the gospel spread throughout the world giving the final evidence that Christ was indeed risen from the grave and that the power of His Resurrection was the creative power of God transforming the lives of those who put their trust in the Savior who died and rose again.

The epistles build upon the certainty of the Resurrection of Christ. From this evidence we can be assured that if we as Christians die we will rise again. More important in our modern day is the assurance that if we believe that Christ died and rose again we also can believe that He might come before we die, that we might be caught up to meet the Lord in the air. "If we believe that Jesus died and rose again, even so them also who believe in Jesus will God bring with Him" (1 Thess. 4: 14). When this occurs, the Lord will descend from heaven with a shout; the dead in Christ shall rise and those believers in Christ who are alive and remain will be raptured, caught up to be with the Lord forever.

The transforming power of God that is manifest in the lives of those who have put their trust in Christ is seen in that empty tomb, the resurrected Christ Himself, and in the promises that are assured because of His Resurrection.

Some day, perhaps very soon, other tombs will be empty. The church will rise triumphantly to meet the Lord in the air, and those living and remaining in earth who have trusted in Christ will be caught up to meet Him and be forever with Him. The Resurrection to which the Scriptures bear witness first revealed in the soft light of that early resurrection morn, points to another resurrection which may be very near as we look for the coming of our Lord.

—John F. Walvoord

Experiencing God's Word

ঞ৴৲

In Psalm 119, the Psalmist writes,

> I delight in your decrees;
> I will not neglect your word... (v. 16)

> Your statutes are my delight;
> They are my counselors... (v. 24)

> Oh, how I love your law!
> I meditate on it all day long... (v. 97)

> Your statutes are my heritage forever;
> They are the joy of my heart. (v. 111)

What is your attitude about the Scriptures? Are you spending significant time in the Word, or do you only manage to get your Bible out on Sundays? Can you join with the Psalmist in saying, "I delight in your decrees," or are your feelings better expressed, "I'm dulled by your documents"? Friend, nothing will make a more significant impact on your spiritual life than devoting time to God's Word. In this section you'll not only find practical ideas for delving into the Scriptures, but encouragement to help you get started. Don't delay. Pick up that Bible now!

Your Bible Can Help You Grow

A common reason that people do not dive into Scripture for themselves is that nobody ever told them what they'd gain by it. What are the benefits of Bible study? What's in it for me? If I invest my time in this manner, what's the payoff? What difference will it make in my life?

I want to suggest three benefits you can expect when you invest in a study of God's Word, which are available nowhere else. And frankly, they're not luxuries, but necessities. Let's look at three passages that conspire to build a convincing case for why we must study the Bible. It's not an option—it's an essential.

BIBLE STUDY IS ESSENTIAL TO GROWTH

The first passage is found in 1 Peter 2:2: "As newborn babes, long for the pure milk of the word, that by it you may grow in respect to salvation." Let me give you three words to unpack the truth contained here. Write them in the margin of your Bible, next to this verse. The first one is "attitude." Peter is describing the attitude of a newborn baby. Just as the baby grabs for the bottle, so you grab for the Book. The baby has to have milk to sustain its life physically; you have to have the Scriptures to sustain your life spiritually.

I had four children, and I learned early that about every three or four hours a timer goes off inside an infant—and you'd better not ignore it. You'd better get a bottle of milk there fast. As soon as you do, there's a great calm. Peter picks up that expressive figure and says that's to be your attitude toward Scripture.

But he also says a word about your appetite for the Word. You should "long" for it. You're to crave the spiritual milk of God's Word. Now to be honest, that's a cultivated taste. Every now and then somebody will say to me, "You know, Prof, I'm really not getting very much out of the Bible." But that's a greater commentary on the person than it is on the Book.

Psalm 19:10 says that Scripture is sweeter than honey, but you'd never know that judging by some believers. You see, there are three basic kinds of Bible students. There are the "castor oil" types. To them the Word is bitter!— yechh!—but it's good for what ails them. Then there is the "shredded wheat" kind. To them Scripture is nourishing but dry. It's like eating a bale of hay. But the third kind is what I call the "strawberries-and-cream" folks. They just can't get enough of the stuff. How did they acquire that taste? By feasting on the Word. They've cultivated what Peter describes here—an insatiable appetite for spiritual truth. Which of these three types are you?

There's a purpose to all of this, which brings us to the third word, "aim." What is the aim of the Bible? The text tells us: in order that you might grow. Please note, it is not that you may know. Certainly you can't grow without knowing. But you can know and not grow. The Bible was written not to satisfy your curiosity but to help you conform to Christ's image. Not to make you a smarter sinner but to make you like the Savior. Not to fill your head with a collection of biblical facts but to transform your life.

When our kids were small, we set up a growth chart on the back of a closet door. As they grew, they begged us to measure how tall they had gotten and record it on the chart. It didn't matter how small the increments were: they bounced up and down with excitement to see their progress. One time after I measured my daughter, she asked me the sort of question you wish kids wouldn't ask: "Daddy, why do big people stop growing?"

How could I explain that big people don't stop growing— we just grow in a different direction? I don't know what I told her, but to this day the Lord is still asking me, "Hendricks, are you growing old, or are you growing up?"

How about you? How many years have you been a Christian? Nine months? Seven or eight years? Thirty-nine years? The real issue is, how much have you grown? Step up to God's growth chart, and measure your progress. That's what this passage is teaching.

So the first reason for studying Scripture is that it is a means of spiritual growth. There is none apart from the Word. It is God's primary tool to develop you as an individual.

BIBLE STUDY IS ESSENTIAL TO SPIRITUAL MATURITY

The second passage we need to look at is Hebrews 5:11-14: "Concerning Christ we have much to say, and it is hard to explain, since you have become dull of hearing. For though by this time you ought to be teachers, you have need again for someone to teach you the elementary principles of the oracles of God, and you have come to need milk and not solid food. For everyone who partakes only of milk is not accustomed to the word of righteousness, for he is a babe. But solid food is for the mature, who because of practice have their senses trained to discern good and evil."

This is an instructive passage in terms of studying Scripture. The writer says he's got a lot to say, but it's "hard to explain." Why? Is it difficulty of the revelation? No, it's the density of the reception. There's a learning disability: "You have become dull of hearing," meaning "you are slow to learn."

The key word in this passage is time. Underline it in your Bible. The writer tells his readers, when by virtue of the passing of time you ought to go on to the college department, you've got to go back to kindergarten and learn your ABCs all over again. When you should be communicating the truth to others, you need to have someone communicate the truth to you.

In fact, he says, you still need milk, not solid food. Solid food is for the mature. Who are the mature? Are they the people who go to seminary? Who can whip anyone in a theological duel? Who know the most Bible verses?

No, the writer says you are mature if you've trained yourself through constant use of the Scripture to distinguish good from evil. The mark of spiritual maturity is not how much you understand, but how much you use. In the spiritual realm, the opposite of ignorance is not knowledge but obedience.

So that is a second reason Bible study is essential. The Bible is the divine means of developing spiritual maturity. There is no other way.

BIBLE STUDY IS ESSENTIAL TO SPIRITUAL EFFECTIVENESS

There's a third passage, 2 Timothy 3:16-17: All Scripture is inspired by God and profitable for teaching, for reproof, for correction, for training in righteousness; that the man of God may be adequate, equipped for every good work.

"All Scripture." That includes 2 Chronicles. I said that once to an audience, and a guy said, "I didn't even know there was a first one." How about Deuteronomy? Can you even find it? Have you ever had your devotions in it? When Jesus was tempted in the wilderness (Matthew 4:1-11), He defeated the devil three times by saying, "It is written." All three are quotations from the Book of Deuteronomy. I've often thought, If my spiritual life depended on my knowledge of Deuteronomy, how would I make out?

Paul says all Scripture is profitable. But profitable for what? He mentions four things. First, for doctrine, or teaching. That is, it will structure your thinking. That's crucial, because if you are not thinking correctly, you are not living correctly. What you believe will determine how you behave.

He also says the Bible is profitable for rebuke. That is, it will tell you where you are out-of-bounds. It's like an umpire who cries, "Out!" or, "Safe!" It tells you what is sin. It tells you what God wants for your life. He provides your standards.

Third, it is profitable for correction. Do you have a closet where you put all the junk you can't find room for anywhere else? You cram it in, and then one day you forget and open the door and—Whoosh!—it all comes out. "Good night," you say, "I'd better clean this thing up." The Bible is like that. It opens up the doors in your life and provides a purifying dynamic to help you clean out sin and learn to conform to God's will.

A fourth advantage of the Bible is that it is profitable for training in righteous living. God uses it to show you how to live. Having corrected you on the negatives, He gives you positive guidelines to follow in life.

What is the overall purpose? In order that you might be equipped for every good work. Have you ever said, "I wish my life were more effective for Jesus Christ?" If so, what have you done to prepare yourself? Bible study is a primary means to becoming an effective servant of Jesus Christ.

One time I asked a group of businessmen, "If you didn't know any more about your business or profession than you know about Christianity after the same number of years of exposure, what would happen?"

One guy blurted out, "They'd ship me." He was right, you know. The reason God can't use you more than He does may well be that you are not prepared. Maybe you've attended church for five, ten, or even twenty years, but you've never cracked open the Bible to prepare yourself for effectiveness as His instrument. You've been under the Word but not in it for yourself.

Now the ball is in your court. God wants to communicate with you in the twentieth century. he wrote his message in a Book. He asks you to come and study that Book for three compelling reasons: It's essential to growth. It's essential to maturity. It's essential for equipping you, training you, so that you might be an available, clean, sharp instrument in His hands to accomplish His purposes.

So the Question facing you now is: How can you afford to stay out of it?

—Howard G. Hendricks
with William D. Hendricks

Why I Trust the Bible

The earliest memories from my childhood remind me that I have always recognized the Bible as a very special book. In Sunday school, as well as in our home, the Bible had a place given to no other book. While I cannot recall my father ever reading a newspaper at the dinner table, it was our family custom to read a portion of Scripture and have family prayer each day. Even before I could read I was taught to memorize short verses of the Bible. Later I joined with the rest of the family in reciting almost daily some portion of Scripture, such as Psalm 1, Psalm 23, or Psalm 103, which were favorite Psalms. The Bible was presented to me as a holy book, the Word of God.

THE BIBLE IS BELIEVED

In my middle teens we moved to a new city and situation. For the first time, I came in contact with some of the great Bible teachers of the last generation. Dr. William F. McCarrell, then pastor of the Cicero Bible Church, held a Thursday night Bible class that I attended regularly, which was my first exposure to verse-by-verse expository preaching. Other famous Bible expositors also preached in our city during my high school days: R.A. Torrey, H.A. Ironside, A.C. Gaebelein, Paul Rader, William Pettingill, and Lewis S. Chafer, the first president of Dallas Seminary. While I did not completely understand all their teaching, one fact was very clear: They all believed the Bible to be the Word of God and trusted it implicitly as setting forth divine Truth. If the Bible taught a doctrine, it was true. As great biblical truths gradually unfolded to me, the Bible became like a trusted friend, tried and true, which could always be depended on to tell the truth.

I was also introduced for the first time to the Scofield Reference Bible and had begun to read the Bible daily. With the help of Scofield notes I began to comprehend something of the tremendous scope of biblical revelation.

While I was dimly aware of the fact that there were others who denied that the Bible was the Word of God, I was not confronted with detailed arguments against the Scriptures until enrolling in college. There I read and evaluated the viewpoints of critics who blatantly denied the trustworthiness of the Word of God. In Bible courses, questions of whether books should actually be included in the Bible were faced, along with questions about authorship, date of writing, and textual problems. Was the Bible indeed the Word of God? Here, struggling with a mass of contradictory information, I enjoyed the clear thinking and cogent scholarship of Dr. J. Oliver Buswell, president of Wheaton College and teacher of my Bible introduction courses there. His skillful handling of various problems made it clear that a person could believe the Bible to be the Word of God and do so on intelligent and logical grounds. I discovered that some of the finest biblical scholars in the world, while fully acquainted with all the attacks that have been made on the Bible, still found the Bible absolutely trustworthy as the Word of God without error.

In the years that followed, which included the years of study at Dallas Seminary and graduate studies in philosophy at Texas Christian University, I found no cogent reasons to depart from my original conclusion that the Bible was indeed God's book, inspired of the Holy Spirit and supernaturally kept from error. It was God's declaratory revelation to man containing the great truths about God, about man, about history, about salvation, and about prophecy that God wanted us to know. The Bible could be trusted just as much as if God had taken the pen and written the words Himself.

In more that forty years of preaching and teaching scriptural truth, I have been impressed with the comprehensive evidence supporting the conclusion that the Bible is indeed the Word of God, absolutely accurate in its statements, a book that can be trusted to teach us spiritual truth. Many large volumes have been written in support of the inspiration and inerrancy of the Bible, but certain facts stand out in my own experience.

The Bible is Inspired

First of all, the Bible clearly claims to be inspired of God. According to 2 Timothy 3:16-17, "All scripture is God-breathed and is useful for teaching, rebuking, correcting and training in righteousness, so that the man of God may be thoroughly equipped for every good work." Peter expressed the same concept in 2 Peter 1:21, "For prophecy never had its origin in the will of man, but men spoke from God as they were carried along by the Holy Spirit." These direct statements of the inspiration of the Bible are confirmed by Dozens of references throughout the Old and New Testaments. The Bible is "the Word of the Lord" and "thy Word," an assertion made in various ways over one hundred times in the Old Testament alone.

In the New Testament, Christ and the apostles, whenever they quoted the Bible quoted it as absolute authority and often indicated that the writers of Scripture had been guided in what they wrote by the Spirit of God. Illustrations of this are found in Matthew 22:42-43 and in frequent quotations of the Old Testament in the New Testament. For instance, in Acts 1:16 Peter refers to the Psalms, "Brothers, the Scripture had to be fulfilled which the Holy Spirit spoke long ago through the mouth of David concerning Judas."

One of the most dramatic texts comes from the lips of Christ Himself: "I tell you the truth, until heaven and earth disappear, not the smallest letter, not the least stroke of pen, will by any means disappear from the Law until everything is accomplished" (Matt. 5:18). In this reference Christ is referring to the smallest letter of the Hebrew alphabet—and the smallest part of a letter that would change its meaning. It would be difficult to have a stronger or more detailed statement of the absolute truth of the Bible than that which came from the lips of Christ Himself.

This points to an important conclusion: those who attack the written Word of God also attack the incarnate Word of God, Jesus Christ. If the Bible is in error, then Christ is in error, too. The two stand or fall together. It is for the reason that evangelical Christians are so insistent that the Bible is indeed the inspired Word of God and that the authors were guided by the Spirit so that they wrote the Truth without any error.

THE BIBLE IS UNIQUE

Even a casual reader of the Bible becomes impressed with its uniqueness. Where in all the world could sixty-books be collected from more than forty authors, be written over a period of more than sixteen hundred years, and yet form one united and continual presentation of divine truth? If the Bible is not inspired of God, it would be a greater miracle than its own inspiration. The unity of Scripture is one of the convincing evidences that the Bible is not a natural book, but a book which God Himself directed and produced through human authors.

Most Christians, while unfamiliar with many of the technical arguments for the inspiration of the Bible, are convinced that the Bible is the Word of God because of what it has done in their own life. The influence of the Bible on millions of those who have put their trust in it is an attested fact of history. Those who have been moral wrecks and victims of drink and drugs have been marvelously redeemed through the power of the Word of God. They have been made new into intelligent, useful citizens and members of the church. The power of Scripture is described in Hebrews 4:12, "The word of God is living and active. Sharper than any double-edged sword, it penetrates even to dividing soul and spirit, joints and marrow; it judges the thoughts and attitudes of the heart."

Wherever the Bible has been consistently applied, it has dramatically changed the civilization and culture of those who have accepted its teaching. It has raised women from debased slavery to a position of honor, love, and purity. The Bible has recognized, on the one hand, man's innate sinfulness and depravity, and on the other hand, the value of human life and the dignity of humanity. In civilizations where even a small portion of the population were consistent Christians, it had the effect of influencing the entire social and political struc-ture. No other book has ever so dramatically changed the individual lives and society in general.

If the Bible is indeed the Word of God, those who read it are confronted with moral decisions. The truth of the Word of God must first be believed and comprehended, and this requires careful Bible study, proper methods of interpretation, and understanding how one portion of Scripture casts light on another. If the Bible is indeed the Word of God, it is as essen-tial to our spiritual life as food is to our physical life. The Bible should be read every day, and its truth allowed to cast its light on our path.

The Bible, however, is more than a book to be admired and revered, more than a book to be placed in a special category as a holy book. Its moral commands and its spiritual values demand commitment. You cannot really believe the Bible without the Scriptures leading you to faith in Jesus Christ as Savior and commitment to Jesus Christ as Lord. The comprehensive sweep of the Bible, as it looks at history from God's point of view and then presents the glorious future that is awaiting the child of God, gives the Christian a life of meaningful activity, a system of values that transcends the materialism of our day, and a glorious hope in a world where there is much hopelessness.

The Bible was written for men as they are, but points the way to what men can be by the grace of God. In direct proportion as we meditate on it and profit by our study of Scripture, so our spiritual lives will grow, our lives will become fruitful in the service of the Lord, and we will be preparing for our eternal destiny. In a day of great confusion and uncertainty about the future, the Bible gives its plain revelation as to where we are in God's program and where we will be going. No other book can do more for those who put their trust in its truth. No other book is inspired of God, given by inspiration of the Holy Spirit, revealing God's truth without any mixture of error. The Bible is as trustworthy as God Himself.

—John F. Walvoord

Reading God's Word

The story is told of a young lady who was lent a book by a close friend. She tried very hard to understand and enjoy it, but she failed completely. Then one day she met a young man. They became acquainted, fell in love with each other, and were soon engaged to be married. It turned out that he was the author of the book she thought was so dull and difficult! With a completely different outlook she again took up the book, discovering that her changed relationship with the author made the book both interesting and understandable. Furthermore, where the book was not clear to her, she could consult the author as to the meaning.

To begin to understand and appreciate the Bible you must first come to know and love the Author through the new birth (John 1:11-13; 3:3, 7), then always and at any time, you can consult Him about the meaning of His Word. However, even to many Christians the Bible is a dull Book, yet it should be read in order that it might become to you personally the living and powerful Book that it is.

DAILY

How many meals do you have in a week? Two? Of course not! Generally, we all have three meals a day and often some in-between snacks. Just as we daily and at set times minister to our physical needs, we should in a similar way minister to our spiritual needs by feeding on the Word of God, and thereby feeding on Christ Himself, the "Bread of Life" (John 6:51-58). Some people just enjoy the Bible on Sunday, but they are not by any means strong Christians. If we would be strong Christians we must daily, preferably at the beginning of the day, feed on God's Word. To get a few snacks through the day as time permits and then to close out the day by reading some portion from it will serve further to enlighten, enrich, and enable us in our individual lives in Christ (cf. 1 Pet. 2:2). The Bible alone is the Book to live by, and it is the only sure and safe written Guide in life, especially in this present day and age when there are so many false guides abroad throughout the world.

INDEPENDENTLY

The moment a sinner is born again through simple faith in Christ, the Holy Spirit comes to indwell him forever. We should be completely yielded to the Spirit of God and ready to hear His voice when we open God's Word, and our reading should be characterized by at least three things. First, we should read with reverence. In other words, we should respect and regard the Bible for what it is—the Word of God. Second, we should read with expectation. There is an old saying which goes something like this: "Blessed is he that expecteth nothing, for he shall not be disappointed." This adage may have its place in some areas of life, for instance, in the area of political promises made by vote-conscious candidates. But it had absolutely no place in the life of the Christian as he opens the pages of his Bible. When we come to God's Word it should always be with the realization that it is His revealed will, the Word of Truth. Read and receive it in an attitude of simple childlike trust, expecting the Lord to speak. Finally, we should read with prayer. Christ has promised, "Ask and it will be given to you..." (Matt 7:7), and the practically minded James has admonished "You do not have, because you do not ask God" (James 4:2b). A good verse to use prayerfully on opening the Word of God is Psalm 119:18: "Open my eyes that I may see wonderful things in your law."

DELIBERATELY

By this we mean read the Bible slowly. Plenty of time should be allowed for reading the Bible. To read it hurriedly is like rushing through a meal—it is but half digested and assimilated. Learn a lesson from the cow. She slowly chews her cud, passing her food from one stomach to the other for digestion. Slow digestion of God's Word is necessary. True, it is a good idea to read the Bible through every year by taking two chapters in the Old Testament and one in the New Testament every weekday, and three of the Old and two of the New on Sundays. But it is more important to read it slowly and systematically in small portions, and thereby avoid haphazard, random reading.

One of my university professors once told us about an older man who to him seemed especially wise in all his ways. When he asked the elderly man his secret the old gentleman said that during his life he had read the Bible through several times, meditating at least a minute on every verse.

DILIGENTLY

Particular care should be taken in our reading of God's Word. Just as a scholar ponders a weighty and impressive looking secular textbook, so the Christian must carefully ponder his sacred Textbook, the Bible. The Bible is not all bread and milk; much of it is "solid food" (Heb. 5:13-14). Therefore, in our reading of it, surely no less diligence should be applied than in our reading of textbooks dealing with mathematics, chemistry, physics, the classics, language study, and the like (2 Pet. 3:16).

Also, as we read, it's a good idea to keep a notebook in order to jot down at least some of the fruits of our reading. I have learned the hard way that "the world's worst ink is better than the world's best memory."

DIRECTLY

Always seek to obtain God's message to you personally. Like Jacob of old who wrestled with God at the brook Jabbok, we also need to wrestle, as it were, with God. Do not cease reading or meditating on a particular passage until the Lord has spoken and given you something to think about and fortify you through the day. Keep in mind an especially important truth as you read: the Old Testament is God's illustration book of the New Testament lesson book (1 Cor. 10:11).

DUTIFULLY

When God has spoken to you in and through His written Word, remember that it is your responsibility to obey and carry out His Word in your everyday conduct and conversation.

Over the past decade or so there has been an avalanche of new translations of the Scriptures, and they are still coming off the presses. On my study desk I keep no less than seven translations, plus my Greek New Testament. In Christian circles the question often comes up, "What is the best translation of the Bible?" Unequivocally, the best translation of the Bible is a man or woman living a godly life in obedience to God's Word (Heb. 5:8 with 1 Pet. 2:21). Also, let us remember that as we carry out His Word, the Lord Jesus Christ always goes with us (Matt. 28:20; Heb. 13:8).

In response to the questioning of a young Christian who earnestly confided to G.R. Harding Wood of Great Britain that he found the Bible dull, Mr. Wood came forth with a splendid yet simple answer centering around four of the many relationships the believer enters into with the Lord Jesus Christ at the moment of salvation. To all, whether or not this young person's problem has been yours as well, he has suggested that we should read the Bible:

1. COMPLETELY, as part of the bride of Jesus (just as a bride reads a love letter.)

2. CONSTANTLY, as a traveler to the home of Jesus.

3. CAREFULLY, as a scholar in the school of Jesus.

4. CONSCIENTIOUSLY, as a soldier in the army of Jesus.

The saintly and gifted F.B. Meyer gave this word of advice:

"Read the Bible, not as a newspaper, but as a home letter. If a cluster of heavenly fruit hangs within reach, gather it. If a promise lies upon the page as a blank check, cash it. If a prayer is recorded, appropriate it, and launch it as a feathered arrow from the bow of your desire. If an example of holiness gleams before you, ask God to do as much for you. If the truth is revealed in all its intrinsic splendor, entreat that its brilliance may ever irradiate the hemisphere of your life." (From "Choice Gleanings" Calendar)

If these suggestions on how to read the Bible are really put to use, the reading of the Bible will not be dull but truly delightful, resulting in genuine spiritual dividends.

—*W. Ross Rainey*

Discovering God's Word

Bible study. What do the words mean to you? Chapter after chapter of ideas that won't fit together easily? Lists of unpronounceable names? Long books that don't seem to relate to each other or to you?

Nonsense! That's not Bible study. Bible study is discovery. It's finding exciting ideas. It's learning life changing concepts. It's making God's Word plain. And you by yourself can open the Word of God and find that it has special meaning for you and that is has answers for your daily needs. But for this to happen you must know what the Bible says.

GETTING STARTED

Flip through your Bible right now. Which books are most familiar to you? Mark? The Gospel of John? Psalms maybe? Well, don't start your study with any of those familiar books. Take one of the longest and hardest to understand. Try Job.

There are many ways to study the Bible, but here's one way to make a book open up for you, even a long book like Job. Begin by slashing a straight line across the middle of a typing size sheet of paper. No, not a faint, timid line but a bold one like this:

Now open to the Book of Job and skim chapters one and two. What happens in them? Look at the last chapter. What happens there? If you've read the book at all, you know that Job went through a lot of trouble and then lived happily ever after.

Mark off the first and last chapters on your line and put down some words to describe them. You might use "Job

Before" and "Job After." Or get fancy and call them Prologue and Epilogue. Like this:

PROLOGUE	EPILOGUE
1-2	42

How is it organized?

The problem is that the beginning and ending of Job aren't what bother us. It's what comes in the middle that's hard to sort out. But the book itself helps us understand. Look at the way the chapters begin. They identify Job's friends by name and tell which one is talking. Skim the first verse of each chapter from 3 to 14 to find the conversation sequence between Job and his three friends. Call that the first cycle and transfer it to your chart.

PROLOGUE	1st CYCLE	EPILOGUE
1-2	3-14	42

WHAT IS THE FLOW?

As you continue looking at the first verses of the chapters that follow, you'll find the pattern repeats itself to chapter 21 as Job answers the second speeches of his friends. Then the pattern is followed again through chapter 31. Later, as you study the words more thoroughly, you'll find the friends get increasingly angry at Job and you sense a crescendo of accusation. You'll want to illustrate that in some way, perhaps like this:

PROLOGUE	1st CYCLE	2nd CYCLE	3rd CYCLE	EPILOGUE
1-2	3-14	15-21	22-31	42

WHAT IS THE THEME?

Another person enters the picture in chapter 32 and talks nonstop to chapter 38. Then he is interrupted by God, who gives Job all the explanation he needs about why he is suffering. And that, of course, is the theme of the book. So the skeleton of the book on your page now looks like this:

PROLOGUE	1st CYCLE	2nd CYCLE	3rd CYCLE	ELIHU SPEAKS	GOD ANSWERS	EPILOGUE
1-2	3-14	15-21	22-31	32-37	38-41	42
PROBLEM — Why do the righteous suffer?				ANSWER — Job sees God's majesty		

HOW WOULD YOU DIVIDE IT?

Of course there is much more to know about the contents of this magnificent book. But the first step in Bible study is to see the overall structure and purpose of a book and have it before you in a manageable form.

This method works with a short book as well. For instance, Galatians falls logically into three divisions.

PERSONAL EXPLANATION	DOCTRINAL TEACHING	PRACTICAL APPLICATION
1-2	3-4	5-6

As you study the book from this basic outline, you'll see how each section leads into the next to give a beautiful mosaic of truth.

The book of Acts begins to open to you as you chart it from the key verse in Acts 1:8. See how the witness spreads from Jerusalem to the uttermost parts of the earth. And from Acts flow the marvelous letters of the New Testament. Romans, Ephesians, Philippians, the Thessalonians letters all waiting for you to explore!

Think of Exodus with its laws and its rules for the priests and the sacrifices. Why were they given? Well, those former slaves coming out of Egypt had to be welded into a nation under God as they faced an unknown future. The stringent instructions were vital for their growth and security.

But why should we bother to study them? The Book of Hebrews gives the answer: because it speaks of Christ who is the believer's Priest and Sacrifice. Exodus and Hebrews each explains the other.

Then there's the reference in the Gospel of John to Numbers. Numbers? The book with so many chapters that are lists of names and figures? Yes, we see a wonderful connection between Numbers and the familiar, beloved Gospel of John. In John 3 Jesus says, "As Moses lifted up the serpent in the wilderness…" (That's from Numbers) "even so must the son of Man be lifted up." That's the explanation for the scene in Numbers.

You see, knowing the Bible is more than just being familiar with a few favorite portions or being able to quote verses. Bible study is observation seeing the purpose of God. It's interpretation seeing the meaning of that purpose in history. It's application seeing the relevancy of that purpose to your life right now.

Don't wait any longer to find the method of Bible study that best opens God's Word to you. The Bible is living, it's powerful, and it will change your life.

—Dorothy Martin

Meditating on God's Word

As I stood five months pregnant, peering into a peculiarly warm and smelly refrigerator, I wondered, "Why do things break down around the house at such inopportune times?" Tuition bills and maternity payments had left us precious little margin for an unplanned refrigerator purchase. "Lord this isn't fair," I mumbled. "Either you have the wrong timing or the wrong people!"

For the next few days a royal battle ebbed and flowed inside of me. As I prayed and thanked the Lord for allowing this event, a measure of peace ruled within me. But when I returned to cooking with warm milk and steamy lettuce, anxiety and doubt invariable supplanted the temporary peace.

My exit off this emotional roller coaster came within a few days. I was reading in the Psalms and became impressed with one particular verse: "A righteous man may have many troubles, but the Lord delivers him from them all" (Ps. 34:19). I quickly committed it to memory. Then whenever the tide of frustration rolled in I found that be reviewing the verse I was able to claim God's deliverance. We also continued our search for a working refrigerator.

God's deliverance came unexpectedly in the form of a young couple from our church. "We've been wondering what to do with this empty refrigerator sitting in our garage for a year and a half," they told us. "You'd do us a favor if you'd come over and get it." Would we ever!

The Lord, in His own sense of humor, replaced our decrepit refrigerator with a newer, frost-free model just in time for company that was unaware of our frenzied week. But lasting peace and victory did not come with the arrival of that refrigerator but rather days before when I meditated on that promise in His Word.

Many people approach Scripture memory and meditation as though it were the entry ticket into the Spiritual Olympics. The casual implication is that Scripture memory is something reserved for preachers and super Christians. Granted, consistent Scripture meditation does require at least an ounce of discipline. Reviewing selected verses until their truths are both easily recalled and readily applied takes concerted effort. However, Scripture memorization is actually the most cost-efficient means of influencing your life with God's Word. Studies tell us that no matter how effective a speaker is, we'll only retain about five percent of what he says. And we'll only recall about one-third of what we read. But the time invested in memorization and meditation pays the rich dividend of one hundred percent recall.

Why is the expenditure of time and energy so worth the effort entailed in memorizing Scripture? Because our life is lived in our mind. More than 10,000 thoughts a day pass through that gray matter neatly tucked between our ears. Theologian A.W. Tozer once said, "Our thoughts not only reveal what we are, they predict what we will become. We will soon be the sum total of our thoughts." The Holy Spirit feeds on the spiritual nourishment of the Word to rewire our mental computer, thereby effectively changing our attitudes and actions.

How does this process take place? Picture your life as a hilltop on which rain falls and, as the water drains off, rivulets are formed. But deeper and deeper by the flow of water, some rivulets eventually become chasms. These rivulets represent the habit patterns of our lives. Little by little, constant exposure makes big changes.

Much of the value of Scripture memory is the result of repetition. Memorizing and then reviewing verses allows God to instill truths in our minds that we might otherwise miss if we only gave a cursory glance to a passage. With more exposure comes greater potential for change.

Recently, I interviewed an older woman who illustrates this process. She is such a dynamic Christian that you would never guess her family background is the bleak picture she reports. Raised primarily by brothers and sisters during the Great Depression, she developed a profound sense of inferiority and lovelessness.

"How then did you find that your background influenced your ability to give and receive love as an adult?" I asked her, "How were you able to overcome those feelings from your past?"

Her answer was, to me, a real support for Scripture memory. "When John and I were married," she said, "I found myself unable to express love. Those feelings lay bottled up inside me and the cork was too tight for words to escape. In my daily reading God impressed me with the verse, 'For in him you have been enriched in every way in all your speaking and in all your knowledge' (1 Cor. 1:5). As I reviewed and claimed that promise, God gave me words to express the feelings buried so long inside of me." She then related many other aspects of her background that the Lord had changed through her persistent claims of promises in the Bible.

LINKING KNOWLEDGE WITH PRACTICE

Scripture memory can be the missing link between the truth we know and the truth we practice. For instance, we all know that as Christians our relationships should be characterized by love. But when God brings a specific verse to mind such as "...live a life worthy of the calling you have received. Be completely humble and gentle; be patient, bearing with one another in love" (Eph. 4:1,2), relationships can take on a new dimension. God replaces an abstract idea on the back burner of our minds with concrete practical applications.

How does someone begin the habit of memorizing Scripture and sticking with it? I must confess that my husband was my greatest motivation to take Scripture memorization seriously. When I first met him I was amazed at his spiritual understanding. And I was equally amazed that he'd only been a Christian for half the time that I had known the Lord! As I got to know him, it became apparent that the difference was his consistent and deliberate intake of scriptural truth. The day after he trusted Christ he began a Scripture memory program through the encouragement of another Christian, and he's still going strong today.

My growth in this discipline, however, was far more sporadic. I started with a topically arranged system of verses but I felt as though I was just repeating nice words. Then I started memorizing verses that were pertinent to my set of circumstances—usually verses that impressed me from my devotional time. As I saw God overhaul some of my attitudes through His Word, my motivation to memorize and meditate increased and I eventually became hooked.

GOD USES HIS WORD

Over the years I've seen God use memorized Scripture as preventive medicine, correcting me before I hit the brick wall of a more devastating experience. Anger is a classic example. As I feel my nerves fraying and the temptation rising to verbally clobber one of my children, God sometimes stops me short with a verse such as: "A gentle answer turns away wrath, but a harsh word stirs up anger" (Prov. 15:1). Since anger only begets more anger, I'm then motivated toward self-control and a softer response. Whether I end the day with a lighthearted attitude or with a tension headache is determined by a series of truths God has faithfully brought to my mind.

Just as often God uses His Word as a salve to heal, comfort, and encourage. One young Christian shared with me his repeated experiences with feelings of defeat and rejection. What brought him out of his downward spiral was meditating on the verses, "The Lord delights in the way of the man whose steps he has made firm; though he stumble, he will not fall, for the Lord upholds him with his hand" (Psalm 37:23-24). As he was able to lay hold of God's forgiveness and acceptance, the Lord began to give him victory.

Scripture memorization also prepares us for the inevitable times of crises and difficulties. Evangelist Billy Graham recently said, "If we have not learned to trust God's Word when times are easy, we will not trust His Word when we face difficulties. I am convinced that one of the greatest things we can do is memorize Scripture. The Scriptures speak to us in those moments when we look to the Lord for sustenance and strength."

Scripture memorization allows God's truth to gain more than just a toehold on our lives. It can be the catalyst for change, comfort, and growth. It's like building a spiritual bank account with interest compounded daily. As we invest consistent time and energy in meditation, our appetite for the Word grows and our understanding deepens. We can say with Jeremiah, "When your words came, I ate them; they were my joy and my heart's delight, for I bear your name, O Lord God Almighty" (Jer. 15:16).

—Paula Rinehart

Spending Time in God's Word

Medically speaking there is a condition we call anemia. It is defined as "a condition in which the circulating red blood cells are deficient in number or in total hemoglobin content per unit of blood volume." Its symptoms are weakness, vertigo, headaches, easy fatigability, irritability, etc. Many times the symptoms are barely noticeable and the condition can be present without being detected. The prescribed treatment is a diet adequate in essential blood-building materials, especially protein. On the lighter side, one man was described as being so anemic he had to get a transfusion before he could bleed.

As we look around today and observe believers in Christ, it seems a very high percentage of these believers is afflicted with a spiritual malady which very closely resembles the physical condition of anemia. There seem to be symptoms which indicate a serious deficiency in the spiritual condition of many believers; weakness, lethargy, lack of power and accomplishment, easy fatigability, ineffectiveness, irritability, and many related problems.

Spiritual Anemia

Upon careful examination it appears quite evident that this condition which I have chosen to call "spiritual anemia", is brought on by an improper spiritual diet. Many believers are just simply undernourished and ill-fed and are seeking to eke out a spiritual existence on a bread and water diet.

A further startling observation is that this condition of spiritual anemia is not just limited to the layperson, the man in the pew, the run-of-the-mill Christian. It also afflicts those who are involved in active ministry of all sorts—pastors, pastor's wives, missionaries, Christian educators, and on and on. It would seem that even these so-called spiritual giants and leaders fall prey to this weakening disease.

Two objectives challenge us in this discussion: (1) to determine what constitutes a deficient spiritual diet and brings on a spiritually anemic condition; (2) to discuss what makes up a well-balanced spiritual diet that will prevent as well as cure this spiritual anemia.

When we approach the subject of diet we realize that we are discussing one of the most common subjects of conversation in our lives today. All of us are conscious about our diets. Some worry about eating the right kinds of food as opposed to "junk" foods. The health food fad is one of the longest standing fads ever to hit our culture. "Junk" food diets are really looked at with disdain—diet drinks, Big Macs, chips, dips, donuts, chocolate turtles, eclairs. Others worry constantly about eating too much. In our culture fat is not considered beautiful but ugly and many of us literally starve ourselves to get rid of blubber and bulges. We have the Atkins diet, the grapefruit diet, the Cambridge diet, the Shaklee diet…on and on ad infinitum.

YOUR SPIRITUAL DIET

But what about the spiritual diet? What are believers trying to exist on spiritually? What is a deficient spiritual diet? Possibly the best way to understand a deficient spiritual diet is to look at some samples or examples. Here are four:

1. Believers who subsist on one Sunday sermon a week. Sunday morning from 11 to 12 they are in church. The message of the morning runs all the way from 30 minutes to 45 minutes—and many times much of that is taken up with froth or foam or at best spiritual milk. We might designate some of this as "sermonettes"; perhaps a Scriptural text from which some thoughts are suggested. The amount of good solid teaching from the Scriptures is negligible. These believers get no further exposure to the Scriptures throughout the next seven-day period. They do not attend Sunday school. They do not attend Sunday night service or Wednesday night, they are not involved in any type of home Bible study class. They do not open their Bibles at home from one Sunday to the next.

2. Believers who hear three sermons a week. Sunday morning, Sunday evening, Wednesday evening. These three sermons or studies are the diet for our second group. But there is no further exposure to the Scriptures throughout the week, no private study or other concentrated instruction of any sort.

3. Christian workers who hurriedly prepare an "assignment." Some who teach Sunday school, who work in junior churches or in nurseries, do not even hear the sermons.

Neither do they open their Bibles privately from one Sunday to the next except for scanty preparation for a lesson or perhaps the quick scanning of a quarterly.

4. Believers who read a chapter of the Bible a day or perhaps a daily devotional book such as *Daily Bread* or *Daily Light*. This is possibly very meaningful but very hurried, light, surface, cursory reading. There is little time or thought given to assimilating the truths of the passages.

There are light readers who touch a verse here and a chapter there. There are lounging readers who start out to read with diligence but who with a yawn sprawl out over three or four sentences. There are few who read with eagerness.

These four examples probably describe at least 75% of all believers.

A SPIRITUAL PRESCRIPTION

Our second objective is to discuss what constitutes a sufficient, well-balanced spiritual diet:

1. Regular, meaningful, personal exposure to the Word of God. At the risk of being labeled "legalistic" I would venture to say this exposure should be daily, just as our physical meals are on a daily basis.

The Bible very clearly teaches the necessity for personal, consistent exposure to the Scriptures in passages such as Joshua 1:8, Jeremiah 15:16, Psalms 1 and 19. First Peter 2:2 exhorts believers to have a hunger for the Scriptures like little babies crave milk in order that they might grow. There is an assortment of proven methods of getting into the Scriptures:

a. Systematic reading for content, not just hurried reading with no interaction.

b. Deep study with a workbook or a notebook. Questions and answers, surveys or outlining, and writing paraphrases are examples.

c. Studying a specific book of the Bible with the help of a good commentary (a teacher in print).

d. Systematic Scripture memorization. There are many choices such as Bible Memory Association, Campus Crusade, or Navigators.

e. Series of cassettes on books of the Bible. Not just topical subjects such as rearing children or husband/wife relationships, as commendable as these are, but actual study of Scriptures.

2. Concentrated time set aside and provided for meditation on the Scriptures.

Psalm 1 exhorts the blessed man to meditate day and night on the Law of the Lord. How few believers today experience the delight and benefit of allowing a truth from the Scripture to monopolize their thoughts. How rarely we allow a verse or a passage to pervade our minds for an extended period of time until its meaning becomes a part of our very being. The Scriptures are not really feeding us and nourishing us until we cultivate the habit and art of concentrating on them and meditating on them.

3. Personal, private, and regular prayer life.

This acts as a catalyst for the working of the Scriptures in the life. Time spent in prayer seals the work of the Scriptures in the heart. This gives time for self-analysis and allowing the Word to work. Prayer and Bible study are inseparable. Either one without the other is ineffective.

And so the problem of spiritual anemia. The proper remedy and diet are within the easy reach of every one of us. I once heard someone say, "Under-nourishment is perhaps the most common ailment of Christians. Our food supply is the Word of God. To neglect the Word is to starve the soul. We cannot grow strong without feeding regularly on the Word."

George Mueller is said to have made the following comments: "I saw more clearly than ever that the first great and primary business to which I ought to attend every day was to have my soul happy in the Lord. The first thing to be concerned about was not how much I might serve the Lord, or how I might glorify the Lord, but how I might get my soul into a happy state, and how my inner man might be nourished.

The first thing I did after having asked in a few words the Lord's blessing upon His precious Word was to begin to meditate upon the Word of God, searching into every verse to get blessing out of it; not for the sake of the public ministry of the Word; not for the sake of preaching on what I had meditated upon; but for the sake of obtaining food for my own soul."

Spiritual anemia —its cure is saturation with and meaningful exposure to the Scriptures. And this is for every believer.

—*Maxine Toussaint*

Wisdom From God's Word

It was late Friday evening and still Sam hadn't come to a decision. He had to give the company an answer Monday morning whether he would accept the position of Vice-president of Operations. Though he had wrestled with this matter for almost three weeks, he was no closer to a decision now than the day they approached him with the offer.

Sam came to Christ nearly five years ago. He had been taught that God makes His will known through the inward leading of the Holy Spirit. Often in the past when faced with a decision, there had been a deep conviction or a strong feeling regarding a matter which Sam interpreted as the leading of the Holy Spirit. But not every time. There were occasions when he made decision without this strong impression and afterward he would spend days worrying that he "had run ahead of God."

Sam had been in his present position for 19 years and had excellent job security. The company wanted him to stay; in fact, they were prepared to give him a substantial raise. Yet he had advanced as far as he could. The new job, on the other hand, presented a challenge and an opportunity for advancement. But it lacked the security of his present position. The last two men who held the job had each lasted less than a year and Sam wasn't sure he had any more to offer. Deep within there was a desire to try, but he couldn't bring himself to say "yes".

What do you do when you must make a decision and there is no inner leading? Most would agree that God can, and sometime does, give direct, supernatural guidance to a believer. But what do you do, as in Sam's case, when there is no "voice" from heaven?

Three key words in the Book of Proverbs provide an answer to that often-asked question and serve as the basis for solid biblical principles for decision-making.

WISDOM

The first word is wisdom. Proverbs repeatedly challenges us to make wisdom our primary pursuit in life: "Blessed is the man who finds wisdom, the man who gains understanding, for she is more profitable than silver and yields better returns than gold. She is more precious than rubies; nothing you desire can compare with her. Long life is in her right hand; in her left hand are riches and honor. Her ways are pleasant ways, and all her paths are peace" (Prov. 3:13-17). Scripture is emphatic: the pursuit of wisdom must be the number one priority for those who want the best in life.

The wisdom of which the Book of Proverbs speaks is not the skillful use of human reason. In fact it has little to do with keenness of intellect. It is, instead, divine revelation applied to human experience. How does one acquire this most prized of life's possessions? Proverbs 9:10 informs us that, "The fear of the Lord is the beginning of wisdom." This "fear of the Lord" is not a cringing dread but rather a reverence for God that leads to a submission to His Word. In short, we acquire wisdom as we surrender to His Word. The first and most important step in decision-making, then, requires us to come to the point at which we say to God, "Your will, made known through Your Word, will be the authority in all my decision. I am committed to living my life according to your Word."

If we are committed to the wisdom of God's Word, then we can have confidence that our decisions will honor Him. Whatever decision we make, as long as it does not contradict God's will revealed in the Bible, is in the will of God. This does not mean, however, that every option in that broad expanse is of equal benefit. Nor is it to say that it would be wise for Sam to flip a coin casually and let the chance fall of "heads or tails" be the decision about which job he would take. How one handles several choices of seemingly equal value introduces another important principle in decision-making.

PRUDENCE

In addition to the wisdom that leads to a surrendered heart, there must also be an informed mind. This principle grows out of the biblical word "prudence." "I, wisdom, dwell together with prudence; I possess knowledge and discretion (Prov. 8:12). In a sense wisdom says, "Prudence and I are best friends. We are always together. Where you find one of us, you will find the other."

The word "prudence" simply means "good judgment". Proverbs 15:5 informs us: "A fool spurns his father's discipline, but whoever heeds correction shows prudence." When a person manifests the good judgment of accepting his father's correction, he shows that he possesses prudence.

Prudence differs from wisdom. Wisdom springs from a divine source, prudence from a human source. Wisdom comes through the Scriptures, prudence through human effort. The two dwell together but their origins are different.

Manifesting prudence through an informed mind necessitates gathering and evaluating data. Jesus underscored this when He said: "Suppose one of you want to build a tower. Will he not first sit down and estimate the cost to see if he has enough money to complete it? For if he lays the foundation and is not able to finish it, everyone who sees it will ridicule him, saying, 'This fellow began to build and was not able to finish'" (Luke 14:28-29). Jesus stressed the importance of getting all the information you can before making a decision.

Another aspect of the informed mind principle is to seek wise counsel. An insightful verse relating to decision-making says: "Plans fail for lack of counsel, but with many advisers they succeed" (Prov. 15:22). Sometimes we make unwise choices simply because we do not take the time or make the effort to talk to the right people.

The primary task of the President of the United States is to make decisions. His effectiveness as the Chief Executive depends on this ability more than any other. Those close to President Bush say that in decision-making he relied more heavily on reliable counsel than any president in recent history.

One method he used in seeking counsel is what his inner circle called "multiple advocacy." Experts with strong opinions on both sides of an issue were asked to share their viewpoints with the President or a close adviser who reported to him. Sometimes he used the "scheduled train wreck," which was simply a debate by the president's staff and members of the cabinet. During such debates the president took copious notes and then he "shopped the options around." After phoning various legislators to share a tentative decision, he would ask, "Would you buy this?" To look at a matter from another's point of view is the essence of wise counsel.

When seeking prudence through an informed mind, we must face the danger that our minds are often unduly influenced by our emotions. Sometimes in the kingdom of the soul, emotion leads a silent coup that deposes reason and revelation from the throne. Confusion prevails whenever emotion rules.

Relying on inner impressions and emotions for guidance can become a decision-making quagmire. Some have made serious mistakes in equating a feeling with the voice of God. Who has not heard some dear Christian confidently state, "God told me to do this" (meaning: "I strongly feel that I should do it") only later to discover it was a disastrous mistake?

Nearly 200 years ago John Wesley spoke very pointedly to this issue:

> "Do not hastily ascribe things to God. Do not easily suppose dreams, voices, impressions, visions or revelations to be from God. They may be from Him. They may be nature. They may be from the devil. Therefore, 'believe not every spirit, but test the spirits whether they be from God.'"

DILIGENCE

Another essential joins with wisdom and prudence to complete the triad for wise decisions: diligence. Making a decision constitutes only the first step. Making that decision work is equally important. Twice the book of Proverbs uses the phrase "diligent hands" to express determination or persistence: "diligent hands bring wealth" (10:4), "diligent hands will rule" (12:24).

Proverbs uses the phrase "diligent hands" in the sense of someone who grasps a task and refuses to release it until completed. In the area of decision-making diligent, determined, unwavering hands are of utmost importance.

Munich, Germany hosted the 1972 Olympic Games. Jim Ryan from the United States had previously broken the four-minute mile and had the fastest Olympic qualifying time for the mile. Most observers expected Ryan to take the gold medal.

When the time for his race finally arrived the runners waited tensely in place. When the gun sounded Jim exploded out of the blocks. He was well ahead when tragedy struck. Somehow Jim tripped and crashed into the cinders. The other runners passed him in a flash and he was out of the race. But to everyone's amazement, he didn't quit. With knees and elbows scuffed and bleeding he finished the race. The fans stood and roared their approval as Ryan came limping across the finish line. Jim Ryan was the hero of the '72 Olympics. Not because he won, but because he refused to quit. That's diligence.

A heart surrendered to God's wisdom, prudence that results in a mind informed with the insights from investigation, and hands diligently committed to the decision that has been made—these are the essentials of wise decision-making.

—Donald G. Shoff

Practicing God's Word

Of the 640 chapels I attended during my student years at Dallas Seminary, the most memorable service was the very first one. The speaker was Dr. John F. Walvoord, president of the Seminary. His message did not contain an overwhelming or even a new thought. But after twelve years in the ministry I still marvel at his simple and yet profound discourse. Quite simply, Dr. Walvoord emphasized that mature Christian living is built upon the foundation of a consistent personal study of the Bible.

D.L. Moody captures this same idea in his little classic of 1895, *Pleasure and Profit of Bible Study*: "A man stood up in one of our meetings and said he hoped for enough out of the series of meetings I was having to last him all of his life. I told him he might as well try to eat enough breakfast at one time to last his lifetime."

Consistent personal Bible study doesn't sound difficult, but without it Christians can't experience the abundant spiritual life. Billy Graham recently noted a survey that indicated only 12% of the people who say they believe the Bible actually read it every day, 34% read it only once a week, and 42% read it sporadically. Passivity seems to be the theme of the day. Most Christians aren't involved beyond the typical spoon-feeding that takes place on Sunday morning.

It is a fact that most Christians spend more time with their daily newspapers than they do with the Scriptures. "Not enough time" is the excuse. Studies indicate that 80% of the U.S. population receives a newspaper at home and that 69% of these people spend over thirty minutes a day reading that paper. If this same amount of time was spent reading the Bible, the entire Bible could be read once a year and the New Testament could be covered twice!

The average American believes in the Bible but if you tried to determine the amount of his belief by the amount of Scripture read between Sundays, you would find that the amount could be printed on the back cover of a church bulletin. Apparently, temporal interests outrank eternal truths.

Perhaps blame could be placed on the scientific gadget-filled generation in which we live. The media generates on-time solutions to on-going problems. We've come to expect and even rely on instant coffee and immediate answers. So why not have "instant spirituality" and "immediate wisdom"? It's obvious that a deep chasm has developed between belief and behavior.

Unfortunately the result of this contradiction between belief and behavior is guilt. Guilt tells us that something is morally or spiritually wrong. It serves as a warning signal that, when not heeded, may lead to crisis. This means that many people study the Word of God out of duty in response to guilt, and not out of devotion in response to love. This is negative motivation and is almost never a forceful or enduring motivation. In fact, if the positive motivation methods Paul used in the Book of Romans were followed, we would have many more tuned-in Bible students today. According to Paul, doctrine is first and duty is second. We need to understand "why we should do" before we pursue "what we should do." The solution to the motivation needed for personal Bible study lies in the rearrangement of belief and behavior.

WHY STUDY THE BIBLE?

Why should we study the Bible? Perhaps the best way to discover this is to examine what it would be like if we did not have the Bible. What would be different in our lives if the impact of the Word of God was gone?

First we would lose God's standards for what is right and wrong. What would be ethical, moral, or immoral? We would quickly become a lawless society. Why shouldn't we cheat if we could get away with it? Why shouldn't we steal if we had the opportunity? Why shouldn't we murder?

Several years ago I had the opportunity to see firsthand how precious and powerful the Word of God is. I was ministering with a group of friends in a remote village in the jungles of Bolivia. One night a missionary asked me if I would like to attend a service.

"Sure," I said. "Where is the church?

"Oh, its right here," he replied with a knowing smile. He told me the service would begin at eight.

A few minutes went by and I looked at my watch. "It's past eight."

"Don't worry. The people will come."

And they did. For the next half hour men, women, children, and even a few dogs began to come and sit together.

"When is the service going to begin?" I asked.

"Why it's already begun."

Presently, a little man unwrapped a small object he had been holding close to his breast. It was a copy of First Corinthians. He stood and preached for half an hour as my friend interpreted for me. It was a moving message. Then a second man stood and spoke from the village's only copy of Ephesians. Finally a third man stood and preached still another sermon. Three sermons in one service!

Suddenly a lady on my left began to weep. God was dealing with her. She stood and openly confessed that she had been unfaithful to her husband, had repented, and had asked him to forgive her. Now she was crying out for forgiveness from her brothers and sisters in Christ. She was restored and then received in love by that church. The scene was straight from the Book of Acts. Two years earlier that church had no standards, no means of reconciliation, no Bible, and no idea of right and wrong!

DISCOVERING GOD'S SOLUTIONS

Second, if we didn't have the Bible, we would lose God's solution to life's ultimate questions. We would ask several unanswerable questions. Who am I? Where did I come from? Where am I going? Why am I here? Any solutions offered would have to come as a result of our own theories and cosmic guessing games. Perhaps we would seek for answers in a test tube. Imagine waking up every morning and wondering why you are here. We would be lost.

The great philosophers of our age who don't believe the truths of the Bible come to the conclusion that life is absurd. We happened by accident; our lives have no meaning and what happens to us after death has no significance. I remember one of these philosophers surmising that the only logical thing to do with that kind of absurdity is to end everything. He committed suicide. God's Word is true but where there is no revelation the people will perish.

Without the Word of God we not only lose the solution to life's problems, we also lose God's syllabus for successful living. The world defines success as productivity measured by return on investments, market share, and new products. If you do well in these areas you are considered a success. But without the Bible I would never have known that in God's estimation profits, investments, market share, and new products have nothing to do with how I am to measure my success.

Giving to the poor, caring for the sick, helping the widowed and orphaned, and loving others as I love myself are the measures of my success. The world's definition of success is temporal; it is man's way and it's changeable. God's definition is eternal and unchangeable.

DISCOVERING GOD THROUGH THE SCRIPTURES

If we didn't have the Bible what else would we lose? We would lose God's stimulation for evangelism, revival, and reformation. Without the Bible we would never share the gospel message that Jesus Christ died on the cross for our sins. People would never be saved because we would never know they were lost. We would have no message. Our churches would pass along social messages from sources like Time and Newsweek. We'd be up-to-date on current issues about the economy, the oil crisis, and world conditions but there would be no preaching against sin, there would be no accountability, and there would be no salvation.

If we had no Bible the greatest loss would be God's secret for knowing Him. Our hearts would yearn for God but the pathway to the Father would not have the light of the Scriptures to point the way. A sense of dread and despair would settle on us.

I have spent hours reading the book of Psalms. God has used this book to break me down, build me up, and give me the assurance that someone has walked this way before. But how could I have experienced these precious moments in a world that had no Bible? The world 's loss would be great indeed.

The point is, however, that we do have a Bible. And we need to be developing a daily walk with God. I believe in the power of God to change lives through His Word.

While serving on the faculty at Multnomah Bible College, I asked a colleague if he would meet with me weekly to pass along the insights he had gained from his eighty-seven years as a Christian. I assured him that if he would meet with me I would faithfully share his insights with the next generation. His response surprised me. "No, Bruce. But I will help you to use the Word of God to become more like Christ." To him, knowing the content was not enough. Applying the principles was the key.

For all practical purposes, most people live in a world with no Bible. Even Christians ignore the Scriptures, remaining content to have someone else read a few passages from the pulpit on Sundays. Nonbelievers are rarely challenged by biblical truth. Instead, they are offered a slick, packaged "gospel" that emphasizes the good life while ignoring the Good Book.

I, like Dr. Walvoord, believe that consistent daily Bible study is the path to spiritual growth. How about you?

—*Bruce H. Wilkinson*

Equipping for the Christian Life

Lord, who may dwell in your sanctuary?
Who may live on your holy hill?
He whose walk is blameless and who does what is righteous,
Who speaks the truth from his heart and has no slander on his tongue,
Who does his neighbor no wrong and casts no slur on his fellow man,
Who despises a vile man and honors those who fear the Lord,
Who keeps his oath, even when it hurts,
Who lends his money without usury and does not accept a bribe
against the innocent.
He who does these things will never be shaken.
(PSALM 15)

King David understood the importance of maturity. Would you like to have a mature spiritual leader to help you along in your spiritual growth? Well, you will find in this section of the book a variety of excellent articles written by wise, experienced Christians. Rely on them! They want to help equip you for the Christian life.

Is the Holy Spirit Transforming You?

Was it some crash course they took, some upbeat seminar on leadership? No. Then maybe it was really the work of angels, but the disciples were given credit for it? No, the biblical record clearly states that it was the same group of once-timid men Jesus had trained. Perhaps some high-powered "heavenly drug," some miracle-inducing chemical, was inserted into their bodies that changed the men overnight? Enough!

There is only one intelligent answer: It was the arrival and the empowerment of the Holy Spirit. He alone transformed those frightened, awkward, reluctant men into strong-hearted, unintimidated, invincible prophets of God. Instead of feeling abandoned and orphaned, they became directly involved in changing the world. Once the Spirit took up residence with them, once He was given complete control of their lives, He put His agenda into full operation, and they were never the same. They embodied His dynamic. They no longer held back or stood in the shadows or looked for excuses not to be engaged in obeying their Lord's mandate to "go and make disciples of all nations." Once "another Helper" came, transformation occurred—immediate transformation.

To appreciate this transformation as fully as we should, we need a "before and after" portrait of the men who walked with Christ. Let's start with the scene at the Last Supper.

Judas had left. The meal had been eaten. The taste of bread and wine was still on their tongues as their Lord began to unveil the reality of His departure. Their stomachs churned with the thought of going on without Him. They were troubled, even though He urged them, "Let not your heart be troubled…" (John 14:1). They were confused, as Thomas's question reveals, "Lord, we do not know where You are going, how do we know the way? "(John 14:5). Later, Peter denied Him…and he was the leader of the group (Mark 14:53-72)! Ultimately, when push came to shove, "all the disciples left Him and fled" (Matt. 26:56). Every last one of them deserted their Master.

At His resurrection they were surprised at the thought of His body not being in the tomb. And that same evening, after knowing of His resurrection, the disciples were hiding out together behind closed doors. Why? They were hiding "for fear of the Jews" (John 20:10). If that were not enough, even after He came among some of them, Thomas firmly resisted, declaring he had to witness everything firsthand or (in his own words) "I will not believe" (John 20:25).

Troubled, confused, bothered, disloyal, fearful, doubting… these men were anything but valiant warriors for Christ. Prior to the Spirit's transforming work, they were wimps! Prior to the coming of the Spirit and His transforming presence in their lives, they bore all the marks of men least likely to survive, to say nothing of succeed.

PERSONAL TRANSFORMATION

Jesus knew His men much better than they knew themselves. He knew Judas was deceptive and Peter was rash. He knew Thomas struggled with doubt and that John was a dreamer. He knew how petty and competitive they were… how selfish and fragile. He knew the final 11 thought of themselves as fiercely loyal, but when the chips were down, they would slink into the shadows. He knew that a new dynamic was imperative if His mission of the establishment of the church and the evangelization of the world had any hope of being accomplished. Therefore, when He promised "another Helper," He meant One who would transform them from the inside out. He knew that the only way they would ultimately do "greater works" than He had accomplished would be through the Spirit's presence and power.

Little did the disciples realize how much they lacked. Most of them (perhaps all of them) thought they had more going for them than was the case. Peter, remember, assured his Lord, "I will lay down my life for You," and "Even though all may fall away, yet I will not (John 13:37; Mark 14:29). What a comedown when they later realized that they were not nearly as resilient or loyal or courageous as they had assured Him they would be.

We've all been there, haven't we? About the time we get out on a limb thinking we're pretty capable, we get sawed off by a sudden and embarrassing discovery. At that point we realize we aren't as effective or competent as we had convinced ourselves we were.

When the Spirit of God bore His way into the lives of those awaiting His arrival in that upstairs room somewhere in Jerusalem, His transforming presence was immediately evident. As I read what transpired in the early part of the Book of Acts, I am able to identify at least four transforming changes among those who received the Spirit.

First, their human frailties were transformed into supernatural gifts and abilities.

From the moment the Holy Spirit arrived, nothing about the disciples remained the same. When His power, His dynamic (the Greek term is dunamis, from which we get "dynamite") fell upon them, they even spoke in another language (Acts 2:1-4).

This experience completely revolutionized their lives. Those who had been troubled and fearful no longer struggled with those feelings. The once frightened, unsure, confused, timid men never again evidence such inadequacies. From that time on they were faithful and confident in their God. They were transformed.

Suddenly they were able to speak in languages not their own. So clear and accurate were those languages that those who heard them were shocked (Acts 2:6-11). It is noteworthy that the original term used for "language" in verses 6 and 8 is the Greek word dialektos, from which we get "dialect." Remarkable! Those untrained, monolingual Galileans were suddenly able to communicate in the native dialects of individuals from regions far removed from Palestine. And if that were not enough, some in the group were given the supernatural ability to touch another life and restore physical health (3:1-8).

Before we get the idea that these men suddenly "glowed" with some kind of aura or in some other way appeared different, however, let's hear the testimony of Peter:

> "Men of Israel, why do you marvel at this, or why do you gaze at us, as if by our own power or piety we had made him walk?" (3:12).

Clearly, Peter and John were still "just plain Peter and John." They didn't promote themselves as miracle workers or divine healers. They seemed to be as amazed over this as those who witnessed what had happened. Having been transformed by the Helper whom Jesus had sent, the disciples did not turn the scene into a man-glorifying sideshow.

Second, their fearful reluctance was transformed into bold confidence.

Remember an earlier scene when these same men, afraid of being found out by the Jews, hid silently behind closed doors? The last thing they wanted was to be pointed out as followers of Jesus. They were frozen in fear.

No longer. According to this narrative, they poured into the public streets of Jerusalem preaching Christ and urging total strangers to repent and to believe in the name of Jesus (Acts 2:38-40). Later, when Peter and John had been arrested and were being interrogated, their quiet confidence did not go unnoticed:

"Now as they observed the confidence of Peter and John, and understood that they were uneducated and untrained men, they were marveling, and began to recognize them as having been with Jesus" (Acts 4:13).

The followers of Jesus didn't look any different physically. They didn't suddenly become learned men. Nor were they abruptly made cultured and sophisticated. No, they remained rawboned fishermen and a couple of "good ol' boys." But deep within their beings, down inside, they were nothing like they had been. They were transformed.

Third, their fears and intimidation were transformed into a sense of invincibility.

Webster states that intimidation is timidity, being afraid, overawed, deterred with threats. These men, having been invaded by God's Spirit, were none of the above.

Instead of running from the public, they ran toward them.

Instead of hoping not to be seen, they exhorted total strangers to repent.

Instead of being frightened by insults, warnings, and threats, they stood face-to-face with their accusers and did not blink. When told to keep it quiet, they answered unflinchingly, "We must obey God rather than men" (Acts 5:29).

Even when called before the Council, the supreme ruling body of the Jews, this handful of "uneducated and untrained men" stood like steers in a blizzard. They weren't about to back down, even if they were forced to stand before some of the same prejudiced and cruel judges who had unjustly manipulated the trials against Jesus of Nazareth. They refused to be overawed. Such invincible courage!

Where does one get such boldness today? From studying at Oxford or Yale or Harvard? Hardly. How about from reading the biographies of great men and women? That may stimulate our minds, but it cannot transform our lives. Then perhaps the secret of such boldness is a mentor, someone whose walk with

God is admirable and consistent? Again, as helpful as heroes and models may be, their influence cannot suddenly infuse us with invincible courage. The Spirit of God alone is able to make that happen.

It was not until He came and filled those frail and frightened men with His supernatural "dynamic" that they were genuinely (and permanently) changed deep within—transformed.

Fourth, their lonely, grim feelings of abandonment were transformed into joyful perseverance.

On the heels of their second arrest, Peter and John let out all the stops! Refusing to tell their frowning accusers what they wanted to hear, they looked them squarely in the eye and pulled no punches.

I find it absolutely amazing that those men, once so petty and competitive and self-centered, are now so strong-hearted, so incredibly confident. So did the officials.

The Jewish leaders must have thought, "A firm warning, a bloody flogging, and this strong threat ought to shut them up for good!"

It didn't.

The flogging, the warning, and the threat merely fueled the fire of their determination. In fact, they left "rejoicing." And upon their return to the company of their friends, joy filled everyone's hearts, not sadness, not disillusionment. The wimps had become warriors! (Acts 5:41-42).

Why? Because the disciples had been radically changed. Not merely motivated or momentarily mesmerized—they were transformed.

HOW IT HAPPENED

But how? What did it? How could these same men who had earlier run for cover now stand tall, refusing to be backed down or even whipped down?

No course was taught. No cheerleader led the disciples in mindbending chants that gave them a positive attitude. No change in environment brought about their transformation. It was the Spirit of God and nothing else. It was the life-changing, attitude-altering, dynamic power of the living Lord that swept over them and became permanently resident within them.

Remember Jesus' promises? Let me quickly review several of them:

"Truly, truly, I say to you; he who believes in Me, the works that I do shall he do also; and greater works than these shall he do; because I go to the Father" (John 14:12).

"And I will ask the Father, and He will give you another Helper, that He may be with you forever; that is the Spirit of truth, whom the world cannot receive, because it does not hold Him or know Him, but you know Him because He abides with you and will be in you. I will not leave you as orphans; I will come to you" (John 14:16-18).

"But the Helper, the Holy Spirit, whom the Father will send in My name, He will teach you all things, and bring to your remembrance all that I said to you" (John 14:26).

"But you shall receive power when the Holy Spirit has come upon you; and you shall be My witnesses both in Jerusalem, and in all Judea and Samaria, and even to the remotest part of the earth" (Acts 1:8).

God kept His word. And the disciples were never the same.

ARE YOU BEING TRANSFORMED?

Is the Spirit of God being allowed to transform your life? In case you think that's an irrelevant question, read the opening words of Romans 12:

"I urge you therefore, brethren, by the mercies of God, to present your bodies a living and holy sacrifice, acceptable to God, which is your spiritual service of worship. And do not be conformed to this world, but be transformed by the renewing of your mind, that you may prove what the will of God is, that which is good and acceptable and perfect."

Don't miss the twofold command: "Do not be conformed...but be *transformed* (italics mine).

Are you honest enough with yourself to answer my question? Is the Holy Spirit being allowed to transform your life?

There are only two possible answers: yes or no. If your answer is no, there are two possible reasons. Either you do not have the Spirit within you (i.e., you're not a Christian), or He is there but you prefer to live life on your own. Let me urge you to do some soul-searching.

Speaking in tongues or healing the lame or explaining the supernatural phenomena recorded in the early section of the Book of Acts are intriguing subjects and, or course, important. But they can so easily become theological smoke screens, points of debate, and safe places in which to hide from the hard, probing question regarding you and your personal life.

My main concern is the Spirit's main agenda: Are you allowing Him to transform your life? If not, why not?

Flying closer to the flame may seem risky. . .but it is the best place to be. In fact, it is the only way to live.

—*Charles R. Swindoll*

Are You Out of Balance?

"I see the light!"

"No, I see the light!"

"You both missed it, I see the light!"

Unfortunately, many discussions of biblical truth and Christian conduct follow this sad pattern of absolute authority and mutual condemnation.

But looking at the Bible is like looking at the facets of a diamond—they reflect light from every angle and every side. To truly appreciate a diamond, you must stand above it and see all the light the diamond is reflecting.

So it is with our understanding and application of the Word of God. We need to understand and apply the whole counsel of God as revealed to us in the Scriptures, to balance Scripture against Scripture in order to achieve balance in our walk with God.

If you are like me, you strive for balance in your Christian life. Yet we all frequently seem to miss the center of the pendulum's swing. At times we are either on the left or right—some just slightly, some a little more.

Why can't we hit center and stay on it? What is the balanced Christian life?

Defining a balanced Christian life is not easy, and it's difficult to pursue what we cannot define. The dictionary doesn't give us much help. Even theologians and Bible scholars frequently fail to add significant insight because often they are trying to teach essential doctrines or interpret Bible passages that have been neglected or misinterpreted.

THE BALANCED CHRISTIAN LIFE

What is the balanced Christian life? Is it a life of do's and don'ts? Is it a "free" life of exercising the liberty we have in Christ with no restrictions? Or is it an excruciatingly disciplined existence of emulating the perfection of a sinless saint?

Recently I asked several believers, "What do you think is the balanced Christian life?" One person responded, "God, family, work, play." Another person said, "Less emphasis on Bible knowledge and more emphasis on Christlike character." A third suggested, "Knowledge, character, and skills."

While each of these answers is excellent, each applies to the person giving it and not necessarily to other Christians. What one person needs for a balanced Christian life might be completely different from the needs of another.

Perhaps we could compare living a balanced Christian life to eating a balanced diet. Such a diet would have the correct amounts of all kinds of foods necessary for proper health. It would be simple to follow by planning menus which contain foods from the basic food groups.

In the same way, the balanced Christian life requires the correct amounts of the right kinds of "foods" necessary for spiritual health. However, the difficulty lies in the fact that God has not given us a simplified list of the basic "food" groups from which to plan our lives.

Because Proverbs commands us to search for truth as for hidden treasure, it's not surprising that we don't find such explicit lists in Scripture. What we discover through an investment of time and effort will be of far greater value—with greater motivation to follow in our lives—than something handed to us on a silver platter.

Still, the analogy of the balanced diet is useful. We need a variety of activities and attitudes to maintain a healthy Christian life and exhibit balanced, mature behavior, as well as an acceptable testimony.

Basically, I believe Scripture reveals there are four things each believer must practice on a daily and regular basis to maintain the balanced Christian life. And even though these activities are the same for each believer, they may be practiced in different ways, different styles, and different settings.

What's amazing is that these activities most often will reveal the exact daily "menu" to be followed to ensure good spiritual health. These four concepts are quite simple and rather basic. They don't sound overly exciting and are definitely nothing new. Perhaps you've heard them countless times before. But the question is, have you been practicing them? The key to their success in one's life is that they be consistently applied.

A recent study showed that regular physical exercise of even the mild variety of a slow walk proved to be of greater value than marathon running and jogging. Our spiritual needs are similar. During a crisis, many of us find great bursts of spiritual energy—but they soon pass. Our great need is for daily, consistent fellowship with God through practice of these four essential concepts.

Consistent Prayer

1. First on my list for a balanced Christian life is prayer—simple but sincere communion with God. When we come to the Lord daily in quiet prayer with a spirit open to learn, we frequently will leave with the Christlike attitudes and convictions needed for that day. I heartily suggest that this "quiet time" with the Lord be spent at the beginning of the day, though each person must determine what is best for his or her schedule and needs. The key, as mentioned before, is that it be consistent.

I would like to suggest a format that has proved effective for many. First, begin with an attitude of prayer that will prepare your heart to meet God and to receive your spiritual food for the day.

Then, an easy plan to follow would be to pattern your prayer time from the acronym "ACTS." A is for "adoration,"

C for "confession, " T for "thanksgiving", and S for "supplication".

This simple guide is in no way inspired, but the activities it includes are. Scripture teaches us that we are to come into the Lord's courts with praise and into His gates with thanksgiving (Ps. 100:4-5). If we confess our sins God will cleanse us from all unrighteousness (1 John 1:9) so that no wall will come between God and us in our communication. And in Philippians 4:6 we are enjoined to be anxious for nothing but in everything by prayer and supplication with thanksgiving make our requests known to God.

Obviously, the practice of consistent prayer will help mold our thoughts and hearts to conform with the character of Christ, and will, on a daily basis, prepare us for the second essential concept.

CONCENTRATED BIBLE STUDY

2. Having communed with God, we're ready in mind and heart to come to His Word for direction and enablement on a daily basis. And we should come prepared to learn.

No one would dream of going to a class or an important meeting without paper and pencil or perhaps even a tape recorder. Likewise we should be prepared to record the message God gives us from His Word.

Perhaps it will be a new understanding of a problem in your life. Maybe a conviction needs to be dealt with in order to maintain purity. Possibly God's Spirit will shed light on a passage of Scripture that seemed a mystery before.

Regardless, we need to take seriously the promise that all Scripture is inspired (literally, God-breathed) and is profitable for doctrine, reproof, correction, and training in righteousness (2 Tim. 3:16). And let's not forget that God's Word will never return to Him void. It always will accomplish something in our lives.

Remember, too, that the Bible is the best commentary on itself. It is, therefore, critical that we interpret the Bible in light of itself. We can only do this as we become familiar with the whole Bible from beginning to end, Genesis 1:1 to Revelation 22:21.

I would recommend in your daily program of Bible reading that you start at the beginning of the Bible and set a reasonable goal that will enable you to maintain steady progress through the Scriptures. Read through the entire Bible, from beginning to end, then start over again. You'll be amazed how knowledgeable you become about God's Word.

As we concentrate, day by day, on our study of God's Word, it will be inevitable that we will come upon the third crucial area of a balanced Christian Life.

Continual Obedience

3. Because this is an area in which the keeping of a set of extrabiblical rules sometimes is confused with true biblical obedience, we need to be cautious.

However, for a believer to spend daily, regular time in prayer and in the Scriptures is to ensure that his or her obedience to the Lord will be biblical, from the heart, and motivated by a sincere love for Christ rather than erroneously trying to "earn" God's favor.

In seeking to lovingly obey God from the heart, we need to remember that obedience involves every area of our thoughts, words, and actions. What we do must be consistent with what we say. What we say should reveal how we think. And how we think should be consistent with the nature and character of God.

We need to mindful, too, of our responsibility to obey God's more difficult instructions in Scripture, such as a consistent, verbal witness for Christ, and a life that is centered around the eternal rather than the temporal.

But, most important, our continual obedience must be based in God's enablement rather than our own, and must depend on God's gracious provision for our human weaknesses and shortcomings.

As we learn from Ephesians 2:10, "We are God's workmanship, created in Christ Jesus to do good works, which God prepared in advance for us to do."

The simple fact that all of us, as believers, are included in God's purpose brings us to the fourth and final concept.

CONCERNED FELLOWSHIP

4. As one Christian speaker said with great insight, "There is no such thing as a Lone Ranger Christian." His point, of course, was that it is neither God's design nor His intent that a believer live out a solitary, isolated Christian existence.

The dangers inherent in isolating oneself from other believers characterize imbalance and include a critical or haughty spirit, a legalistic attitude, or pride. Some even may avoid other believers out of guilt of the Holy Spirit's conviction of a specific sin or sins.

But the truth is that God has designed believers to function corporately as His body on earth and has given them various gifts and talents to carry out that purpose for their good and His glory. To forsake the crucial facet of concerned, reciprocal fellowship is to hurt our own balanced walk with Christ as well as hinder the function of Christ's church.

On the other hand, to be consistently involved in a vital body of believers where Christ is honored and His Word taught is to enjoy a balanced, well-rounded Christian experience. This is particularly true when the crucial ingredients of prayer, Bible study, and obedience are also being practiced on a personal basis.

SO WHAT?

Having briefly covered the "how-to's," perhaps a few cautions are in order as a preventive against imbalances. If the procedure for having a balance Christian life is so simple, why are some Christians struggling with it?

The answer is that, generally speaking, we all are more easily influenced by others than by God. It is far easier to read and heed the information and injunctions given by a current popular book, teacher, or philosophy than to faithfully go through God's Word line by line and word by word to listen for His voice. But God never promised it would be easy. Remember that we are searching for hidden treasure.

What God reveals to another person concerning his or her balanced Christian life may be of some interest and value to you, but what God reveals personally to you as you come to Him and His Word is crucial. No one else can do it for you, and there is no substitute.

Leading a balanced Christian life involves a simple but important procedure that allows God to show you daily the different kinds of activities and attitudes needed to ensure a healthy Christian life. Your needs will differ from others and will change with circumstances and time.

But the concepts above are to be lifetime habits, ones which will keep us in balance until we go to be with the Lord.

—Jerry Benjamin

Divine Alternatives!

On both a national and local scale, our society is deteriorating spiritually, ethically, and morally. As Christians, therefore, we are placed in the position of having to confront and address a culture that conflicts with our divine order. For example, our children are no longer being taught the evolutionary "theory" in public schools; they are being taught the evolutionary "fact." Twenty years ago Time magazine would not have printed articles that are pro homosexuality; now they appear as a matter of course.

The problem is compounded when we realize that more is being done in Christian work and more money is being spent on gospel outreach than ever before. Evangelism may not be what it ought to be, but it's reaching more people today and doing it better. There are more radio broadcasts, more written materials, and more Bible-teaching churches than ever before. Even so, the situation in the world keeps getting worse. The valid question is, Why isn't evangelism changing this deteriorating situation? If more is happening evangelistically by Christians, why is the world not getting better?

When you look at what God says in His Word, you learn that He clearly teaches us that this world will not improve. Paul told Timothy that as the latter days approach, mankind is going to become more arrogant, unloving, and brutal, holding to a form of godliness but denying its power (2 Tim. 3:1-5). Although the activities of Christians may produce revivals that deter the eroding process, Scripture teaches that the results of these awakenings are only temporary.

This reality produces a dilemma for the Christian. To state it simply, since the world is going to deteriorate regardless of my efforts to change it, how involved should I get in this world in an attempt to make a difference? The answer is that the Christian should provide an evangelistic alternative so that the deteriorating world system can see what God looks like in the midst.

The goal of the evangelistic alternative is not to save the world from destruction, because that goal can never be achieved. On the other hand, the world must not be left to self-destruct just because we know about its ultimate end. Rather, our goal is to give the world a clear option. We do this by presenting a picture of what the world could be if it operated under divine jurisdiction. The problem is that the world is in darkness—but God wants to establish a lighthouse. He wants to take the light to the darkness rather than waiting for the darkness to assess its own status and seek out the light. That's evangelism!

The Bible validates this philosophy of maintaining an evangelistic presence in the world in Daniel chapter 11. There Daniel is writing about the persecution Israel would endure throughout its history. He taught that Israel would be cast about from one Gentile nation to another, and the Jews would be persecuted and abused. As Daniel moves toward the end of the section, a message from verse 32 jumps out at us because it seems to be totally incongruous with what the content is saying: "…but the people who know their God will firmly resist him." In the midst of a deteriorating situation, if there is a group of people who know their God, they will be able to be strong (internal fortitude) and do great things (external actions). They will be able to live successfully in a deteriorating situation.

One popular example of this is found earlier in the Book of Daniel. This illustration presents a perfect picture of what the Christian stance ought to be whenever he or she is exerting an evangelistic influence on this ungodly culture. The Book of Daniel opens with Daniel out of his religious environment. Nebuchadnezzar had decided that he would re-educate and reform some of the sharper Jewish young men so that he could place them in leadership positions in his kingdom. One of the men he decided to train was Daniel.

The king intended to "Babylonize" these young Israelites so they would forget their past and acquiesce to their new cultural environment. His plan was for them to become Babylonians who reflected a Babylonian world view through the educational process, gainful employment at the "executive level," and heretical religious accommodations. However, verse eight says: "But Daniel resolved not to defile himself with the royal food and wine."

Nebuchadnezzar had offered Daniel the world. Above all his peers, Daniel could have had the best. He could have lived in the king's house, become the king's right-hand administrator, eaten the king's food, and possessed the king's knowledge—things he never could have expected as a slave. However, Daniel determined that he was not going to eat the king's meat.

Why did he decide that? Because God had already said in the Book of Exodus that the Israelites could not eat meat offered to idols (34:15), and that they could not eat certain kinds of meat at all. Daniel, therefore, had a divine perspective. He knew what God had spoken about eating meat. This suggests that God expects His people, who live in a secular society, not to be conformed to this world. What is needed today is a group of people who do not "eat the king's meat," who do not "buy into" the king's system, and who do not go along with the immorality of the day. Our society desperately needs people who do not accept and follow the lifestyle and the deteriorating role of today's system.

Much has been written about the fact that Daniel did not eat the king's meat. But notice what Daniel did do. He did get the king's education, he took the job, and he changed his name. Why would he only go halfway? Why didn't he just look at Nebuchadnezzar and say, "Look, I don't want to be part of this ungodly system. God is going to judge you and the other Gentile nations. So not only will I not eat your meat, I am also going to refuse your job and your salary. I'm not going to wear your clothes and I'm not going to go to your schools. Instead, I'm going to separate myself from your whole system"? The reason Daniel didn't say any of that is because all God commanded was not to eat the meat. God doesn't mind us being in the world; He just wants us to make sure that our influence is on the world. Thus, Daniel provided

Babylon an alternative. He let an ungodly Babylonian king know what God looks like by providing an alternative. This means that a Christian secretary sitting at her desk is not like the other secretaries around her. Nor is the Christian lawyer in his office. God does not forbid us from becoming secretaries, lawyers, doctors, politicians, presidents, or entertainers. All he says is not to eat the meat.

The reason Christianity is not being heard today is because we do not have many "alternatives" in the world. We have churches that are full on Sunday mornings, but that is not how Christianity is lived. Christianity is lived in the marketplace. To the degree that the believer lives for Christ in the world is how much one is counter to the culture. A believer runs against the grain of what may be acceptable to society, and he or she should do so without apology.

An important epilogue to our story is that Daniel offered an alternative to Melzar, who was responsible for the young Jewish men. Daniel requested very politely to be tested. This test consisted of being allowed to go on a vegetable diet that did not include the king's meat. The essence of his request was to show what God could do through His people's obedience. The results of this experiment were staggering: "At the end of the ten days they looked healthier and better nourished than any of the young men who ate the royal food" (Dan. 1:15).

In other words, being God's alterative made God look good, made God's people look good, made Melzar look good, and—of great importance—began the process of establishing a divine testimony before the king.

If men and women are going to come to Christ, it will be because God's people have taken the initiative and "run with the ball." We need to run with it in spite of the opposition and confrontation of an opposing culture. And we need to run with it in love and with the determination to make a difference. If Christians are no different from the cultures of which they are a part, then the people in those cultures will not sense that they are missing anything. Some will reject us; others will accept us. But none should be able to ignore us if we are God's evangelistic alternative. Like Daniel, we too will make a difference by conforming to divine standards in a secular society.

—*Anthony Evans*

And Two at Parbar

I used it only as a joke. I would tell people it was the most familiar and important verse in the Bible, one which would solve all their problems. When someone would want to argue about eternal security or some other point of doctrine, I would facetiously tell him, "Just read I Chronicles 26:18 and it will solve all your problems." Of course, it would. For by the time he had figured out what the verse meant, he had forgotten his problem. In the King James Version it reads, "At Parbar westward, four at the causeway, and two at Parbar." Isn't that beautiful?

One day it occurred to me that if all Scripture is profitable, then I Chronicles 26:18 must be more than just a joke. As I studied the passage, I found that it illustrated some exciting biblical principles. As I took this illustration seriously and put these principles to work, I found that they transformed my life and the life of my church.

The original historical context of the passage finds David giving orders for the temple. With this military genius and organizational ability, David not only designed the temple, he also designed the service for the temple. After he gave orders

concerning the priesthood, he told the rest of the Levites t
they also had work to do. Remember, the Levites were the
holy family. All priests had to be Levites, but not all Levites
were priests. David saw to it that every member of the family
of Levi had a ministry.

In verse 1 of this chapter he talks about the porters. These
were not just gatekeepers. They were temple guards. The
temple's gold and silver utensils and other valuables needed
protection. Verse 17 says, "There were six Levites a day on the
east, four a day on the north, four a day on the south and two
at a time at the storehouse."

It's likely that Parbar was a suburb of Jerusalem. A gate
opened up to that suburb, and since the temple was built up
from the lower land, there was a causeway which led up to the
gate itself. Two guards were stationed at the suburb of Parbar
and four more were at the causeway which adjoined the temple
gate.

That is the basic meaning of the verse. But this passage
also illustrates at least five principles which I believe are
extremely relevant to us today. I trust you will burn them on
the frontal lobes of your brain and never forget them.

First, every believer has a job. Like the Levites, believers
also are a holy family (1 Pet. 2:9). And as part of that holy
family, every believer has work to do within the church of
Jesus Christ. An Italian economist developed a theory that in
any country 20 percent of the people will hold 80 percent of
the work. (Also, 20 percent of the people may give you 80
percent of the problems!)

Unfortunately, the church often has not been able to beat
those averages. In an interview, a coach once defined football
as "22 men running around on a field who desperately need
rest, watched by 50,000 fans who desperately need exercise."
All too often that sounds like a description of the church
today. But God did not design it that way. God has given
every believer a gift. We all have a job to do.

every job is important. In II Chronicles 35:15, [...] not allowed to leave their posts. It was as neces- [...] Parbar as it was to guard the Gate Beautiful. [...] imagine someone thinking Parbar was not that [...]

[...] that General Solomon cannot sleep one night. He makes a tour of the temple to check his guards. As he comes upon the west side through the suburb of Parbar he stops, expecting to be greeted by two guards. Instead, there is silence. As he walks up the causeway to the temple he is met by four flashing spears and a cry, "Who goes there?" He identifies himself and asks, "Where are the two guards at Parbar?" One of the men stammers, "Well...ah...General Solomon...ah...Parbar isn't that big an assignment. Corporal Samuel's wife is having a party tonight, so...we let him off. Oh, and Corporal David had company for the holidays so he couldn't make it either."

The next morning as the sun is pushing away the misty fog, drums roll and bugles sound and two men are put to death. Leaving even an "unimportant" post is treason.

Paul often compared the church to a physical body (1 Cor. 12). Any member of a body has two responsibilities: to be restfully available and to be instantly obedient. If, while speaking and gesturing, my arm refused either one of these, I would look spastic. Yet many believers refuse to be restful, and they object to obedience.

The slightest task can have great significance. You may be a Sunday School teacher with five students, but your job is as important as Billy Graham preaching to millions. Dr. Bob Jones Sr. used to say that the most important light in the house is not the great chandelier in the parlor, it is the little night-light in the hall which keeps you from breaking your neck on the way to the bathroom in the middle of the night.

Whatever your job, God sees it as important.

Third, every believer must be qualified. In I Chronicles 26:4-8 the writer indicates that four qualifications are needed for any job. The first is found in verse five where God blesses Obed-edom. This blessing refers to many offspring. In other words, Obed-edom was fruitful. Every believer ought to be reproducing himself.

The second qualification, found in verse six, is courage—"They were mighty men of valor" (KJV). In many parts of the world, the church is growing in spite of persecution. The courage to risk one's life is a powerful testimony. God needs men and women who have the moral and physical courage to confront a culture steeped in moral decline and theological compromise.

The believer also must be qualified by persistence. That's what the word translated "strong" in verse seven seems to indicate: Strength through long periods of time. I thank God for the men and women who year after year faithfully serve God and never give up. A salesman once read an advertisement which told him that if he would send three hundred dollars, he would be sent the secret of how to increase his income immediately. He sent the three hundred dollars and got the answer in only two words: "Work harder." Often the secret of success is just to "keep on keeping on."

One more qualification is found in verse eight. The sons of Obed-edom were said to be able men, or capable. Remember, consecrated inefficiency is still inefficiency. Dedicated incompetence is still incompetence. God wants believers to sharpen their tools for the task, to become capable servants for Jesus Christ.

The final principle is perhaps the most important. The greatest ability is dependability. It would have been no good to have the greatest guard in the world at Parbar if he did not show up. This is especially meaningful to me because of a faithful bell ringer.

When I was 17, I lived in a little town in West Virginia and had not been in church for about three years. On a

Sunday night in February the continuous ringing of the bells of a small church nearby seemed to pull out of me all the searching unrest of my heart.

I slipped into the service that night, knelt at an altar and asked Jesus Christ to save me and to use my life. About a year later I came back to the church and asked where that faithful bell ringer lived. I climbed a hill to a little cottage and asked the old man there if he was the one who rang the bells that February night. When he assured me he was, I thanked him for his part in my salvation and told him I was going into the ministry. Great tears overflowed his eyes and began to flow down his cheeks. As he grasped my hand he said, "Son, I've been ringing those bells for over 15 years and you are the first person who has ever thanked me." I hope I was not the last. His dependability brought me to Jesus.

May we continually be aware that we each have an important role to play, that every job is important, that we should seek to be qualified, and that the greatest ability is dependability. "At Parbar westward, four at the causeway, and two at Parbar."

—*James A. Borror*

What Are You Doing?

When Nicolo Paganini willed his elegant violin to the city of Genoa, he demanded that it never be used. It was a gift designated for preservation, but not destined for service.

When the resurrected Christ willed His spiritual gifts to the children of God, He commanded that they be used. They were gifts not destined for preservation, but destined for service (Eph. 4:7-16).

If you are a child of God through faith in Jesus Christ, the Bible teaches that the Holy Spirit has given you at least one spiritual gift (see 1 Cor. 12:6, 7, 11). This spiritual gift is a supernaturally bestowed ability to serve God in a particular way. Five key passages list for us these spiritual gifts: 1 Corinthians 12:8-10; 1 Corinthians 12:28; Romans 12:1-8; Ephesians 4:11 and 1 Peter 4:11.

With the exception of those special phenomenal abilities given to reveal and authenticate God's Word before the Bible was completed, we find nine spiritual gifts listed which you and I might possess. Just what are these spiritual gifts?

Spiritual Gifts

The spiritual gift of faith is that God-given ability to trust Him for big things, and to pray consistently with an unusual amount of confidence.

Teaching is the capability of making clear the rich truths of the Word of God with accuracy and simplicity.

Those who have the spiritual gift of service have an unusual capacity for helping others. This might take the form of hospitality in the home, benevolence in someone else's home, or the enduring ability to work happily behind the scenes to the glory of God.

While the gift of service is normally given to followers in the economy of God, the spiritual endowment of administration is given to divinely destined leaders in the work of God. This is the special faculty of organizing, managing, and supervising in Christian service.

The gift of exhortation can take the shape of public speaking or one-to-one counseling, but always has one unique function—the edification of believers. This may include encouragement, comfort, warning, or rebuke.

Giving is also a spiritual gift. It is the special ability to give and to give and to give. Financial giving of significant proportion and regularity is primarily in view, but this gift goes beyond the realm of money. It includes a giving attitude and ability in all areas of life.

Compassion and grace characterize the believer who possesses the gift of mercy. He has the sweet ability to empathize. He has a special care for those who have fallen, those who are going though trials, and those who suffer rejection.

Evangelism is the ability to lead people to Jesus Christ with unusual effectiveness. This may take the form of personal evangelism or mass evangelism.

Finally, the gift of pastoring is the divinely given knack for shepherding the people of God. Feeding, guiding, and protecting are all part of this shepherding care.

DISCOVERING YOUR GIFT

"Great!" you might say, "but how do I know which spiritual gifts God has given to me?" That's a good question.

Many Bible teachers suggest four steps in the discovery of one's spiritual gift(s). I believe these four steps are indeed biblical, and I commend them to you.

1. Consider the desires of your heart. It is the norm that when God bestows a spiritual gift to a believer, He also gives him or her a desire to be actively engaged in that particular facet of service. In other words, if God has given you the gift of teaching, you may well have the desire to teach. If He has given you the gift of service, you could have the desire to offer an unusual amount of help to your fellow believers. In looking over the gifts mentioned in the Bible, which is the area or areas of your strongest desire?

2. Get active in the work of God now. Learning comes by doing. In order to know where you are especially gifted in the body of Christ, you must get actively involved in the body of Christ. Experience is usually a good teacher. Go to it!

3. Listen to the observational comments of Christian friends. Other believers can recognize your gift. If no one else

in the world agrees that you have the gift of teaching, it is probably safe to assume that teaching just isn't your spiritual gift. In the New Testament, a believer's spiritual gift was recognized by his fellow comrades.

4. Evaluate your own success. If you are indeed gifted in a certain area, you will experience some measure of success in that given area of ministry. If you believe that you have the gift of exhortation, and your fellow Christians leave your counsel more defeated and depressed than when they came to you, you should seriously reconsider your gift.

These four steps might sound simplistic, but they are basic. Consider the desires of your heart. Get active in the work of God now. Listen to the comments of Christian friends. Evaluate your own success.

God is not cornering you in a guessing game. As you pursue wisdom in this important matter of discernment, He will give you guidance (James 1:5). Once you have determined your spiritual gift, it is your responsibility to develop it and equip yourself for its most efficient use (2 Tim. 1:6).

USING YOUR GIFT

On the other side of the coin, may I also say that there are some dangers in the discovery and use of spiritual gifts. In considering the doctrine of spiritual gifts we ought not only to ask "What should I do?" but also "What should I not do?"

Here are four points of caution:

1. Do not substitute the use of your spiritual gift in place of love for the brethren. Paul warned in 1 Corinthians 13:1-3 that even if we have a significant spiritual gift, but have not love, the gift is worthless. Someone once said, "Service is love in working clothes." This certainly applies to the correct use of spiritual gifts.

2. Do not neglect other responsibilities by hiding behind your spiritual gift! How often I have heard someone say, "Oh,

no, I don't witness. Evangelism just isn't my spiritual gift!" While it is true that God has given a special unusual ability in evangelism to every Christian, every Christian is responsible to evangelize! Paul even told Timothy, who had the gift of pastoring, to "do the work of an evangelist" (2 Tim. 4:5). In the same way, Christians who do not possess the gift of giving are responsible to uphold the work of God financially; and Christians who do not have the gift of helps are nevertheless responsible to "do good unto all men." We must not hide behind our spiritual gifts. We are to excel in the area of our gift, but we are not free of responsibility in the other areas of service.

3. Do not take pride in your spiritual gift. Remember, a spiritual gift is given by the grace of God and for the ultimate purpose of bringing glory to Him (1 Pet. 4:10-11). "You do not do God a favor by serving Him," said Victor Nyquist, "He honors you by allowing you to serve Him."

4. Do not limit your Christian service to the area of your spiritual gift. Seek to be stretched by the Lord in your consecration.

In summary, then, the discovery and use of one's spiritual gifts are privileges and responsibilities of every believer. They are your privileges and your responsibilities.

Begin now to look for opportunities for service in your local church. It may not be an official position. In all likelihood, it will not be. Make it a point to encourage your discouraged brethren at every opportunity, if you think your gift might be exhortation. If you think your gift might be the gift of helps, you will not need to look very far for an opportunity to serve. If you think your gift is teaching, let your pastor know of your interest.

In the words of T. C. Horton, co-founder of Biola College, "You can measure what you would do for the Lord by what you do."

—Gary L. Hauck

Chosen For a Purpose

The sun had not yet risen over Jerusalem. Fog hung lightly over the ground, resisting a gentle wind's attempt to drive it back toward the sea.

In a small village, not far from the city, a man awoke, yawned widely, and stretched his slightly stiffened body. He sat up listening and concentrating. Satisfied, he nodded his head with a half-smile on his lips. The promise of an unusually mild winter's day filled him with anticipation.

He arose and bound his tunic (in which he had slept) about him with a coarse, cloth girdle. His bare feet made hardly a sound as he made his way toward the kitchen, where he greeted his parents.

Then, with his father, he left the house. As was their custom, they ate their breakfast of a cake of barley bread stuffed with olives while they walked along the Mount of Olives toward Jerusalem. His father found him a strategic place to sit and beg alms, near one of the temple's exit gates, and left him there.

As he sat alone, waiting, listening, he heard the many people approaching. It sounded like a mob. His body stiffened. He hardly breathed, trying to distinguish a word out of the many voices that might tell him the meaning of this great multitude.

Then a man asked, "Rabbi, who sinned, this man or his parents, that he should be born blind?" Another man answered, "It was neither that this man sinned, nor his parents. (John 9:2-3).

The man heard someone spit next to him. Then something warm and wet touched his eyes. A man said to him, "Go, wash in the pool of Siloam" (vv. 6-7). The blind man went and washed his eyes. He could see!

Life is strange. We go on day after day, month after month, year after year doing the same things. We often wonder about life's meaning. We occasionally do things we consider valuable, and we take pride in them. But mostly, we find life routine. We wonder: "Why am I here? Why do I live now and not three hundred years ago? Did God create me for any particular reason, or am I only an accident of birth? A victim of circumstance?"

These are legitimate questions. No one wants to feel like an accident, a fluke of nature. We long to know that we matter. God made us this way. We long to feel wanted, valuable, significant.

When no one affirms our value, we may experience anxiety, depression, and even fear. We may engage in behavior designed to call attention to ourselves. We may develop destructive habits like overeating, smoking, drinking, taking drugs, promiscuity—all in an effort to ease the pain of seemingly meaningless existence.

But we need not despair. God has provided an answer to the deepest needs and longings of our hearts. In His Word, He gave us "precious and magnificent promises "(2 Pet. 1:4).

As we learn these promises and grow in His grace, we discover God created us with and for a purpose. He considers us valuable and gives meaning to our lives. "For we are His workmanship created in Christ Jesus for good works, which God prepared beforehand, that we should walk in them" (Eph. 2:10). Let us consider these truths.

OUR SIGNIFICANCE:

"You did not choose Me, but I chose you" (John 15:16).

I have often struggled with the meaning of my life—why God created me, and why at this point in time. Will I make a mark in history, or will I live only a few troubled years and then pass off the scene, into oblivion—largely unknown and only a little mourned?

God, in His great love and kindness, impressed on me this truth: to Him I am significant. My significance rests in that He has given me eternal life in a relationship with Him. Not all receive it.

On our part, eternal life commences when we, the "whosoever wills may come," turn to Christ for that life. On God's part we are chosen in Christ before the foundation of the world. That God chose us in Christ Jesus and delivered us from the kingdom of darkness for His glory gives us significance. What greater proof of our importance to God can we find than the sacrifice of His Son (Rom. 5:8)?

OUR MEANING:

"And appointed you"

But knowing our significance to God does not always satisfy all the longings of our soul. God's love for me tells me more about Him than about me.

If loving and choosing us sum up all that God has done for us, life might indeed deteriorate into an existence with death as its ultimate end and release. However, Paul tells us in Ephesians 2:10 God created us for doing good works which He preordained for us.

At the beginning of this article, we saw a man blind from birth, sitting in a prominent place outside the temple. Anyone seeing this man begging for a living might not consider that his life held meaning. Jesus revealed to His disciples that this man was blind so God's work might be clearly shown through him. What greater honor can God give to any person than to choose that person before the foundation of the world as a channel to reveal His glory, power, and majesty?

After the blind man believed in and worshipped Jesus, we hear nothing of him again. His moment in the spotlight had passed. His life, though, still has meaning. Almost 2,000 years later, we are talking about how Jesus healed a man born blind. We still wonder at his courage in standing up to the religious rulers. We gain hope for our problems because of what Jesus did for that man whose life appeared to have no meaning. Think too about the implications for our attitudes toward the severely mentally retarded, the terminally ill, the deformed, the handicapped, or even the unborn.

OUR PURPOSE:

"That you should go and bear fruit"

God gives us purpose in living.

Jesus told His disciples He ordained them to go forth and bear fruit. Paul tells us that God created us for the purpose of doing good works. The fruit we bear includes the good works God called us to carry out in the Spirit's power.

It is the Holy Spirit who bears fruit in us—love, joy, peace, self-control. . .(Gal. 5:22). Such fruit shows we partake of God's divine nature. Through the Spirit's enabling we also can cultivate the character qualities (fruit) God commands of us— moral excellence, knowledge, perseverance, godliness, brotherly kindness…Peter tells us if we cultivate these qualities in increasing measure, we will not prove useless or unfruitful (2 Pet. 1:5-8). What we do for God and others also constitutes good works, and again it is by the Holy Spirit's power that we bear such fruit.

Praying for governmental officials, supporting the saints, obeying authorities, paying our income taxes, giving to our church for God's work, supplying the needs of fellow believers, and all such deeds reflect the good works to which God has called us.

His purpose for choosing us and our purpose for living meet and find fullest expression when we reach out to others in the power of the Spirit.

OUR WORKS' VALUE:

"And that your fruit should remain."

When we realize God created us for a purpose, and we

carry out that purpose, our lives have meaning, and the things we do continue to have value. When we live for ourselves, our lives seem meaningless, because we cannot experience our significance apart from God. Whether we dig ditches, drive buses, fly planes, teach school, practice law or medicine, or study economics, without God we cannot see lasting and eternal results of our works.

When Jesus told the blind man to go and wash in the pool of Siloam, the man could have argued with Him—telling Him the impossibility of giving sight to one born blind. He could have debated, as did the Pharisees, the Lord's credentials or the advisability of working on the Sabbath. Instead he obeyed the Lord and received his sight. The telling of this event today shows the lasting nature of the man's obedience.

Remember that God considers faith which leads to obedience a good work. For when the people asked Jesus what they might do to work the works of God, He told them the work of God was to believe on Him whom God had sent. When God's day for judging His people comes, our God will judge our works for enduring quality. Will they be wood, hay, and stubble, or silver, gold, and precious stones?

God wants our works to remain, or endure the test by fire. This will happen only as we seek God's purpose for our lives and live according to that purpose.

OUR SECURITY:

"That whatever you ask of the Father…He may give to you"

What a marvelous God we have! He created us for Himself. He gives us security. His plan is that as we learn to walk in His ways, to bear fruit by His Spirit, we might grow in our confidence in Him. He promises to give us the things we desire of Him. But He gives us our desires only as we order our lives with His purpose for us.

When our lives seem without meaning and purpose, and God does not seem to answer our prayers, the time is right for us to examine our relationship with Him. Are we trying to find significance by the things which we do or possess? Do we look to others for meaning? Are living for ourselves? Are we experiencing failure every time we try something? If so, we cannot expect to receive the things we desire from God. Rather, we can expect that feeling of emptiness, meaninglessness, and futility to continue.

In Ephesians 4:17 Paul tells us not to live as unbelievers live, in the futility of their minds, having their understanding darkened in blindness from hearts hardened against God. We must live in the light of His Word and walk in the Spirit's power. Jesus said we can do nothing without Him, but we can do all things through Him who gives us the ability.

Our lives take shape as we realize that God chose us for Himself, thus giving us significance, and that He created us with a purpose in mind—to live for His praise and glory. As with the man born blind, even though long periods of time pass in which life seems formless, we will find God's purpose for our life when He calls us to step up, front and center, and play our part in His eternal script.

We cannot measure the significance of our part by the time it takes to play or by the size of the role God has written for us. The value of our part can only be measured by the faithfulness with which we play it for His glory and praise.

—Menaja C. Obinali

A Wise Investment

They called it a "sure thing" in the booming Sunbelt city—a multi-million dollar land deal, evenly divided among a dozen businessmen, prime property in an upscale suburb, zoned for a mall. Glamorous architectural drawings tantalized the investors with visions of cruises and ski resorts. Expectations ran high when the deal was done.

Then, predictably, the boom turned bust. Growth slowed. The paper fortunes of the dealers evaporated. Finally only one investor was left, and now he was liable for the entire deal. He sat across the table, tears in his eyes.

"I don't think we'll have anything left, Steve. The house, the car, we'll lose everything. If only ..." His voice trailed off.

"If only I'd invested in God's work, even just a fraction of what I've thrown down this hole! At least that investment would last."

Stewardship seems an antique word. It smells musty, like fundraising drives, pledges, and a way of life that died a generation ago. In light of the rampant materialism of our day and the desperate desire for financial security, perhaps we should reintroduce it to our vocabulary.

Jesus spoke of it often. An honest reading of the gospels reveals that he majored on the theme. Jesus painted a picture of man as a caretaker of life. We hold all assets—time, money, talents, abilities, relationships, truth itself—on loan from God. One day we will stand before God and give account of these loans. In the final analysis, we are managers, not owners; servants, not masters; stewards, not consumers. And a careful look at Luke 12 reveals that stewardship matters greatly: it is a virtual "continental divide" in the spiritual realm.

LIVE RESPONSIBLY TOWARD GOD

We live near the Canadian Rockies, two hours from the Continental Divide. The drive on the TransCanada Highway toward the spine of the mountains follows the Bow River, a beautiful, east-flowing stream. As we approach the Divide, the river bends away from the road into the hills on the right. Suddenly a perceptible change in orientation occurs. A new river appears on the left, the Kootenay. This rapids-strewn mountain river flows west. Our continent divides visibly. Our souls also divide visibly over the issue of stewardship.

Luke 12 begins with a warning against the sham religiosity of the Pharisees and an admonition to fear God (vv. 1-5). Our Lord says, in effect, "You will face the living God at the end of life with nothing to hide you from the naked reality of your own beliefs and choices. Live accordingly."

Following this command to live responsively toward God, Jesus states four assumption-altering facts about life. Then He applies these facts to His disciples. The sum total of this teaching? A lifestyle of stewardship.

Peter's question in Like 12:41 reveals the movement of the passage: "Lord, are You addressing this parable to us or to everyone else as well?" Translation: "Is this teaching about stewardship for disciples or for everyone?" Jesus' answer forces the question back to us. "Who then is the faithful and sensible steward?" The choice is ours. We choose to be stewards instead of Pharisees by our response to the teachings of Luke 12. The issue of stewardship thus becomes a continental divide between spiritual reality and hypocrisy. Some run over the divide toward a sham faith; others run toward discipleship.

A STEWARD'S LIFESTYLE

Four truths establish the framework of a steward's lifestyle. First is the dramatic declaration in verses 6-7 that God, cognizant of the lifespan of every sparrow, knows and values us. As individuals, we are inestimably valuable to God.

We read, "You are of more value than many sparrows." I am convinced a smile played about the Lord's lips as He spoke. As a father, I wouldn't trade the life of one of my children for all the birds in the world. I would endure songless days, teeming insects, rotting carrion, and plagues of rodents rather than lose a child. Our heavenly Father certainly values us more than a bunch of birds. Jesus employs vast understatement to teach powerful truth: God knows and loves us personally, infinitely.

Second, one particular issue determines our experience of this love of God. Our knowledge of God's love turns on the fulcrum of a relationship with Jesus Christ. "And I say to you, everyone who confesses Me before men, the Son of Man shall confess him also before the angels of God; but he who denies Me before men shall be denied before the angels of God " (vv. 8-9).

Jesus adds a third fundamental truth in response to a question from the raucous crowd concerning inheritances. Refusing to arbitrate the matter, the Lord declares, "Not even when one has an abundance does his life consist of his possessions" (v. 15). Life is fundamentally spiritual, not material or physical.

I recall my investor friend. A year after his financial fall we sat at the Thanksgiving table. He thanked God for his trial. "Nothing has every happened to me," he said, "that has more clearly taught me life's essentials." Jesus speaks reality: life does NOT consist of possessions.

Finally, Jesus declares a fourth truth as the punch line of a parable in verses 16-20. Every person will give an account of his life to God. We must answer directly to our Maker for our investment of the assets He has lent us. As the author of Hebrews states bluntly, "It is appointed for men to die once and after this comes judgment" (Heb. 9:27).

PICTURES OF THE STEWARD

We could see these four truths as miscellaneous declarations—important but unconnected: God's infinite love for us; a relationship with Jesus Christ as life's pivotal issue; the definition of life as spiritual, not material; and the reality of eternal accountability before God. Value, destiny, identity, and purpose represent critical truths, but what do they have to do with "stewardship"?

The Lord Jesus makes the connection for us. He applies each of these truths and thereby draws a picture of a steward's lifestyle.

First, He returns to the idea of our value to God. He exhorts us to stop frantically worrying about material possessions and physical well-being. God knows what we need and will supply our needs (vv. 29-30).

A New Testament steward held a position of responsibility over the household assets of his master, exercising as much care over them as if he were the owner. In the deal, the steward's personal needs were met by the master. A man could not properly oversee his master's assets if he focused on meeting his own needs. He fulfilled his stewardship by relaxing in his master's provision.

In exactly the same way, the fact of God's personal love and care releases us from our natural concern for meeting our needs. Freedom from obsessive worry about our own physical and material needs constitutes the first step in a lifestyle of stewardship.

By temperament, I am plagued by worry. Last year, two surgeries to remove a tumor and a protracted battle with mononucleosis bred a climate of anxiety in my life. I found myself obsessed with my own health, constantly playing amateur diagnostician. Over the months of emotional and spiritual warfare, I have learned the truth of Luke 12:22-30: By worry I cannot add a cubit to my life's span. All I can add is fear, unbelief, and self-centeredness!

In the process, although I have been deservedly rebuked by the Lord, I have also seen His unwavering love. My father cares for my needs. That truth releases me from the paralysis of worry. I can serve Him, free from obsessive self-concern. I can be a steward.

Jesus applies the second truth in verses 31-32. If life pivots around a relationship with Jesus Christ, and if God settles the eternal destiny of all men through Jesus, then it stands to reason that God's stewards serve Him by declaring the gospel about Jesus. He has called us to serve Him. We do that by investing ourselves in the kingdom. So Jesus adds, "But seek first His kingdom, and these things shall be added to you" (v. 31).

Seeking the kingdom of God is a broad command that probably covers every aspect of life. But we primarily serve Jesus as King by doing what He did—giving people the opportunity to be reconciled to God through the gospel (see John 17:1-3). Christ has commissioned us to make disciples among all the nations (Matt. 28:18-20). The second step of a lifestyle of stewardship is extending the kingdom of God.

LIFE IS SPIRITUAL, NOT MATERIAL

Back to my friend…he recently had the opportunity to make a cross-country trip to a hospital where another friend lay dying of AIDS. The trip resulted in his seeing his friend put his faith in Jesus Christ a week before his death. My friend was extending the kingdom of God.

At its core, life is spiritual, not physical; and because of this fact, Jesus makes a third admonition to His disciples: "Sell your possessions and give to charity; make yourselves purses which do not wear out, an unfailing treasure in heaven" (v. 33). Controversy rages over His exact meaning, but the general point is clear: Center your investments in treasures that last for eternity. Invest spiritually.

A steward of Jesus Christ sees life as fundamentally spiritual and responds by putting his efforts into spiritual growth. He invests money in spiritual enterprises. He looks for ways to please God. He builds up a spiritual bank account.

Finances, time, assets, and relationships all become means of declaring our basic definition of life—spiritual or material.

As I write, I am interrupted by a phone call from another friend. The world would never deem this man successful. He has worked hard for years in sales, selling little. His biggest handicap? A gifted counselor and evangelist, his sales pitches invariably turn into ministry events. His wife shares his people-passion. Yes, they eat their share of beans (she is one of history's greatest "food-stretchers"), but this couple is eminently successful. They touch people that the church misses; many call this man "pastor"; their four sons are all deeply committed to Jesus Christ. Life is, at its core, spiritual.

Finally, the Lord admonishes us to live in light of unavoidable accountability. Because all of us will stand accountable before God, He urges us, "Be dressed in readiness, and keep your lamps alight. And be like men who are waiting for their master when he returns from the wedding feast, so that they may immediately open the door to him when he comes and knocks" (vv. 35-36). We fulfill this command when we live on the edge of hope, ready at a moment's notice to meet Jesus.

A lifestyle of stewardship, then, involves four distinct choices—a firm rejection of worry about physical well-being, a fierce commitment to extend the kingdom of God, a consistent decision to invest in spiritual treasures, and a constant readiness to meet Jesus Christ. The discourse ends with Peter's question, "To whom does this apply?" And the Lord answers, "The choice is yours."

In the end, little hillocks, rocks lying at particular angles, a twist in a rivulet, another foot of elevation, determine the destiny of water as it runs toward the sea. The cumulative effect of small things adds up to divide a continent. Likewise, our beliefs and corresponding actions add up to divide our lives into one of two basic directions, self or God. Strangely, this old-fashioned word, stewardship, lies close to the heart of life's continental divide. Before caricaturing stewardship as another fundraising drive, read the Bible. Far more than signing a pledge card, stewardship is living in light of the facts of God's love, Christ's Kingship, life's spirituality, and our eternal accountability.

—*Steven A. Breedlove*

The Temptation Trap

Paul wrote, "No temptation has overtaken you but such as is common to man" (1 Cor. 10:13). But Christians often ignore this fact. Dr. Charles Ryrie suggests, "To read or hear some on the spiritual life, one would think that the so-called victorious Christian never experiences temptation; or if he does, it is a slight and fleeting experience which really causes him no problem. I have just perused a half dozen books on the spiritual life. Only one of them mentioned temptation and then in only two paragraphs. Perhaps this unrealistic attitude toward the reality of temptation is the cause of discouragement among some believers who, thinking they have the secret of victory, suddenly find themselves not only confronted with temptation but actually overcome by it" (Balancing the Christian Life, p. 135).

TEMPTATION COMES WITH LIFE

To be tempted is human. Even Jesus Christ was tempted in His humanity. Let's examine Jesus' temptation to see what we can learn from His experience.

The temptation of Jesus occurred in a unique setting. According to Matthew's Gospel, John baptized Jesus in the Jordan, and a voice from heaven said, "This is My beloved

Son, in whom I am well-pleased." Then Jesus was led up by the Spirit into the wilderness to be tempted by the devil (Matt. 3:17-4:1).

It was in our Lord's baptism that He pledged to fulfill every righteous demand of God against sinners. It was His pledge to go to the cross and die for sinners so that God could be just and the justifier of the ungodly. John could then exclaim, "Behold, the Lamb of God who takes away the sin of the world!" (John 1:29). And Satan then came to tempt, to offer the crown without the cross. As G. Campbell Morgan stated, "The temptation is the story of hell's attempt to thwart heaven's purpose."

Luke's account reads, "And Jesus, full of the Holy Spirit, returned from the Jordan and was led about by the Spirit in the wilderness for forty days, being tempted by the devil. And He ate nothing during those days; and when they had ended, He became hungry" (Luke 4:1-2).

It is interesting to note that Jesus faced temptation when He was full of the Holy Spirit and submissive to Him. Thus, led by the Spirit into the wilderness, He faced the devil himself. For 40 days He was led of the Spirit. For 40 days He was tempted by the devil. For 40 days He ate nothing. Satan had no doubt been an invisible spectator at the baptism of Jesus, had heard the words of the Father: "This is My beloved Son," and now responds, "So this is God's Son who has come to crush me and set up the Kingdom of God." He resolved to defeat this divine champion. As he had conquered the first Adam, so would he the last.

Satan then launched what has been called "the great offensive." "And the devil said to Him, 'If You are the Son of God, tell this stone to become bread'" (Luke 4:3). At the baptism, the voice of the Father had said, "This is My beloved Son, in whom I am well-pleased." The devil challenged that, and said, "If indeed You are the Son of God, prove it by commanding the stones to turn into bread." The issue is, will Jesus continue to trust God, or will He obey Satan and turn those stones into something to eat?

Jesus responded in effect, "I will trust the Father who sustained the children of Israel for 40 years in the wilderness." He quoted from Deuteronomy 8 which describes that wilderness experience: "Man shall not live on bread alone" (v. 4). The devil was subtly suggesting that man's total needs are physical. Jesus' basic need at this hour, according to Satan, was physical, and that need could be met by turning the stones into bread.

Today the devil is still saying that man's primary needs are physical, and that if he satisfies the physical needs and drives, he will be totally fulfilled. But the Bible teaches that man is more than a physical being; he is body, soul, and spirit. The satisfaction of just the physical needs of man will not provide a life that is fulfilling.

D. H. Lawrence wrote, "My great religion is a belief in the blood, the flesh, as being wiser than the intellect. We can go wrong with our minds, but what our blood feels or believes and says is always true. The real way of living is to answer one's wants." In other words, as the philosophy of the day expresses it, "If it feels good, do it." But that is a basically pagan statement. Its origin is from Satan himself. Jesus refuted it by quoting Scripture to show the inadequacy of meeting only one's physical needs.

The second great temptation is found in Luke 4:5. "And he led Him up and showed Him all the kingdoms of the world in a moment of time." As the Lord and Satan looked north, south, east, west, somehow all the kingdoms of the earth came into view. "And the devil said to Him, 'I will give You all this domain and its glory; for it has been handed over to me, and I give it to whomever I wish' " (v. 6). Man had been given dominion over the earth, but that dominion had slipped out of his hands because of Adam's disobedience. Satan was quick to seize control and become the prince of this world.

Satan went on to say to Jesus, "Therefore if You will worship before me, it shall all be Yours" (v. 7). His offer was, "I'll make you Messiah by a shortcut. Instead of the cross and then the crown, You can be the King now." The temptation was for Christ to compromise with evil to achieve His goal of the crown. That too is a familiar temptation of Satan. It is heard by the businessman; it is heard by the student; it is heard by the housewife—"Compromise with evil in order to achieve your goal".

Again Jesus answered by quoting the Word of God, "It is written, 'You shall worship the Lord your God and serve Him only' " (v. 8). The devil tried to lure Jesus into violating the first commandment, "You shall have no other gods before Me." Jesus knew that if He bowed to Satan to worship him, He would become his servant, and that was unthinkable.

The third temptation appears in verse 9. "And he led Him to Jerusalem and had Him stand on the pinnacle of the temple, and said to Him, 'If You are the Son of God, throw Yourself down from here.' " Now we see Satan attempting to seize the sword of the Spirit from Jesus' hands, quoting Scripture himself, though not accurately. "For it is written, 'He will give His angels charge concerning You to guard You,' (omitting the words, "in all your ways,") and, 'On their hands they will bear You up, lest You strike Your foot against a stone'" (Luke 4:10-11).

It was a sheer drop of approximately 400-500 feet in that day into the Valley of the Kidron from the pinnacle of the Temple. Satan in effect was saying, "Yes, Jesus, You're right— You can trust God. Now give the people some divine razzle dazzle. Jump from this pinnacle of the Temple. The angels will swoop down from heaven, lift You up, and You will not be injured. Then the people will immediately acclaim You as Messiah."

"Jesus answered and said to him, 'It is said, "You shall not put the Lord your God to the test" ' " (v. 12). Thus, three times Satan tempted Christ, and three times the Son of God responded with a verse of Scripture.

The narrative concludes, "And when the devil had finished every temptation (or as Morgan says, 'When hell had exhausted itself'), he departed from Him until an opportune time" (v. 13). As we know, the devil always has a follow-up program, and he did come back later. He tempted Jesus through Peter, and Jesus had to say to him, "Get behind Me, Satan!" (Matt. 16:23). He also tempted Jesus through Judas in the Garden of Gethsemane, and Jesus said, "This hour and the power of darkness are yours" (Luke 22:53).

Now, what can we as believers learn about temptation from this crucial passage?

First, we learn not to expect to be free from temptation, for not even Jesus was, nor the biblical heroes—Noah, Abraham, Jacob, Moses, David, Jonah, Peter, and others. They experienced it, and some of them yielded. We must accept the reality of temptation.

In the second place, we must distinguish between temptation and sin. I remember when a seminary student came into my office and said, "Prof, I must be a sinful person, because I am tempted so much." I said, "Well, now just a moment, son. The real issue is, do you yield to temptation?" Temptation is not sin; yielding to temptation is. Joseph was tempted in Potiphar's house. He did not yield. David was tempted by the sight of Bathsheba. He did yield and sinned. Temptation and sin, while they seem to offer so very much, yield so very little.

Third, we must understand that we do not face temptation in our own power and strength, but in the power of the Holy Spirit. Jesus, full of the Holy Spirit, was tempted by the devil. And John declared in 1 John 4:4, "Greater is He who is in you than he who is in the world." How encouraging—the Holy Spirit indwelling the Christian is greater than Satan, the prince of the power of the air, our great tempter! God does not intend for us to face the enemy in our own strength.

In the fourth place, we need to realize that the way to victory is to know and use the Word of God. Jesus defeated the devil by quoting three verses from the Book of Deuteronomy. Someone once asked how we would fare against the temptation of the devil today if our victory depended on verses we had memorized from Deuteronomy. Perhaps that is not a fair question, but we should be hiding the Word of God in our hearts that we might not sin against the Lord. In 1 John 2:14, John wrote, "I have written to you, fathers, because you know Him who has been from the beginning. I have written to you, young men, because you are strong, and the word of God abides in you, and you have overcome the evil one." Here we see the secret of victory. The way to overcome the temptations of the devil is to abide in the Word of God and allow that Word to abide in us.

Finally, we must remember that Christ prays for us. Jesus said to Peter, "Simon, Simon, behold, Satan has demanded permission to sift you like wheat; but I have prayed for you, that your faith may not fail" (Luke 22:31-32).

What a comfort to know that in our hour of temptation, Jesus, the great ascended High Priest and intercessor, prays for us that we may not fail.

With God's help, we can be victors and not victims in temptation.

—Donald K. Campbell

The Perfect Mouth

An insurance adjuster recently noted the unique way that people file reports on their claims when asked to describe their accidents in the fewest words possible:

- "I pulled from the side of the road, glanced at my mother-in-law, and headed for the embankment."
- "The pedestrian had no idea which way to run, so I ran over him."
- "The guy was all over the road; I had to swerve a number of times before I hit him."

Communication. It is the process of expressing how we feel and what we think. It is impression as well. It is a tricky, risky piece in the puzzle of existence. Words can confuse, embarrass, and hurt. Conversely, they have the power to heal, encourage, help, and teach. Unfortunately, unless we are under the Holy Spirit's control, our words are more prone to hurt than to heal.

Words are often tragically destructive. Recently my favorite sports writer was analyzing a fine levied on a local baseball manager for verbally chewing out the commissioner. His column defended the manager by saying, "After all, they were just words."

Just words? There's no such thing. Words have tremendous weight. The pen really is mightier than the sword. It is not true that "names will never hurt me." Job said, "How long will you vex my soul and break me in pieces with words?" (Job 19:2, KJV). I must be constantly aware that my words to my children as their father, to my congregation as their pastor, and to my wife as her life partner carry impact. That's why God holds me accountable for my words (Matt. 12:36-37).

Devastating words aren't the only problem we have with our speech. Occasionally, our tongues simply succumb to the cascade of everyday pressures.

In addition to stress from our everyday encounters, our words come under the pressure of our exposure to negative patterns of speech. Many of us are exposed to degrading speech on a daily basis. From the choice words of an angry boss to the crude and shaded language of prime time TV; in casual conversation with a neighbor to careless chatter among Christians; there is a steady exposure to corrupted communication. Unfortunately, our tongues often become a mimic of the input and, to our chagrin, the destructive words are out before we know it—occasionally in front of people who can't believe what they're hearing!

Whether it be well-meant confusion, careless destruction, survival in chaos, or subconscious submission to environmental patterns of speech, words can be destructive in three dimensions. They are able to destroy our relationship with God, our relationship with those we treasure the most, and even our relationship with ourselves. Having a tongue is like having dynamite in our dentures—it must be reckoned with.

Transforming our tongues requires supernatural strength. Victory demands taking up supernatural arms—being "strong in the Lord and in His mighty power" (v. 10). Being strong in the Lord is no mystical, hocus-pocus process. Being strong in the supernatural, victorious strength of the Lord has some solid resources that are available to us. As we discover and digest God's Word, the indwelling Spirit transforms it into growth—growth that produces spiritual, victorious strength.

God has blessed us with a wealth of truth in regard to the tongue—truth that warns, convicts, and transforms us as we permit it to take residence within us. One of the most instructive sections of truth on the tongue is James 3. In this passage, five principles unfold that make us aware of the gravity of our words.

PRINCIPLE 1: THE MEASURE OF MATURITY

"We all stumble in many ways. If anyone is never at fault in what he says, he is a perfect man, able to keep his whole body in check" (James 3:2).

The word stumble means "to fall or to trip." What a graphic picture of immaturity in our speech—tripping. Our seven-week-old sheep dog Paddington, trips over everything in his path. His clumsy stumbling reflects his immaturity. A stumbling tongue reflects our spiritual age as well. Our spiritual maturity is not measured by the communication patterns of those around us, but by the standards of God's Word.

The word perfect literally means complete or mature. This verse asserts that we are not mature until we stumble not in word, being able to bring our entire body under control.

Certain skills are priority skills. If you master them, others come quite naturally. A marathon runner has no difficulty running a mile. A professional golfer can handle the two-foot putts. And so it is with the tongue. If we master the tongue, we have the capacity to master other areas of our lives.

Have you ever seen someone revive a drowning victim with mouth-to-mouth resuscitation? What a thrill it would be to bring renewed life to our relationships by learning the skill of mouth-to-mouth maturity.

PRINCIPLE 2: SMALL BUT SIGNIFICANT

"When we put bits into the mouths of horses to make them obey us, we can turn the whole animal. Or take ships as an example. Although they are so large and are driven by strong winds, they are steered by a very small rudder wherever the pilot wants to go. Likewise the tongue is a small part of the body, but it makes great boasts. Consider what a great forest is set on fire by a small spark" (James 3:3-5).

Wars that have claimed thousands of lives have been ignited by the tongue's spark. Marriages that once set sail on a joyous adventure have been steered onto the rocks by the rudder of a splintered tongues. After several years in the ministry, I cannot recall one counseling situation in which the problem was not either ignited or seriously complicated by negative words.

The kids on our block say it best. The tattletale is called "Mr. Bigmouth." That isn't a reference to the size of his mouth, but rather a pungent description of the heap of trouble that his little mouth produces.

PRINCIPLE 3: CUMBUSTIBLE COMMODITY

"The tongue also is a fire, a world of evil among the parts of the body. It corrupts the whole person, sets the whole course of his life on fire, and is itself set on fire by hell" (James 3:6).

The seriousness of the tongue's activity is revealed in the truth that it is "set on fire by hell." It is a "world of evil," literally an entire network of sin. We have an organized crime syndicate right in our mouths. Our tongues have the capacity to corrupt our entire being - nothing is exempt from the damage our tongues can cause.

Occasionally my wife and I have enjoyed the privilege of being with respected godly people. Though the encounters have always proven beneficial, more than once we have found ourselves surprised by their readiness to share freely the faults of others and thereby unconsciously tarnish their images.

We should remember that fire is one of the few forces that does irreparable damage. Fiery words often destroy relationships that, even when restored, are never the same again. Our families, our businesses, our churches, our friends, our enemies, our wealth, our security, our happiness, and our peace are vulnerable to the defilement of the tongue. We should wear signs that say, "CAUTION: LIFE IS A COMBUSTIBLE COMMODITY - DOUSE YOUR TONGUE!"

PRINCIPLE 4: A WILD AND DEADLY BEAST

"All kinds of animals, birds, reptiles, and creatures of the sea are being tamed and have been tamed by man, but no man can tame the tongue. It is a restless evil, full of deadly poison" (James 3:7-8).

I get a kick out of how much effort we put into taming animals. There is "elephant soccer," dogs that bark "Jingle Bells," chimps that communicate in sign language, birds that talk, and porpoises that "shoot baskets" better than I do.

Taming the tiger in our tongues must be a priority. By the Spirit's power, the tongue can be tamed for God's glory. If we do not bring it under the Spirit's control, it will be "full of deadly poison." When speaking of sinful mankind, Paul wrote, "The poison of vipers is on their lips" (Rom. 3:13).

In regions of South America there is a snake called the "Two-Step" snake. If it bites you, you take two steps and die. Its venom swiftly paralyzes your nervous system which stops your heart. Words can be like that. They have the potential to kill swiftly a relationship, paralyze love, poison minds, destroy faith, stain purity, and deface reputations.

PRINCIPLE 5: THE DOUBLE-TROUBLE TONGUE

"With the tongue we praise our Lord and Father, and with it we curse men, who have been made in God's likeness. Out of the same mouth come praise and cursing. My brothers, this should not be. Can both fresh water and salt water flow from the same spring? My brothers, can a fig tree bear olives, or a grapevine bear figs? Neither can a salt spring produce fresh water" (James 3:9-12).

Someone has said that most tongues are tied in the middle, wagging at both ends. God's Word pictures it as a double tongue (1 Tim. 3:8). It's amazing how we can verbally poison one another all the way to church and as soon as we turn into the parking lot begin to speak out of the pious side of our mouths! We hardly finish singing the doxology and we are complaining about the usher who didn't put us in our favorite pew. "My brethren, these things ought not so to be" (James 3:10, KJV)

Even nature doesn't act so incongruously. It would be impossible for our wells to send forth salt and fresh water, and for our fig trees to bear olives! If they did, we would reject them with disappointment. God might well ask us, "Can a 'new creation'(2 Cor. 5:17) send forth 'old words'?"

In these five principles James has categorized the tragic and shifty potential of the tongue. Step one to victory is to permit these truths to penetrate us. James rings a clear warning: A transformed tongue must be a top priority for those on the growth edge of discipleship.

James' warning, however, takes on added weight when we realize that many Christians are insensitive to the problems of destructive speech. We excuse one another with rationalizations such as, "Well, it's the truth, isn't it?" or "If they didn't want people to talk, they never should done it." The most subtle excuse among Christians is, "Let me share this with you that we might pray more intelligently." This desensitization process has opened the floodgates to communication sins.

I understand that if you put a frog in a pan of cold water and place the pan on the stove, the frog will not jump out—but will slowly boil to death. It's not that the frog is dumb. It's that his nerve endings become desensitized in the heated water. The hotter the water becomes, the more numb his nerve endings become—until finally he is cooked.

Like the frog, we too can numb our spiritual nerve endings. By making careless communication an acceptable part of our lives, we assume that a carnal tongue is par for the spiritual course. When that happens, our churches, schools, homes, friendships, and relationships with God will all be victimized—cooked to death by our lack of sensitivity. Our foremost commitment, then, should be to nurture and protect the inward development of humility, patience, and love. These are skills that grow and develop. They are taught by the Spirit through His Word and engrafted into our lives by attentive application and continued commitment.

In order to aid in the development of these skills, we should:

Define accurately and practically, in our own words, the essence of humility, patience, and love. Make these definitions concise, biblical, interesting, and relevant. Be creative.

Memorize our definitions and key Scripture passages that fortify our sensitivity to the essence and importance of genuine humility and patience.

Pray regularly (several times a day) for the developing work of the Spirit in each of the three areas. Prayer will not only unlock the Spirit's work, but will also help remind us of our commitment.

Speak less and listen more, permitting the principles of humility, patience, and love to guard the door of our lips. David prayed, "Set a guard over my mouth, O Lord; keep watch over the door of my lips" (Ps. 141:3).

Evaluate what we have said by the standards of the three principles that we are now committed to, not by the standards of others.

Be patient. Our spirit and our speech cannot be transformed in a day. Patiently persist!

Nurturing our inner maturity will not only fortify and stimulate our growth but will also infect others with an awareness of the positive benefit of a tongue in check.

—*Joseph M. Stowell III*

Thou Shalt Not!

A couple of years ago, reverberations were felt throughout the professional basketball world as the "twin towers" of Akeem Olajuwon and Ralph Sampson teamed up in Houston to become one of the most feared frontline tandems in the NBA. The combination of these two giants of the sports world presented a potential of awesome proportions as they shut down opposing players and inhibited opposing teams.

Unfortunately, in the realm of Christian experience the "twin towers" of legalism and license already have demonstrated their imposing presence in the life and practice of countless believers, frustrating spiritual growth and inhibiting the spread of the gospel. For the church as well as individual believers, I believe they represent a potential problem of awesome proportions.

But how can we as believers cope with these two extremes of Christian behavior? I believe a couple of definitions at this point would be helpful. On the one hand, legalism is the tendency to reduce one's relationship with God to a set of rules which can in turn be used as a standard to measure spirituality. On the other hand, license is the improper application of our liberty whereby we gratify the flesh rather than allow the Holy Spirit to control our lives.

All of us at some time or another have had the experience of being under club memberships, church covenants, college rules, or Christian "standards of behavior" that we or someone else would criticize as being legalistic. Likewise, in our churches and Christian organizations, the battle of license and legalism is waged over topics ranging from television to holidays, from diet to dress, from movies to children's education.

Originally fought in the arena of salvation, this battle between legalism and license in our century has entered into the arena of sanctification. Accordingly, I think we will find that the answer to legalism in relation to salvation is an accurate understanding of the doctrine of justification, while the corrective to license is provided by the doctrine of sanctification.

The purpose of this article is to look at three passages in the Gospels in which Jesus Christ exposes the liabilities of imposing a system of legalism which hinders our belief and frustrates of our spirituality.

The Pattern of Legalism: Matthew 15:1-9

In the time of Christ, the most notable legalists were the Pharisees. The Pharisees were known for their attention to the "oral law," which was added and accepted alongside the Mosaic Law as equally inspired and authoritative. Some 365 laws were added as a sort of "fence" to protect people from violating the written Law, either through oversight or accident.

The problem with these "fences", as well as any other additions one might make to the Word of God today, is the loyalty one gives to man-made standards over the Word of God. Hence, the pattern of legalism is one which sets up an external standard, beyond the Word of God, which measures personal righteousness.

In Matthew 15:1-9 the Pharisees asked why the disciples ate with unwashed hands. In His answer Jesus exposed three downward steps in the pattern leading to the substitution of a man-made standard of legalism in the place of—or in addition to—God's Word. The first step in this pattern is the violation of the written laws of God for the sake of tradition (v. 3).

Though many times they originate out of a sincere motivation, codes of conduct often strain at gnats to specify what God has communicated in general principles or to make specific applications of a concrete command into any and all situations. In this case, the ceremonial washings prescribed in the Book of Leviticus were supplemented by the traditions of the Pharisees until they ultimately prescribed the occasions, the amount of water, the number of rinsings, and the use of one or both hands at the time when these washings were considered necessary! This tendency is one in which personal beliefs are translated into prescribed behavior.

The second step in the pattern of legalism is the invalidation of the Word of God for the sake of tradition (v. 6).

Jesus taught that the Pharisees were guilty of setting aside the commands of Moses which taught that children are to honor their parents (Exodus 20:12 and 21:17). By a practice known as "corban" (which meant "devoted as a gift to God"), the Pharisees had developed an excuse for not helping support their aging parents. They simply claimed that their money was dedicated to the temple. Jesus strongly condemned such a practice as nullifying the Word of God.

This second pitfall is also what causes us to be selective in the application of the Word of God to our lives today. How often is the clear biblical teaching concerning the tongue bypassed even as judgment is pronounced against those who don't echo our personal opinions of Christian behavior?

Likewise, the unfortunate fall of anther believer into sin often allows for the setting aside of the New Testament commands regarding gossip or restoration. Too frequently, the action items on our agenda take priority over those of the Lord, and they invalidate what He has clearly commanded.

The third step in the pattern, substituting the teachings of men for the truth of God, completes the downward spiral into traditionalism (Matt. 15:9).

Jesus condemned the Pharisees and teachers of the Law by calling them hypocrites and quoting Isaiah 29:13: "These people honor Me with their lips, but their hearts are far away from me. Their worship of me is made up only of rules taught by men."

Someone has said, "The hypocrite tries to appear before men as he ought to be before God and yet is not." Another has said, "The worst form of hypocrisy is that which carries its self-deception to the point where it thinks that it really is what it only pretends to be."

In Christ's day as in our own, the unmistakable pattern of legalism is that it substitutes a false standard for the infallible Word of God.

THE PROBLEMS OF LEGALISM: MATTHEW 23:13-28

On another occasion in His life, Jesus announced a series of woes upon the hypocritical system of the Scribes and Pharisees in which He identified legalism as the setting up of a superficial standard of righteousness (Matt. 23:13-28).

He also showed that superficial standards are the result of five basic errors of discernment as demonstrated by the Jewish leaders at that time. Too often these errors determine the modern mentality of passing judgment on others today.

Briefly, these five basic error are:

1. Legalism obscures the simplicity of salvation both for the one who preaches and for the one who would seek to practice such a standard. Here, Pharisees and the teachers of the Law actually became an obstruction at the entrance to the kingdom of heaven (v.13).

2. The internal reality is ignored for the sake of external appearances. Jesus used the example here (as at other times in the Gospels) of long public prayers which were a masquerade or façade to cover private sins (v. 14).

3. The physical is a higher priority than the eternal. The Pharisees confused the gold for the temple, the offering for the alter, and the throne for God Himself in their obligatory observances (vv. 15-23).

4. The minutiae is mistaken for the monumental. Tithes of the mint, dill, and cumin were calculated while the principles of justice, mercy, and faithfulness upon which the Old Testament offerings were grounded were neglected (vv. 23-24).

5. Actions are emphasized above attitudes. Like washing only the outside of the cups and painting the tombs with whitewash, the spiritual reality of the Pharisees' legalism revealed lives of hypocrisy and lawlessness (vv. 25-28).

It becomes clear, then that legalism sets up a superficial standard of external rituals which tend to fog the biblical focus on the internal reality of a genuine relationship with God.

PRINCIPLES OF RIGHTEOUSNESS: LUKE 18:9-14

Probably the clearest example of the liabilities of legalism comes by way of a parable Jesus told "to certain ones who trusted in themselves that they were righteous, and viewed others with contempt" (Luke 18:9-14).

In the parable, two men went up to the temple to pray; but only one went away justified. Both claimed to believe in the same God and both came to worship in the same place. Why was it that only one of the prayers was heard and not the other?

This parable of the Pharisee and the publican became more vivid to me during a trip to the Middle East where the three great monotheistic religions of the world converge and often collide. Our tour happened to coincide with the Moslem Fast of Ramadan and the Jewish anniversary of independence. Jewish, Muslim, and Christian prayers were being expressed in synagogues and at the Wailing Wall, in mosques and in the streets, and in churches and even on the bus. Thousands of prayers were being offered, but not all those praying were "going away justified."

In providing this contrast of two extremes in Jewish society, Jesus offered four principles of righteousness which will protect us from legalism.

The first principle is that religious activity is no guarantee of spirituality. Two men went to the temple to pray but only one went away justified. Just because a person may go to church, give money in the offering, sing the hymns, say the prayers, and attentively listen to the sermon does not mean that he or she is manifesting a righteous relationship with God.

The second principle taught in the parable is that righteousness is not the result of self righteous activities one might perform. The Pharisee was used as an example by Jesus to teach that righteousness is not the result of what one does or doesn't do.

The proud comparisons and commendations of character which the Pharisee advanced were nothing more than the self righteous activities of one who trusted in himself while viewing others with contempt.

Conversely, as one of the most despised by his fellowman, the Publican (tax collector) was the model for the third principle which taught how one can stand righteous before a holy God: justification is the means whereby a sinner who comes to God in faith is declared to be righteous. The faith of the publican was demonstrated in his desire for God to extend His mercy toward him. In contrast to the pride of the Pharisee, the Publican manifested a humility of heart which served as the foundation for the fourth principle which concluded the parable. That is, present humility is the prerequisite for future exaltation. The reverse is also stated in the passage. "Everyone who exalts himself shall be humbled" (v.14).

Humility is necessary to avoid the pitfalls of legalism that come from substituting human regulations in place of the revelation of God in the Scriptures; from establishing a superficial list of external rituals instead of emphasizing the internal realities; and from sacrificing the biblical doctrine of righteousness for a relative degree of self-righteousness.

To avoid legalism entirely is probably impossible. Yet if we are careful to recognize the liabilities of legalism as they creep into our individual lives and collective congregations, and are willing to depend wholly upon the authority of God's Word for our freedom as will as our righteous behavior, I believe we will see an accelerated spread of the gospel and a new dimension of personal spiritual growth.

—*Mark L. Bailey*

Savoring Your Age

Explaining to a young man what it was like to be old, a woman revealed a picture of herself as a debutante, glowing with youth and beauty. He smiled.

"So you think I was pretty?" she asked.

He nodded good-humoredly.

"But how can you tell?" she asked. "When you meet a dragon that has eaten a swan, do you guess by the few feathers around the mouth? That's what it is—a body like this is a dragon, all scales and folds. So the dragon ate the white swan. I haven't seen her for years. I can't even remember what she looks like. I feel her, though. She's safe inside, still alive; the essential swan hasn't changed a feather. Do you know, there are some mornings in spring or fall, when I wake and think, I'll run across the fields into the woods and pick wild straw-berries! Or I'll swim in the lake, or I'll dance all night tonight until dawn! And, then , in a rage, discover I'm in this old and ruined dragon. I'm the princess in the crumbled tower, no way out, waiting for her Prince Charming."

Perhaps you are a kindred spirit with this woman. When we grow old we often lose physical beauty and strength, loved ones, and financial security. The pain can be very real and deeply felt.

In the United States, these losses are accentuated by a cul-ture which prizes the glamorous, the young, and the produc-tive—and discards the old. Since work and financial success too often establish a person's worth, it's easy to feel like a non-person when you pass sixty-five.

Look at the fear with which young people face turning forty. Birthday cards joke about adding another year. We use hair coloring, wrinkle potions, and face-lifts to stay youthful.

It all makes one point: Avoid old age at all costs. It's ugly. Even the word "old" connotes such fearful thoughts you hesitate to use it—and so do I.

As an older American, how affected are you by our culture's attitude? Do you feel a sense of accomplishment and pride, or embarrassment and shame when you describe yourself as old? Let's turn our eyes away from what the world is telling us and look at what God has said.

GOD'S PERSPECTIVE ON AGING

In the Scriptures it is clear that the aging have high priority. In patriarchal times, the elderly held undisputed sway in all areas of family life. Israel depended on the elderly to give direction during times of trouble and transition. They were the priests, judges, and scribes. King David wrote Psalm 3, 18, and 37 in his later years. And in Proverbs, the book of wisdom, old age is the prize of life.

Solomon says gray hair is a crown of splendor (Prov. 16:31) and that parents are the pride of their children (Prov. 17:6). Yet our culture says gray hair should be hidden and parents are a burden. But old age is not a burden. It is a reward from God (Prov. 3:2, 16; 4:10; 9:11; 10:27).

In the first century, again it was the elders who were most revered. Age signified deep-seated maturity and wisdom. Peter wrote his letters in his seventies; John wrote his in his eighties and nineties! Nicodemus was born again when he was up in years.

It is clear that in God's eyes, life does not end at sixty-five. In fact, David says that the righteous will still bear fruit in old age, they will stay fresh and green (Ps. 92:14).

But our culture is often the measure by which we evaluate our successes and failures over a lifetime. Its materialistic standard and values either build us up or shove us aside. We don't live in Japan or other Eastern cultures where character and wisdom are highly valued, and it takes courage and faith to believe an invisible God when today's values seem so much more powerful.

WHAT DO YOU NEED?

The older man or woman without God is a victim of our society. Although increasing numbers of organizations serve the elderly, when an old person reaches out for some sense of identity and worth, he is often met with a wall of intolerance for his condition. As a result, he shrinks into his own private world, wounded by the reflection he sees of himself in the eyes of "valuable" people. Many see no hope at all, evidenced in one man's comment:

"What is the sound I make when I am old? Shuffling for sustenance, napping for strength, dressing for no one, waiting for one certain visitor, I am a diminished me. No capital I. No self to fling free, a bird sailing skyward. There is only a small i, shriveling within the layers of the years."

What are the needs of older Americans? Surprisingly enough, your needs are identical to those of the young. All need to be loved and to belong. This is what gives us purpose in life and reason for living. Psychologists say there is no greater psychic shock than to feel useless. If this is true, we have two deadly forces against us when we are old, culture and losses. Society's rejection of anything but beauty, energy, and financial success causes enough problems. But when we lose a spouse, a meaningful career, or the children who once needed us, we have a good reason to feel useless. The things that make us feel worthwhile in our youth can be cruelly snatched from life.

Is there any question why we find old people who are sick, withdrawn, and cynical, almost welcoming death? Even one-year-old children withdraw and get physically ill when love and affection are taken away.

Studies conclusively prove that the healthiest, happiest old people are those who have a good self-image and strong religious beliefs, both of which lead them into meaningful activity, filling the void created by losses. It's not surprising that self-image and religious beliefs are linked.

If we see ourselves through the eyes of culture or in light of our losses, our self-image will undoubtedly shrink. But if we look into the eyes of our Creator and in the pages of the Bible, we will find plenty of reason to feel good about ourselves.

VALUE IS FOUND IN GOD

To begin with, the Creator of the universe made us in His image and longs for a personal relationship with us. If our relationship with God has not been growing over years of trust and friendship, this is the first place to start. Remember Nicodemus, born again as an old man? New life had just begun for him. We only need to acknowledge our helplessness and sin, and trust Christ for forgiveness. Our slate will be clean and a new life is possible. Yes, even if you're eighty!

Or, maybe there was a time in life when we had zeal for God and many intimate moments with Him. But for some reason or another we walked on without Him. In God's eyes every day is a new day with new hope. Forgiveness is free for the asking, but renewal takes work, just as it would with any old friend. Get to know Him again. Bask in His forgiveness. Enjoy the warmth of His love and acceptance.

Worth, value, and a proper self-image come from God. But the way to reinforce those truths is to act on them. If you like yourself, you probably think you have something to offer a hurting world. Christian psychologists have an interesting comment for those who don't like themselves. The prescription for developing their self-esteem is in "giving." So whether or not you feel good about yourself, involvement in other people's lives reinforces a sense of personal value. And there's no question that people need someone like you. We could all give our lives to others every day for the next twenty years and still find unmet needs in our own community.

We have countless excuses for avoiding social and organizational involvement. Maybe your biggest fear is the risk. The risk of rejection, failure, disappointment. But once you find your niche, you can discover the joy of giving yourself to others, and the frightening risk you took will be long forgotten.

What are some of the ways you can use your life to meet people's needs? One eight year-old girl put it this way:

"A grandmother is a lady who has no children of her own. She likes other people's little girls. A grandfather is a man grandmother. He goes for walks with the boys and they talk about fishing and tractors and things like that. Grandmothers don't have to do anything but be there. They slow down passing things like pretty leaves or caterpillars. They never say 'hurry up.' When they read to us they don't skip words or mind if it's the same story over again and again. Everybody should try to have one, especially if you don't have a television; because grandmothers are the only grown-ups who have got time."

FINDING A MINISTRY

There are countless children whose parents don't have time... or don't even exist. Orphanages need volunteers, churches need Sunday school teachers, working women need babysitters. The government sponsors a foster grandparent program for men and women like you. Foster grandparents work with children in hospitals, homes for neglected children, public schools, day care centers, and private homes. What do they do? Just what a grandparent should: give love, guidance, and companionship to children with special needs. The intimacy and love which are exchanged are therapeutic for both the child and the foster grandparent. You could even start your own foster grandparent program, using your church as a base.

As a Christian, your church might be the most rewarding place to give your life to others. Talk to your pastor about ways you can minister to your brothers and sisters in Christ. Visit ill or handicapped people at home and in the hospital. If you are confined to your home, encourage others over the phone. Read the Bible to believers who are blind, tutor or teach crafts to young people in the church, organize your own social group. In my church there is a group called Three-Score-and-More who meet for a potluck supper and fellowship. They also stay in touch with the needs in the church, filling in where they can help.

What is your particular burden and gift? Are you compassionate and understanding? Start a free counseling service. Time for listening to others is a precious commodity which few young people own. Are you concerned about government? Campaign for your favorite candidate. Are you troubled over juvenile delinquency? Lobby for new city playgrounds. Do you have opinions on issues of today? Put your wisdom up front by writing letters to editors. Be creative. Take a risk and get involved where you care. You have a wealth of experience and wisdom built over valuable years of living. The living isn't over. It's time to invest. If you use what God has given you, your later years can be even richer than your youth—and God will be glorified through your life. But remember—all these activities take on greater meanings when you are involved closely with people. Intimate relationships with God and people are without a doubt the key to fulfilling activity. If that isn't there you're right back in the cultural rut of pure achievement.

I've suggested many ways for you to give your life to others. You can invest your time and yourself, but you can also invest your possessions. You may not have much money to give to the church. Christian organizations, or charities, especially in these inflationary times. But your estate may be worth a lot more than you think, and you can invest it through a thoughtfully planned will. A wise investment of your estate can help build ministries which will continue for years and years. And that is a wonderful way to make the work of a lifetime count for eternity!

God entrusts each of us with one life. Some of us have more time than others to use it. Don't buy the world's view that older people are useless and helpless. God has clearly refuted that story. Yes, pain, grief, and loneliness are often intensified in our later years. And even Christ was tempted to shy away from them. But He has walked that path before us and promises never to leave us in the dark. The power and strength which was freely given when we put our faith in Christ is still there. But only we can choose to use it.

—Peggy Wehmeyer

God's Waiting Room

Whenever I visit my doctor, I always set aside extra time for each visit. I generally have to wait in the waiting room before I'm summoned to be examined. And then I have to wait again in the examination room before the doctor comes in!

The waiting room, a land where time seemingly stands still. It is a place where life is put on hold. In my doctor's office, it feels like hours have passed, and yet when I look at my watch, it's been only 20 minutes. When we are in the waiting room, it seems as if progress has come to a screeching halt.

Perhaps you feel like you're in the waiting room. Maybe one of your loved ones is ill and you're praying that God would heal them. Maybe you're in a job situation that you consider unbearable, and yet you have no other choice than to endure it. Maybe you're single, and you're searching for Mr. or Miss "Right." Maybe your children are in preschool, and you can hardly wait for them to grow up so that you can have more freedom. Maybe you're a teenage and you just can't wait until you learn how to drive or are old enough to move out on your own. Maybe it's a family situation where your spouse or your kids are causing you grief and you are begging God to change them.

You feel like you are in the midst of a crisis, and it seems as if God has led you down a long hallway and has ushered you into a room with a huge sign over it that says "Waiting Room." And you enter that room, and you wait, and you wait, and you wait. Time, for you, has now stopped. You have entered the waiting room and you have no idea how long you'll be there.

Well-meaning friends stop by and say, "I'm so sorry. Wait for the Lord. Yes, wait for the Lord." In your anguish and frustration, you feel like crying out, "How long, O Lord? When are You going to do something? I don't know how much more I can take!"

Any time we enter the waiting room, we have an abundance of questions: Who? What? Why? How? How long? In God's waiting room, on the coffee table by the door, there is a manual that helps us to understand the waiting room. It discusses many questions. What does it mean to wait? How do we do it? Who are we waiting for? Why are we waiting for Him? What happens when we wait? What do we expect to happen?

In that manual there are three main questions: What does it mean to wait for the Lord? Why are we to wait for Him? What happens when we wait for Him? Let's examine the manual to see what it says about these questions.

What Does It Mean to Wait for the Lord?

When we think of waiting, we usually think of waiting for time to pass. When you come to a red light, you wait for the light to turn green. If you want to watch the 6 o'clock news and it's only 5:30, you wait for a half hour to pass. If your son or daughter is 12 or 13 and they ask you for the keys to the car, you tell them to wait until they're 16 and they can get their driver's license. We wait for time to pass.

But waiting involves more than simply the passage of time. It also means to anticipate or expect something to happen. Psalm 130:5-6 says, "I wait for the Lord, my soul does wait, And in His word do I hope. My soul waits for the Lord more than the watchmen for the morning; Indeed, more than the watchmen for the morning."

If you have ever worked a graveyard shift, or if you've ever been camping, you know what it means to wait for the morning. It is more than just waiting for time to pass. You anticipate the sun coming up. It will be light soon. It will be warm again. Waiting involves anticipation, expectation.

Waiting also involves being confident of what God is going to do. Psalm 52:8-9 says, "But as for me, I am like a green olive tree in the house of God; I trust in the loving kindness of God forever and ever. I will give Thee thanks forever, because Thou has done it, And I will wait on Thy name, for it is good, in the presence of Thy godly ones."

Psalm 52 was written while David was being pursued by King Saul. You can read the account in 1 Samuel 22. It tells about how he was betrayed and how he had to flee. In spite of that situation, David says in verse 8-9 of Psalm 52 that he will wait on the Lord. Not only will he wait, but he will trust in God's loving kindness and he will give thanks for what God will do in the future.

When we think of waiting, we think of just sitting back, waiting for something to happen. Waiting is something which happens to us, not something that we do. It is a passive activity. However, Scripture points out that waiting is active, rather than passive. Lamentations 3:25 tells us this, "The Lord is good to those who wait for Him, To the person who seeks Him."

One of the ways that we wait for the Lord is by seeking Him. Whenever we enter the waiting room, we need to spend time seeking God. We need to dive into His Word, looking for answers about our situation, about prayer, about walking with God. We need to spend time on our knees, pouring our hearts out to God in prayer. We need to seek the Lord actively as we wait.

If you're anything like me, waiting involves a great struggle, namely, being patient. Psalm 37:7-8 talks about this struggle when it says, "Rest in the Lord and wait patiently for Him; Do not fret because of him who prospers in his way, Because of the man who carries out wicked schemes. Cease from anger, and forsake wrath; Do not fret, it leads only to evil-doing."

While we may agree with God that we will wait for Him, it is extremely hard for us to be patient. Waiting chafes at us. We fidget and squirm to try to get out of the situation. Then we begin to look around and compare ourselves with other people. We become envious and we worry. It bothers us that these people don't have to wait. One of the great struggles is looking at other people my age and seeing what they have and what I don't have. I feel like saying, "God, it's not fair that we have to put life on hold. Why can't we be like them?"

Waiting contains five basic elements. Obviously, one is the passage of time. But waiting is more than that. It means having the expectation that God will do great things in your life and being confident that He will do what is best for you. It also means actively seeking Him. Finally, it means being patient while He is working.

WHY SHOULD WE WAIT ON THE LORD?

Knowing what it means to wait on the Lord is not enough. We must also understand why we should wait on Him. Psalm 52:8-9 tells us that we are to "wait on Thy name." To us, a name doesn't mean much. We pick names for our children on the basis of what sounds good with our last name. Or we pick a preppy name, or the name of a famous person. But in the Old Testament, a person's name indicated their character. Think of some of the names of God: Jehovah, "the self-existent One who reveals Himself"; El Shaddai, "Almighty God"; El Elyon, "Most High God"; Jehovah-jireh, "the Lord will provide."

We could look at many other names of God and discover that He is loving, kind, faithful, just, true, and everlasting. We can wait thinking about God's name because it reveals His character. It lets us know that God is who He says He is and that He can be trusted.

Perhaps you are in a situation that seems impossible and you feel like there's no hope for the future. Knowing that God's name is El Shaddai, "Almighty God," can remind you that no problem is too hard for God. Corrie Ten Boom used to say that no matter how deep the pit, God was deeper still. Knowing that God is Jehovah-jireh, "the Lord will provide," can help you to understand that God will provide for and meet your every need, even in the midst of your loneliness and longing. Knowing that God is kind and that He does whatever is best for us can help us cope with the illness or death of a loved one. Knowing that God is just can help us to endure a job situation where we are being discriminated against. We can wait on the Lord because He is true to His name.

We can also wait on God because He is the source of our security. In Psalm 62:5-6 David expresses it this way, "My soul, wait in silence for God only, For my hope is from Him. He only is my rock and my salvation, My stronghold; I shall not be shaken."

For David, a man involved in many battles, a rock and a stronghold were extremely important. They were his front line of defense. He was dependent on them for security. When he was behind the rock or inside the stronghold, he was safe from his enemies. He was safe as long as he took advantage of his defense system. Once he ventured outside the stronghold and in front of the rock, he was vulnerable to attack.

Just as the rock and the stronghold protected David in battle, so God is the source of our security when we face our daily battles. As long as we are depending on Him for security, we are safe and we will not be shaken. But when we start depending on money, possessions, jobs, or relationships, we are on shaky ground.

What happens when we wait on the Lord?

Why bother waiting on the Lord? What happens when we wait for Him? Scripture tells us that three benefits come to those who wait for the Lord. Psalm 145:14-16 describes the first of these benefits.

"The LORD sustains all who fall, and raises up all who are bowed down. The eyes of all look to Thee, and Thou dost give them their food in due time. Thou dost open Thy hand, And dost satisfy the desire of every living thing."

The first benefit is that God provides for and meets the needs of those who wait for Him. He sustains and encourages. He gives them their food in due time. He opens His hand and satisfies the person's desire. He meets each person's daily needs.

Do these verses describe you as you sit in the waiting room? Fallen? Bowed down? Looking to God? If you are waiting on Him, He will raise you up and meet your needs in His time. However, be very careful about setting time limits for

God. God meets our needs and answers our requests in His time, not ours. He operates on His schedule, not ours.

When we encounter a problem situation, we have to make a choice whether or not to wait on the Lord. When we choose not to wait on God, we become impatient and we worry. We doubt that God is good and loving. We doubt His ability to provide for us and to solve our problems. When we respond like this, we are prime candidates for ulcers, migraine headaches, high blood pressure, and even heart attacks.

We suffer physical problems when we take these burdens upon ourselves. God doesn't want that for us. The second benefit that He wants to give us is refreshment. Isaiah 40:31 describes what God does for those who wait: "Yet those who wait for the LORD will gain new strength; They will mount up with wings like eagles, They will run and not get tired, They will walk and not become weary."

While people all around are collapsing due to exhaustion, the people who wait on the Lord will be refreshed. When your business associates suffer from ulcers due to worry, you can experience God's peace if you wait on Him. God can refresh and renew those who are weary because He Himself does not become tired or weary. And He wants to give that refreshment to those who are willing to wait on Him.

Probably one of our greatest fears in waiting on the Lord is that we'll come to the end of our time period and discover that we wasted our time. We'll find out that there was something else we could have been doing. However, God not only provides for and refreshes those who wait on Him, but He also promises that waiting will be worth the time spent doing it.

In Psalm 25:3, David says confidently, "Indeed, none of those who wait for Thee will be ashamed." In this psalm, David is asking God to teach him His ways and to lead him in truth. He confesses his dependence on God, and he asks God to protect, guide, and pardon him. As he reflects on his request, he declares confidently that the time he has spent with God has been worth whatever he sacrificed to do it. He knows that God will not allow him to be ashamed.

Are you in the waiting room? Are you facing what seems to be an impossible situation? Are you lonely, crying out for companionship and comfort? Are you asking God to meet your needs? When you pray, does it seem like you're getting a busy signal from God? Do you wonder if He hears and answers?

If you are asking these questions, my answer is the same as the psalmist, Wait for the Lord. As you sit in the waiting room, take the time to read the manual. Spend time seeking God. Find out who He is and what he has promised to do in your life. Find out what He wants you to do. Continue to pray, confidently expecting Him to do great things in your life. Be patient and allow Him to work in His time. He can be trusted because He is true to His name. We can wait for Him because He is our source of security. As we wait for Him, He will refresh us and renew our strength. He will give us the grace and strength that we need in order to soar like an eagle above the problem.

—*Mark S. Wheeler*

Where Is God When Bad Things Happen?

On October 23, 1989 a Pasadena, Texas chemical plant exploded, killing or injuring several workers and destroying property around the area. That evening the press interviewed Mrs. Jose Gonzales, whose husband was critically injured and in intensive care. "We've always trusted in God," she said, "and He never let us down before." The next day Jose Gonzales died.

Mrs. Gonzales spoke for millions of Christians when she affirmed her faith in God. And like most of us, she struggled to hold on to that reality when God did not respond in the way she asked. Few Christians lack an intellectual sense of God's power and presence. The difficulty comes when we try to transfer that knowledge into practical and emotional reality during times of crisis. We all know God is in His heaven controlling the world as He wills. But still we ask, where is God when I need Him?

WHERE IS GOD DURING DANGER?

On October 17 I had lunch in the Pacific Garden Mall in Santa Cruz, California. Four hours later it was leveled; six persons died and over 600 were injured in Santa Cruz County as the great World Series earthquake hit San Francisco and dozens of miles around. Who can forget the televised pictures of collapsed Highway I-880 or the dropping of a 50-foot long panel on the Bay Bridge?

Where is God during natural disasters? Many people asked that during 1989, a year that saw 14 major storms, 9 floods, 3 tornadoes, and 3 hurricanes, in addition to the earthquake.

Perhaps that's the question David asked the day he discovered the Amalekites had raided Ziklag (1 Sam. 30:1-6). It was certainly not a natural disaster, but it did represent clear-cut danger. The possibility of losing wives and families created internal strife within his ranks. Yet the text tells us, "David strengthened himself in the Lord his God" (v. 6). How did he do that? The next two verses answer the question: "David inquired of the Lord."

In times of danger, especially those times in which we seem powerless to do anything for ourselves, Christians must review and affirm one of the major life principles of the Bible: God alone can be counted upon in times of total helplessness, even those times when friends turn against us.

Unfortunately, turning to God is often the last option many Christians consider. Some turn inward believing they can conquer anything that comes along, and only when God stretches them out in utter hopelessness do they turn to Him. Others respond to a crisis by looking for human help—family, friends, pastors, counselors.

Natural disasters and other kinds of danger are difficult to explain and most of them contain riddles we will not solve until we get to heaven. But one principle stands firm— through that kind of experience God calls us to look up and trust Him with the outcome, however bizarre it might seem at the time.

WHERE IS GOD DURING ILLNESS?

Jim Conway is a familiar name among evangelicals who connect him with research and writing on male mid-life crisis. At the age of 16, Jim's daughter, Becki, entered the hospital for testing on a malignant tumor on her leg. Each day the family laid hands on her leg and asked God to heal her; each day the tumor remained. One morning the doctor wheeled her into surgery and at Jim's request, took one more look to make sure the tumor was still there. Two hours and forty-five minutes later he came out and told the family he had taken Becki's leg off above mid-thigh. Jim writes:

> In my anguish, I cried out to God, "Why? What's Your reason? Why would You allow a beautiful girl to have her leg cut off when You could stop it? She is only a junior in high school." ...I felt as if my whole world had fallen apart. My confidence in God was gone (*CLR Vision*, October 1989, p. 1).

Jehovah's people crying out to Him for healing was a familiar sound in Bible times as well as now. In 2 Kings 20:1-3, King Hezekiah lay ill to the point of death and the prophet Isaiah told him, "'Thus says the Lord, 'Set your house in order, for you shall die and not live.' Then he turned his face to the wall and prayed. ...And Hezekiah wept bitterly."

Some suggest that Hezekiah's tears were shed for the nation, worrying that his death would give the Assyrian Sennecherib something to boast about. I think he was tired of being sick and afraid of dying. He reminded God of his own personal righteousness and, unlike many similar situations in both Old and New Testaments, God responded by adding 15 years to his life. One commentator writes that "Hezekiah's prayer (what he said) and his tears (how he felt about what he said) moved God to heal him."

What is the life principle here? We might word it something like this: For reasons we often do not understand, God sometimes chooses to heal His people on the basis of prayer. That's the positive side and we all rejoice in affirming it. The negative side? Sometimes He chooses not to. The history of the church to the present hour is replete with examples of "thorns in the flesh" God chose not to take away.

Jim and Sally Conway searched for answers about Becki. They all sounded like hollow advice from Job's comforters until they finally admitted they did not need an answer; no answer other than that God loves them. Somehow in His sovereignty everything fits together, even when we're sure it never can. How did Job put it? "Though He slay me, I will hope in Him" (Job 13:15). To put it another way, I'm committed to God even if it kills me.

WHERE IS GOD DURING TROUBLE?

Where is God when we get into trouble? Many Bible characters could have asked that question. Some, like Joseph, more than once. Consider the trouble a teenage boy must feel when his brothers throw him into a cistern, then a few hours later, sell him to a wandering caravan of Ishmaelites (Gen. 37:12-28). We know the outcome so we can read the account in the light of Joseph's rise to leadership in Egypt. But I suspect it was somewhat difficult to make that kind of positive analysis from the bottom of the cistern.

Sometimes the financial blood drains out of a business and a good Christian goes bankrupt. Sometimes Christians lose their jobs or get sued. Sometimes marriages break up or teenagers get hooked on drugs. So where is God when we get into trouble?

Perhaps the life principle in the Joseph epic reminds us that the struggles of life, even when maliciously caused by other people (or by our own stupidity), cannot thwart God's ultimate goals. Joseph's youthful struggles were only complicated by a doting father and hateful brothers. Yet years later he could look at those brothers and recall that afternoon at the cistern: "You meant evil against me, but God meant it for good in order to bring about this present result, to preserve many people alive" (Gen. 50:20).

WHERE IS GOD DURING SORROW?

I will always remember Sunday afternoon September 11, 1977. My mother lay dying in a hospital and there was nothing I could do. In fact, the next day she did die and those 48 hours were among the darkest of my entire life. To be sure, sorrow can be connected with illness or trouble but most often we focus primarily on the agony of the heart.

The outstanding biblical example has to be Jesus in the Garden of Gethsemane just before the Cross. The text tells us He "began to be very distressed and troubled" and told the disciples, "My soul is deeply grieved to the point of death" (Mark 14:32-34). His soul, His inner self-conscious life, was overwhelmed with grief so much that it almost killed Him before He got to the cross. The full impact of the spiritual consequences of His death had staggered the Son of God Himself. The possibility of alienation from the Father horrified Him.

There are numerous life principles which jump out of the text at us. Perhaps the one most important for our present focus reminds us that God's plan for our lives may be at times incomprehensively and desperately painful, but will always work out for our own good. The sorrow of the Garden turned into the death of the Cross. But that awful tragedy gave way to resurrection and glory, defeating Satan and opening the doors of heaven to all who trust the Savior.

I'm impressed that in sorrow prayer was necessary even for Jesus. That prayer focused on obedience; it required sacrifice and hard work. I'm impressed too, and not just a little bit frightened, that sometimes the worst crises of life have to be faced alone with only God to hear that prayer The disciples were asleep and would have been little help awake. In the darkest pit of personal agony, sometimes God alone can hear our cries.

WHERE IS GOD DURING DEATH?

In late fall 1989, teenager Amy Lynn Thatcher of Duncanville, Texas was kidnapped and killed. She was a believer, apparently from a strong Christian family. What did the face of God look like to them at that girl's funeral? An automobile accident or drowning hurts badly but kidnapping and abuse followed by murder surely reaches a higher level of pain. Where is God when we need Him at the time of death? God's plan for our lives may be at times, incomprehensible.

Another Christian family once struggled with that question. When Jesus reached Bethany, Martha reminded Him, "Lord, if You had been here, my brother would not have died" (John 11:21). Moments later Mary echoed exactly the same sentiment. Martha's faith in the Lord was strong; she understood the Old Testament and affirmed, "I know that he will rise again in the resurrection on the last day" (v. 24).

That day to Martha, God's Messiah offered a promise the like of which people never heard before or since:

> I am the resurrection and the life; he who believes in
> Me shall live even if he dies, and everyone who lives
> and believes in Me shall never die (John 11:25-26).

Life principle? You know it well: For Christians, as ugly and painful as it is, death is temporary. Life is permanent because life is eternal. The life of the ages has been made available through Jesus the Lord of life. His true spiritual life is of such a quality that the spirits of believers will never die.

But our question persists—where is God when I need Him? The answer persists too. he is precisely where He has always been—in His heaven taking complete charge of everything that happens in His world.

As we said at the beginning, the problem lies not in understanding what the Bible says, or even believing it. We must allow God's Holy Spirit to activate the truth of His Word in our lives when we need it. That kind of reality doesn't just occur, and it rarely takes hold after the fact. The spiritual strength of our lives on a day-to-day basis—before danger, illness, trouble, sorrow, and death strike—makes the difference in a time of crisis.

Remember we don't have to understand God's plan and it doesn't have to make sense in human logic. God who allowed the doors of China to remain tightly closed to the gospel, with the other hand tore down the Berlin Wall. God who allows Moslem lands to stay hard and cold has opened the Iron Curtain in ways the most optimistic missionary could not have predicted five years ago.

Our only attitude to the omnipotent King of Heaven must be that of Shadrach, Meshack and Abednego. Our God is able to deliver us from any crisis. But even if He chooses not to, we will still serve Him.

—Kenneth O. Gangel

Hoping for the Best

"Is this all there is to life?"

I admit that, while lying awake in bed one night, I wrestled with this question.

After being a Christian for 15 years, I could no longer ignore the fact that I felt a desolate emptiness in my soul. The exuberant optimism of earlier days as a new Christian seemed all but to evaporate with the passing of time. Relationships that fell short of expectations, setbacks in reaching life goals, and the ongoing tedium of uneventful days, forced me to ask myself, "What am I really hoping for in this life?"

The answers I came up with that night were not uncommon for someone preparing to enter an academic ministry. I hoped to teach in a Christian college or seminary. I hoped I would one day be able to write some helpful books and articles. I hoped to impact the lives of many. I hoped to marry a godly woman who would serve as a co-heir with me in "the gracious gift of life." I also hoped that one day my missionary parents would return to the States so we could spend the rest of our days together as a family. As I weighed these hopes in my mind, I was struck by how immediate and earthbound my priorities seemed.

Since that day I have learned two valuable lessons bout the aching abyss in my soul.

WHAT ARE YOU HOPING FOR?

First, the things Christians hope for often pertain to this world, and we want these things now. Because the return of Christ seems remote and future, we tend to put our hope in fulfilling those immediate concerns of our lives: productive careers, satisfying marriage and family relationships, lasting friendships, and secure retirements. Consequently, we tend to misplace the Object of our long-term hope (Christ) with short-term hopes.

A second lesson I have learned is that the lingering emptiness we all experience is a normal and indispensable part of our growth into Christlikeness. Admittedly, this may run counter to many popular ideas of the Christian life. Moreover, as Christians we might be afraid to admit to others that we are less than fulfilled with life. Still, it is only in a world where disappointment, relational incompleteness, and imperfection abound that the need for hope arises. If the emptiness in our hearts could be filled adequately in this life, what would happen to our hope?

The preceding thoughts raise a key question: Can the Christian virtue of hope find legitimate fulfillment in the here-and-now as well as in the hereafter?

In the Old Testament, hope often speaks of a waiting or longing for the promise of God, even when obstacles seem to frustrate the fulfillment of those promises. In the Psalms, the objects of hope often included God's gracious acts of deliverance and His consequent blessing in the near future. Hope, in its long-term aspect, arises in the anticipation of Messiah's return and the future emotional restoration of Israel.

In the majority of contexts where the word hope appears in the New Testament, it generally anticipates the return of Christ, the resurrection of the body, and the restoration of the cosmos, or created order. Hope then is the desire and confident expectancy of God's future promises in Christ. However, the idea of immediate hope fulfilled in the here-and-now appears far less frequently in the New Testament. For example, Paul hopes to see fellow Christians (1 Tim. 3:14); he hopes for the favorable outcome of those to whom he has ministered (1 Thess. 2:19); and he states his short-term ministerial desires (Phil. 2:23). Likewise, the author of the Epistle to the Hebrews expresses confidence that his readers will pull through the difficult trials that they had experienced (Heb. 6:9-12). Although other words are used in the New Testament to communicate the idea of hope (desire, expectation, waiting, confidence), in the majority of instances, hope is for (1) eternal life after death, (2) the return of Christ, and (3) Christ's accompanying blessings of cosmic transformation.

HOPING TO MEET JESUS

What may we gather from these observations?

First, the New Testament's focus on distant hope indicates that hope, a Christian virtue, should have its focus not on the concerns of this life, but on "the blessed hope—the glorious appearing of our great God and Savior, Jesus Christ" (Titus 2:13, NIV). To regard ourselves at home in the here-and-now invites disappointment and disillusionment. Granted, the Bible does suggest obedience on our part is a prerequisite for God's answers to our prayers (Ps. 37:4-5; 1 John 3:21-22; 1 Pet. 3:10-12). So, hope for the here-and-now is not wrong if coupled with motives that honor Christ. But what if the things we hope and pray for do not come to pass? To be sure, "Hope deferred makes the heart sick" (Prov. 13:12). Consequently, we must read the Bible with the understanding that we cannot order God's agenda for our lives. As a loving, sovereign, and all-wise God, He decides which good gifts to give to His children.

Second, as startling as the emotion might seem, death is the Christian's sweetest friend; it is the blessed corridor into the fulfillment of our hope (2 Cor. 5:8). It is the precious "gain" about which the Apostle Paul wrote (Phil. 1:21). This understanding of death leads us then, not to a fascination with death, but to a focus upon the return of Him who will resurrect the dead. For this reason, the return of Christ is regarded as the blessed hope since those who do not die will experience a total renovation of being in that day. Perhaps this is why Paul commands believers to be "rejoicing in hope" (Rom. 12:12).

Third, if the ultimate fulfillment of hope occurs with the radical transformation of our bodies upon the return of Christ, sin will accompany and perplex us all the days of our mortality. Addictive behaviors, selfishness, inner pain, and relational deficiencies can be overcome in this life—but only in measure. Total recovery and victory are yet future. So, our ongoing struggle with sin serves as a vital stimulus not only for hope, but for faith and love as well. This struggle with sin compels us to hope with fellow pilgrims who, in "one hope of [our] calling" (Eph. 4:4), share that same inner-most yearning for a better day. In the meantime, perseverance, as an ingredient of hope, is the order of the day (Rom. 5:4).

HOPING FOR A GLORIOUS FUTURE

Can we have hope in the transforming power of God for the here-and-now? Yes! But we perceive God's transforming power by the way we grow in our relationships with God and with one another through increased faith, hope, and love (1 Cor. 13:7; 2 Thess. 1:3-4). Hope in the here-and-now must be hope for maturity, specifically, the enriching of our relationships with Christ and with people. Christian hope at its very core, whether it is long-term or short-term hope, is hope of relationship.

Can we have hope in God for favorable outcomes in the here-and-now? Yes! Yet we must do so with an attitude that says, "If it is the Lord's will, we will live and do this or that" (James 4:15, NIV).

Through hope, perplexing disappointments will not cause us to be taken captive by defeatism or cynical indifference. Christian hope is not a form of escapism, but a realistic perception of life and of the future. Hope is an active waiting that appropriates the spiritual resources we have in Christ to overcome the despair that we are prone to fall into whenever we are confronted with the misfortunes and inequities of life.

Hope is a memory of the future that drives us to communion with God and with fellow believers, and aids us in our ultimate triumph over the paralysis of despair. Until the day we are united with "Christ Jesus our hope" (1 Tim. 1:1, NIV), the emptiness in our souls will remain. At times the ache will be acute and unrelenting. This is the gist of Paul's thought when he writes, "We ourselves, having the first fruits of the Spirit, even we ourselves groan within ourselves, waiting eagerly for our adoption as sons, the redemption of our body" (Rom. 8:23).

So then, hope and faith in Gods' promises in Christ will sustain us and provide the confidence that, however bleak things may seem, the gnawing emptiness we all experience is not final: A glorious day is coming!

"Hope does not disappoint us, because God has poured out his love into our hearts by the Holy Spirit whom he has given us" (Rom. 5:5).

—*Gary L. Nebeker*

When the Excitement Fades

Quitters. Nobody wants to be one; yet all of us have been disappointed by them. Are you a quitter? I suspect that most of you would answer "Absolutely not!" But one of the most discouraging realities in the church is the average believer's inability to stick it out. When the going gets tough, the ranks thin quickly.

The dropout rate in Christianity is alarming. Few believers follow through on their initial zeal for the Savior, and the loss to the church in potential ministry is great. Most of us assume that sin or bad doctrine is responsible. A closer look reveals that many of us simply quit. When the excitement fades so do we.

Jim is one of those who quit. When I first trusted Christ as Savior Jim was my closest Christian friend. What fond memories I have of those years. We were partners in the leadership at a local Young Life Club. Our days were full of spiritual excitement and eternal significance as we led Bible studies, took kids to camp, prepared evangelistic messages, prayed together, and talked theology for hours. It seemed we couldn't get enough.

I have always looked forward to spending some time with my old friend when I go home. He's still a great guy. He runs an honest business, devotes himself to his family, lives a balanced life, and even goes to church. He knows he's a Christian, that Jesus died for his sins, and he could probably hold his own in most conversations about the Bible. But it's not the same. Somewhere along the way Jim just gave up.

What happens to people like Jim? Why do so many of us who begin so zealously become so zeal-less? Maybe you feel like quitting. You're not alone.

The first believer who felt like quitting was Peter. It was after the resurrection when an angel had promised that Jesus would meet with His disciples in the north (Matt. 28:7). They went to Galilee and waited. But Jesus didn't show. Peter, disappointed by the delay, announced that he was going fishing. He must have been pretty persuasive because seven of the disciples went with him, and three of those weren't even fishermen! John records the event in chapter 21 of his gospel. It's a touching story God has used many times to speak to His children who want to give up. The passage revolves around the three major mistakes Christian quitters make.

Don't Look Back! (John 21:1-14)

The first mistake Christian quitters make is looking in the wrong direction. When we walk with Christ our entire orientation is to the future. We are new creatures in Him and all things have become new (2 Cor. 5:17). When we begin to look back at our comfort zone we get into trouble.

Peter tried returning to his comfort zone. You really can't blame him. Jesus had been talking about a coming kingdom and glory with Messiah for three years. But each time they asked the Lord if "this was it," they were told to wait. Now, exhausted from the trauma of the crucifixion and the turmoil following the resurrection, Peter and his friends were discouraged. They remembered the good old days when life was uncomplicated: the daily routine of fishing, the security of knowing what was next, the satisfaction of running your own life. So Peter announced to his friends, "I'm going fishing" (vv. 1-3)!

I remember a time when I was tired and almost quit. It was my second year of seminary. The bills were piling up and the workload seemed unbearable. I hated my menial job and never had enough time for studies or family. I began looking back at the "good old days" when we had been in the Army: good pay, significant duties, exciting travel, great friends. Why did I ever resign my commission? Then I received an inquiry from Uncle Sam. There was a shortage of officers and they were offering special incentives to those who would come back in.

I almost quit seminary. The military was my comfort zone. I would simply pick up where I left off. Then the story of Peter in verses 1-14 reminded me that I could never go back.

Peter was tired of waiting. He would just pick up where he left off. But the Lord wanted him to know that he would never just be a fisherman again. In fact, without Jesus Peter couldn't even fish well anymore. It wasn't until the Lord showed up to give them specific instructions on fishing that these professional fishermen even got a bite. With the Lord's guidance their net overflowed.

Do you ever ask yourself, "Why do I put up with all this?" Being a serious Christian adds a lot of pressure to our schedules. And serving with other believers often results in strained relationships, disappointment, even pain. All of us will sometimes dream of what life was like before we were so committed. But we need to know that we can never simply pick up where we left off.

I know a couple who always look ahead excitedly. Talented, professional, good looking, articulate, with no children, Mark and Peggy moved to Oregon to get away from the rat race of Southern California. Their mountain home provided a perfect base camp for the lifestyle of their dreams. Skiing, backpacking, rafting, hunting, and fishing filled their lives.

But it didn't take long for them to see that these beautiful Cascades were full of hurting people who needed their Savior. They traded their mountain hide-away for a house closer to the new church they helped start in the valley. Their skis, fishing poles, packs, and hiking boots now gather dust in the garage. But they don't care. You see this garage is attached to a home full of God's love, and the dust never settles there. Tonight's the party for the junior high gang. Tomorrow they will lead a home Bible study. Then there's that couple they're discipling, and the new believers who want to know how Jesus Christ can rebuild their marriage, and the friend who doesn't know Christ yet, and....

Thank God for people like Mark and Peggy who never look back.

The lesson for quitters in verse 1-14 is clear. Don't look back. You belong to Jesus now and things can never be the same. Your future is with the Lord and full of exciting significance if only you will follow Him. For those who will follow there is the assurance of a Savior who will provide an intimate and personal way. He even cooks breakfast!

Don't Look for Perks

At the center of the quitter's problem is a lack of motivation. When it comes to serving God the only sustaining force is a deep love for the Savior. When we consider the mercies of God, the only reasonable response is to present our bodies as living sacrifices (Rom. 12:1). If we are following our Lord for any reason other than love we will run out of steam.

The heart of this passage records Peter's threefold lesson on proper motivation. The Lord makes sure that His disciple made the connection between love for the Savior and service to Him. Whatever else was cluttering Peter's desire to follow Christ, it was jettisoned on that day. His Lord left no room for selfish goals. Only the pure motivation of love for the Chief Shepherd qualified Peter to care for His sheep.

The pattern never varies. Dropouts betray their inner motives the moment they quit. Each year our church presents many opportunities to serve. Initially, the euphoria of all that is new and exciting carries people through. Then, as the year wears on, the rationalizations begin to trickle in: "I don't think I am cut out for teaching small children; it simply isn't fulfilling." "I just cannot work with this man anymore; our differences are too great." "Our family is just too stressed out over this." "I really don't have the time to put in on this class." At the end of the year the only ones left standing are those who volunteered for the right reason in the first place—love for their Lord.

I wish you could meet Dirk. He's the CEO of a global firm, a renowned researcher and inventor, and a world-class Sunday school teacher. All employees know that he must not be disturbed when he is preparing next week's lesson. Executives, engineers, competitors, and customers are all put on hold until Dirk has complete confidence he is teaching the best class he can.

Many have commented to me how odd it is that such an important man spends so much time preparing for Sunday school. Sometimes only a handful show up. But they don't know my friend. Dirk isn't teaching this class to attract great crowds. The class is a weekly love offering to a Savior who died for the teacher...when he was still a sinner!

The believer who is looking to get something out of service to Jesus Christ never lasts. The Christian who volunteers because of a deep love and commitment to Jesus Christ never fails.

What about you? What strings are you attaching to your service for the Savior? Be careful. God will stretch those strings until they break. Don't look for perks. Do it for love, or don't do it.

DON'T LOOK AT OTHERS (JOHN 21:18-22)

The third error believers who throw in the towel make is looking at the wrong person. Christianity is a personal relationship with Jesus Christ. God has unique plans for each of us. When we compare ourselves to others we usually get ticked off at God.

One of the most interesting dynamics in the gospel accounts is the relationship between Peter, John, and Jesus Christ. Peter is the Lord's obvious choice as leader of the disciples, but John is Christ's closest friend. Surely the memory of the Last Supper is fresh in Peter's mind. The future leader of the church had to depend upon John to find out who would betray their Lord (John 13:21-26). So when Jesus solemnly predicts Peter's future execution on the cross (21:18-19) Peter's immediate reaction is, "But what about John?" Jesus' rebuke is sharp. "If I want him to remain until I come, what is that to you?" You follow Me" (21:22)! Peter had to learn to trust Jesus to take care of John while he concentrated on what Jesus was saying to him.

Did you ever fall into the comparison trap? My closest friend, one of the most effective men of God I know, has been haunted by this problem. He grew up under the ministry of a very talented pastor who now heads up an international ministry. My friend, though equally gifted, has never gained the high-profile status of his mentor. His assignments from God have taken him through two very painful pastorates. While his role model was on tours behind the Iron Curtain, this young pastor was settling disputes over the color of the cloth curtains in dingy Sunday school rooms. This contrast has been one of the greatest challenges to his attitude. He often commented to me during the toughest times, "I bet Joe never has to put up with trivial, petty problems like this!"

Let me ask you this: Who is your "Joe"? Who is it that you present before the Lord and ask, "What about this person? Why does he or she have it so good when I've got it so bad?" Their marriage is marvelous, but yours is miserable. His career is soaring while your stalls. She gets all the attention at church, but nobody even notices you. It seems they never have the problems we have. It just isn't fair! So I'm just going to quit.

Jesus would no more put up with that attitude today than

He did on the shores of Galilee hundreds of years ago. Don't look at others. Christ is more than capable of dealing with each saint. He doesn't need any help from us to make sure every believer gets a fair deal. The cancer of comparison will eat at your attitude until you quit. But Jesus says, "Stop worrying about others; you follow Me."

Don't Miss God's Best (Matt. 28:16-20)

The timing of Jesus' visit with his disciples that morning causes us to consider the enormous cost of quitting. The events recorded in John 21 follow the disciples' arrival in Galilee to wait for their Lord (Matt. 28:16). It was during this time of waiting that Jesus met His discouraged disciples for breakfast and taught them these vital lessons on quitting. But look at what follows: The Great Commission (Matt. 28:18-20)! Think of all they would have missed if they had quit that morning. These were the men Jesus had chosen to change the world, not to go fishing.

I often wonder what my friend might have accomplished for God. He was a phenomenal evangelist and disciple. He had a way about him. His pattern was simple but effective. He would move into your life, earn your trust, then challenge you with the eternal truths from Scripture. God used him to bring many to Jesus in those few short years before he faded.

We may not know exactly what God has in store for us. But His best will never happen if we quit. Don't miss God's best. God has great plans for you. But you will never know that exciting future of growing significance for your Savior if you quit.

Don't look back; the comfort zone is a myth. Don't look for perks; the compelling force in your life must be love for Christ. And don't look at others; the comparison game always disappoints.

Don't quit.

—R. Edward Underwood, Jr.

Expressing Praise and Prayer

Ascribe to the Lord, O mighty ones,
Ascribe to the Lord glory and strength,
Ascribe to the Lord the glory due His name;
Worship the Lord in the splendor of His holiness!
(PSALM 29:1-2)

How do you respond when your hear somebody shout, "Praise the Lord!" Be honest. Do you sometimes feel uncomfortable? Do you ever wonder where they got their excitement from, and what you need to do to get yours back? This next section will prepare your hearts for worship. Be warned, though: The pages you are about to read could change your heart. You'll find yourself joining David in saying, "How good it is to sing praises to our God! How pleasant and fitting to praise Him!"

Encountering His Holiness

Imagine suddenly being ushered into a room filled with unusual expectation. Your attention immediately focuses on activity surrounding a throne. Someone sits on the throne, lofty and exalted, seated and sovereign. Thousands of attendants adore him unendingly. You have been invited to observe.

The attendants appear inhibited. They blush, veiling their faces for what they are not. They humbly, even cautiously, participate in the experience. They shroud their feet, scattering any hint of casualness. And yet, they possess a freedom. They can soar on wings through the heavens in their worship.

A hush comes over the room, hovering like a thick cloud. And then the silence is shattered. In a perfectly choreographed cadence, the adoring attendants sing, "Holy, Holy, Holy is the Lord of Hosts." "The whole earth is full of His glory," they chime. Without a dissenting note among them, they all sing as one. The foundation shakes. The room rumbles. You then clue in. "I have been invited to observe God! I have witnessed the worship of majesty."

No longer able to remain silent, you then cry out, "Woe is me, for I am ruined! Because I am a man of unclean lips, and I live among a people of unclean lips; for my eyes have seen the King, the LORD of hosts" (Isa. 6:5).

INTO THE PRESENCE OF GOD

Scripture portrays vivid images of those invited into the presence of God. Isaiah was not alone in his experience. On another occasion a shepherd named Moses, on a mountain called Horeb, received an invitation through a bush all in flames. The ground on which he stood was holy. So he RSVP'd by removing his sandals. On this occasion, God came down (Exod. 3:1-5).

On yet another occasion, man went up.

He was alone on a remote island forced into early retirement. Old and near death, and at a time when some might write their memoirs, he would soon live out the epilogue of his life. His name? John. His occupation? Apostle.

Moments before, he sat counting relentless waves as they snuggled the sandy beach. The cry of the sea gull soon faded as the roar of the surf gave way to the voice of rushing waters. Before John stood One with wooly white hair, flaming red eyes, and glowing bronze feet. Launched from his mouth was a sword. Two edges. Both sharp. John heard the echo of praise thrice repeated. "Holy, Holy, Holy." His response? He fell down as a dead man. He passed out cold. The voice of many waters extended a tender hand. "Do not be afraid; I am..." (Rev. 1:9-20).

THE MISSING JEWEL

Writing to his generation, A.W. Tozer called worship the "missing jewel." Sadly enough, our generation still searches in vain for this rare gem. We have traded the practice of internal retreat for the product of external hoopla. The entertainment generation has little patience for genuine worship.

The church today is inflated and prosperous. It even has political clout. But the practice of worship, both corporate and private, often lies neglected along the roadside of our Christian experience.

True worship, though, was the experience of Isaiah, Moses, John, and countless others in Scripture. They, having been invited to a heavenly worship service, left the experience moved, shaken, even broken—yet renewed. They had been in the presence of God. They had experienced His holiness. Not one of them left puffed up with pride.

Isaiah is an oasis of help in times like these. In his observations, he reminds us of the results of true worship. His experience shines like a beacon, announcing that we too can experience God's presence in true worship.

What happens, though, when we worship? First, Isaiah reminds us that our worship experience can rearrange our perspective.

Isaiah first sees the Lord seated on a throne. Take note, the Lord is seated. He is not frantically running about trying to keep his creation in order. He is neither panicked nor worried. Rather He is seated and sovereign.

When we worship the Lord, let's remember that He is in control. Nothing alarms Him, or takes Him by surprise. Nothing is too big for Him to handle, or so small it escapes His attention.

When the winds of my world begin to blow, He remains seated. When raging waves surround me, He governs their temper. If the report from the doctor reveals the need for emergency surgery, I need not be moved. If the cogs of free enterprise eliminate my job, I don't have to fret. Why? Because the Lord is seated and sovereign. Isaiah's worship experience begins by seeing the Lord high and lifted up above His created order. He alone is sovereign.

FOCUSED ON OUR GOD

Isaiah not only sees the Lord, but he hears the choreographed voices of the angelic host. They sing, "Holy, Holy, Holy." Notice they do not sing, "Righteous, Righteous, Righteous," or "Just, Just, Just."

When we worship the Lord, remember too that His nature is altogether different from ours. He is holy. He is unspotted by the pollutants of this world. He is unstained by evil. He is everything I am not. His eyes are too pure to behold evil. Mine, if given the chance, are prone to drink in the intoxicants of this life.

The holiness of God cannot co-exist with sin. Though He

is long-suffering, He is never tolerant. He never folds a frustrated arm, or shakes a despairing finger. He never winks like a doting old grandfather and says, "Boys will be boys." And so when I come to worship the Lord, I cannot be casual with sin. The presence of God demands holiness. The presence of God demands that we confess our sin.

On another occasion the angels are heard singing to the One "who was, and is, and is to come." The Lord is not only sovereign and holy, He is also eternal. "From everlasting to everlasting, Thou art God" (Ps. 90:2).

If we turn and gaze into yesterday, exhausting our mind's eye, and then do an about-face and drink in tomorrow until we can consume no more, God is beyond both ends. He is eternal. Never beginning. Never ending.

Scripture warns us that "all flesh is like grass, and all its glory like the flower of grass. The grass withers, and the flower falls off, but the word of the LORD abides forever" (1 Pet. 1:24-25). But most of us live life for the fading glory. The next promotion. The big deal. A house, or two. A car, or three. A membership. A pat on the back. The glory of it all dissipates. It is a puff of mist, gone when touched by the scorch of eternity.

But when our mind is focused on the eternal Lord of Heaven, we are reminded that our temporal days are not futile. Our time-shackled nights are not hopeless. The Ancient of Days is the One who numbers our days. He transforms our fading glory into surpassing glory. He confirms the work of our hands. He gives purpose to our existence. By reminding us that He has made us to live with Him forever He gives us, in a word, hope.

When we truly worship the Lord, we absorb His person. We drink in His attributes. When we do, He realigns our reality. He rearranges our perspective.

Further, Isaiah reminds us that our worship experience can

renew our purpose. Isaiah saw the Lord seated on a throne. He heard the angelic host sing of His holiness. He then cried, "woe is me!" The prophet was undone, shackled by the reality of his sin. And so he took his seat on the sideline. He relinquished his ambition under the brutal slaying of holiness.

But the Lord had plans for the prophet. An angel bearing a searing coal flies to touch Isaiah's unclean lips. Isaiah is about to be knighted into the Lord's service. A commissioning call echoes through the halls of eternity. "Whom shall I send, and who will go for Us?" A prophet humbly steps forward with renewed purpose. "Here am I. Send me!" The Lord replies, "Go!"

Throughout Scripture we are privy to sneak previews of the main event. Isaiah's experience is only one. By the time Scripture crescendos in John's Revelation of Jesus Christ, the heavenly choir and orchestra are pregnant with worship. The basses boom in glory's basement. The sopranos skip through hallowed halls of majesty. The altos and the baritones blend harmony in the parlor of praise. The instruments of worship tune with the oil of gladness, anxious to express their joy.

Suddenly there is silence. A hush comes over the scene. Shhhh… The conductor raises his hands. And in one fell swoop he whisks the participants into a furious rendition. His baton crashes through stanza after stanza, announcing to an audience of starry skies, "The Lamb is worthy." The constellations clap their hands. The mountains below shout, "Bravo! Encore!" But the participants are packing their bags. They quietly leave…it's only a rehearsal (Rev. 4:1-5:14).

Eternity will be filled with the echo of worship. The heavenly host is getting ready. Are you?

—Ronald L. Jones

Delighting His Heart

"Go and worship God in the church of your choice!" urged a sign in Beaumont, Texas. Donald Grey Barnhouse and his family passed the sign and pulled to a stop at a traffic light. Another car pulled alongside and a child was overhead to inquire, "Daddy, what does worship mean?" The father replied, "It means to go to church and listen to the preacher preach."

What does worship really mean? The answer supplied by the man would probably be a very common response. But does it provide an adequate model for worship? Comparing it and other popular conceptions of worship with biblical descriptions of worship, there is the gnawing suspicion that something vital is missing. The rich fabric of worship woven by the Scriptures makes these models seem threadbare, frayed, and patched by comparison.

A proper understanding of worship is vital to anyone who would delight the heart of God. The importance of acceptable worship and the dangers of faulty worship are clearly outlined in the Bible. The tragic story of Cain and Abel graphically portrays the awful consequences of inadequate worship. A chain of events that eventually left one brother dead and one a perpetual outcast began with an incident of faulty worship. Genesis 4:5 reports the incident simply by saying: "But for Cain and for his offering He [the Lord] had no regard."

Right from the beginning the Lord wanted man to know that the matter of worship is important. Faulty worship is rejected throughout the pages of Holy Scripture from Cain to the Pharisees It neither pleases God nor satisfies the deepest needs of the worshipper.

As Richard Adams perceptively notes in his novel Shardik, "Worship yields nothing to the slipshod and half-hearted. I have seen worship which if it had been a roof they had built would not have kept out a half-an-hour's rain; not had they the wit to wonder why it left their hearts cold and yielded them neither strength nor comfort."

THE RELATIONSHIP OF THE WORSHIPPER

Worship that pleases God and produces personal benefits ought to follow some sort of established pattern. But what is that pattern? What are we to do in order to avoid the "leaky roof" worship described by Adams?

In sharp contrast to the popular conceptions of worship, the overwhelming testimony of God's Word is that acceptable worship deals more with internal factors than with external functions. As poetic records of true worship, the Psalms reflect this fact. They provide a wealth of information on worship. Psalm 16 in particular seems to summarize beautifully the essentials of worship.

In reading Psalm 16, one discovers that the first component of acceptable worship is found in the relationship the worshipper has with God. David expresses this as the sense of security that he has in God in verse one: "Keep me safe, O God, for in You I take refuge." To David, God, and God alone was ultimately the bedrock of his life. His life was not built on the foundation of his armies, his family, or his wealth.

Apart from this component, worship is smothered before it can even begin. The Pharisees were heaps of faulty worship. They went through the motions meticulously, but Jesus exposed their motives as terribly flawed. They did not know God, nor did they care to know Him. Their worship was designed solely to impress men and gain worldly ends.

A young man will go to any extreme to avoid household chores at his own home. At the home of his sweetheart he will expend great energy just to be close to her. Drying the dishes becomes pure pleasure—provided she is washing. The love relationship turns obligation into delight. The same principle is at the heart of worship that pleases God.

THE OBEDIENCE OF THE WORSHIPPER

The second component of worship that David identifies in Psalm 16 is obedience. In verse two, David confides to God, "Thou art my LORD." He uses the title for God and not the name. He is indicating that God is sovereign in his life. And to acknowledge sovereignty is to recognize that obedience is required.

A compass lines itself up in obedience to the force of the magnetic north pole. Pass a magnet over iron filings and it will cause them to form various configurations in accordance with its magnetic field. Worship, similarly, involves aligning ourselves with God's will for us.

Cain acts as a counterpoint to David's obedience. Apparently, he came to God not as suppliant, but as one trying to set his own terms. He replaced the required blood sacrifice with the produce of his fields. His relationship with God was not enough to displace the proud desire to control his own destiny. Romans 12:1 identifies the acceptable "spiritual service of worship" as the result of yielding one's self as a living sacrifice to God. To be disobedient to the claims of lordship of Jesus Christ or to individual commands of God is to abort worship.

THE VALUES OF THE WORSHIPPER

In the phrase, "I have no good beside Thee" (Ps. 16:2), the third component of worship is encountered. It is the component of value. David could identify nothing in his life he valued more than God. Perhaps it is value that is most definitive of worship. The word worship itself comes from the contraction of the old English word worthship.

In our modern world so many things vie for our attention and affection. Values conflict and it is difficult to set priorities.

Our modern situation is reflected by a special sale sign found in a drug store greeting card section. Over an attractive red valentine card emblazoned hugely "I love you only!" was the sale sign reading "one card—30¢, five cards for a dollar."

Like the purchasers of that card, it is hard for us to be single-minded in the pursuit of a goal. Yet this is the attitude of the true worshipper—the single-minded determination to know God at the expense of anything else that interferes. Like the Old Testament saints with their sacrifices of lambs and bulls and goats, the worshipper must reserve the choicest and the best of his life for God. Nothing else can be allowed to crowd God out.

Perhaps these three components were what our Lord had in mind when He told the Samaritan woman by the well that true worship is "in spirit and in truth." Cain and many others have failed in these crucial matters of the heart. For in worship, it is quite simply more attitude than action, and more motive than motion.

THE BENEFITS OF THE WORSHIPPER

The rest of Psalm 16 adds a whole new dimension to the concept of worship. It paints a luscious word picture of the benefits and enjoyments of worship. Moreover, the benefits correspond beautifully with the three components of worship outlined in the first part or this Psalm. With zest and anticipation, the true worshipper unearths God's richest treasures through productive worship.

The worshipper who has an abiding relationship with God and maintains the vitality of that personal exposure is rewarded in worship with a deeper knowledge and appreciation of God. God Himself is like a refreshing drink of cold, clear water on a hot day to the worshiper (Ps. 16:5). And, the Psalmist says, it is like God has become a choice piece of property which provides a secure dwelling and continual sustenance from its rich soil. The one who looks to God for security will appreciate the benefits of that security through worship.

Corresponding to the second component of worship, obedience, is God's bestowal of direction. David's assurance of guidance is tied, in his own words, to the fact that he had "set the LORD ever before" him (Ps. 16:8). Through a heart that was carefully tuned in to God's frequency, David had the benefit of God's counsel. Even when the path was covered by the darkness of circumstances and obscured by the swirling fog of doubt, David anticipated and received God's guidance through worship. What a promise this is that God holds out to the one who will meet the conditions of worship. It is especially valuable for such a confusing time as ours.

Acknowledging God's worthship also reaps rich benefits. To highly value God and to desire Him is the one craving that can and will be completely satisfied. To know God is not an impossible dream for the true worshipper. All the other things men value highly will crumble and fade. The false gods which compete for our attention and allegiance can only disappoint. But the true worshipper finds abiding satisfaction and fulfillment in God Himself. David sums it up "…my heart is glad, and my glory rejoices; My flesh also will dwell securely" (Ps. 16:9). True worship gives access to God's wealth during the moments of worship. That wealth does not tarnish or rust, nor can it be stolen away. It provides dividends that extend beyond life into eternity (Ps. 16:10-11).

What is acceptable worship? It is any act that proceeds from a heart that is rightly related to God, from a heart that is in submission to God, and from a heart that values God above all else. These are the components of true worship. These attitudes can transform the most mundane activities of life into an enriching experience of worship. They alone can transform time set aside for worship from meaningless mumblings into a vital contact with our Creator.

But these components are not automatic even for the believer. Their intensity will change from time to time. Therefore they must be constantly cultivated by the one who would worship. Our worship delights the heart of God and benefits us when we cultivate our relationship to God, our obedience to God, and our value of God.

—*Alan J. Johnson*

Welcome In His Presence

"Welcome! Come on in! Make yourself at home!" These words are spoken and heard any time friends gather, whether during the holidays or at other times of the year. As people open their homes to family and friends for gatherings and celebrations, guests normally enjoy the benefits that belong to all guests—namely food, friendship and fellowship.

During the Christmas holidays, an analogy often is made in reference to Jesus' being born in a stable. Because there was "no room in the inn," the question often is asked, "Do you have room for Jesus? Is He welcome in your life?"

I'd like to turn that question around. Instead of asking if God is welcome in your life, I'd like to ask, "Are you welcome in His presence?" What kind of man, what kind of woman does God welcome into His presence? And, most important, are you developing in that direction?

This is not a new question. It's one that King David asked thousands of years before the birth of Christ. David too was concerned with the kind of person God would welcome, and in Psalm 15, he asked,

"O Lord, who may abide in Thy tent? Who may dwell on Thy holy hill?"

"Thy tent" and "Thy holy hill" speak of Israel's special place of worship in Jerusalem. From the phrases David uses, we can see that he is asking, "What kind of person will God welcome into His presence to worship Him?"

Today we might answer by replying simply, "A Christian. A man of God. A woman of God." Certainly, any person who has accepted Christ by faith is entirely welcome in God's presence. But in reference to vibrant, ongoing fellowship with God, we need to go further. We need to ask, "What is that person like? How does that person live?"

TRUTHFUL LIVING

Why is this so important? It's important for two reasons. First, it deals with practical living. Interestingly, the qualities David discovers in this psalm closely correspond to the qualifications for elders and deacons as found in the New Testament books of 1 Timothy and Titus. They offer a practical description of the believer and how he should relate to the people around him. It is not a question of salvation—it is a question of how a believer should live life in order to be able to worship God.

Second, it is an important question because of the benefits of being welcome in God's presence. In Old Testament culture, to be welcome in someone's house meant enjoying the benefits of Oriental hospitality—namely protection and sustenance.

A few years ago, a movie told the story of a young boy who went to Arabia in search of a horse that had been stolen from him. While he was there, he learned that if he told someone, "I want to be your guest," that person was obligated to take him in, feed him, and protect him. The host was responsible to sustain and protect his guests.

In Psalm 15, David asks, "Who is welcome in God's presence? Whom will God protect and sustain?" In verses 2-5, he gives a threefold answer to this question. He writes:

(vs. 2) He who walks with integrity, and works right-eousness, And speaks truth in his heart.

(vs. 3) He does not slander with his tongue, Nor does evil to his neighbor, Nor takes up a reproach against his friend;

(vs. 4) In whose eyes a reprobate is despised, But who honors those who fear the Lord; He swears to his own hurt, and does not change;

(vs. 5) He does not put out his money at interest, Nor does he take a bribe against the innocent. He who does these things will never be shaken.

David's answer has a very interesting structure to it. In verse 2, three broad characteristics describe this person. The one who is welcome in God's presence is one who has integrity, one who does righteousness, and one who speaks truth.

Looking farther along in verses 3-5, these three character-istics are explained in more detail. Verse 3 corresponds to the third quality, speaking truth; the first portion of verse 4 corre-sponds to the second quality, working righteousness; and the last part of verse 4 along with most of verse 5 corresponds to the first quality, walking with integrity.

David states that the person who is welcome in God's pres-ence is one who speaks truth in his heart. He doesn't just speak it outwardly. His whole character is truthful. Proverbs 23:7 tells us that as a man speaks in his heart, so is he. What he says inwardly is a characteristic of his entire lifestyle. Instead of merely speaking truth, this psalm is pointing out, the righteous person lives truth.

This kind of truthful living shows itself in several ways. First, the upright person does not "slander with his tongue." When asked for his opinion of a person or an event, he tells the truth without adding to it. He doesn't run others down verbally, whether in their presence or behind their back. He doesn't participate in racial slurs or ethnic jokes. He simply does not slander with his tongue.

In addition, this kind of person does not do "evil to his neighbor." This kind of truthful living shows itself in small ways as well as large. It means that he doesn't take his neighbor's paper when his own wasn't delivered. It means that he doesn't deliberately water his lawn when his neighbor's car is parked in front of his house. He doesn't borrow something and not return it.

Also, speaking truth means that one does not "take up a reproach against his friend." This kind of person doesn't keep a running score of every wrong done against him. He doesn't hold grudges. He doesn't keep reminding others of their past sins. He forgives, and he forgets.

Working Righteousness

David goes on to tell us that the person who is welcome in God's presence is one who "works righteousness." The phrase "works righteousness" refers to personal ethics. It means that the upright person is ethically righteous, that he acts in an honorable manner. He doesn't cheat on his income tax. He returns money at the store when he was inadvertently given too much. His life is governed by personal honesty.

In verse 4, we next see a contrast about this person: "In whose eyes a reprobate is despised, but who honors those who fear the LORD." This person views life and people through God's eyes. He hates what God hates, and he honors what God honors. He is not caught up in a "celebrity" mentality. He doesn't worship the rich and beautiful, the famous and powerful. He places value on people who put God first and who live for Him. He does not make his evaluations based on the world's standard of success and achievement.

Along with being truthful, acting in an ethical manner, being honorable in all his dealings, and viewing life and people through God's eyes, the true worshiper of God—the one welcome in God's presence—is one who "walks with integrity." He is a man who keeps his word. He does what he says he will do, when he says he will do it. If he promises to be somewhere at a certain time, he is there, on time. If his bills are due on the tenth, he doesn't pay them on the fifteenth. A man of integrity keeps his word.

This kind of person keeps his promises even if it costs him something: "He swears to his own hurt, and does not change." This does not mean that he deliberately tries to hurt himself. Rather, it means that once he makes a promise, if circumstances change so that he is at a disadvantage, he still keeps his word.

A general contractor I knew in Texas once signed a contract to build a water park for a large city. After signing the contract however, he discovered that he had left something substantial out of his estimate. Instead of making a profit, he stood to lose $200,000! But because he was a man of integrity, he resolved to fulfill the contract. Fortunately, the city later canceled the contract.

A man of integrity is one who "does not put out his money at interest." This is the idea of exploitation and abuse. In that culture, when one's fellow Israelite borrowed money, it meant that he was absolutely destitute. According to God's law, his fellow countrymen were not to take advantage of him by charging interest that he would never be able to repay.

In the same way, a true worshiper of God is not going to take advantage of others' misfortune by putting out his money at interest. He is not going to be the family loan shark, taking advantage of his brothers and sisters or his parents and his children. He is not going to take a friend out to McDonald's for lunch and the next week expect his friend to take him out for a steak dinner.

A man or woman of integrity also is one who is not influenced by bribes. He does not "take a bribe against the innocent." He is honest in his business deals. He doesn't accept kickbacks. He doesn't make deals based solely upon what benefits he may receive. He is not susceptible to outside influence or corruption. He makes his decision honestly, and then he stands his ground.

SOLID FOUNDATION

David wanted to know who was welcome in God's presence. He wanted to know what the true worshiper of God lived like. He discovered that this person is one who walks with integrity, who does righteous deeds, and who speaks the truth. And he also learned that this kind of person enjoys a special blessing.

David writes, "He who does these things will never be shaken." The phrase "does these things" refers to an entire life based upon integrity, righteousness, and truth. The psalm goes on to say that the person with this kind of lifestyle will never be shaken. Of course, this does not mean that he or she will never have problems, never be out of a job, never experience conflict, nor ever lose a loved one.

But it does mean that life will be absolutely stable all the way. When David says that the upright will never be shaken, it refers to a fundamental stability. It means that they won't be shaken from their high position of godliness. They won't be shaken from the residence of the divine presence. And they will always be welcome in God's presence.

Just north of Los Angeles, there is an amusement park that has a high observation tower. Visitors to the park can ride an elevator to the top and enjoy a magnificent view of the entire park and surrounding area. What many visitors don't know is that the tower was designed to have a sway factor of seven feet in either direction at its highest point. That means that in the event of an earthquake or high winds, the tower has the potential to sway back and forth a total of 14 feet! The tower definitely will be shaken, but the foundation will remain secure. Because of that secure foundation, the tower will last.

David says that the true worshiper of God has that kind of

fundamental stability. Those whose lifestyle is marked by integrity, righteous deeds, and truth can go through hard times knowing that their foundation will remain secure and that they will always be welcome in God's presence.

In the eyes of the world, men and women are measured by their outward actions, by their activities. In God's eyes, however, men and women are measured by their character. David asked, "Who is welcome in God's presence? Whom will God protect and sustain?" The answer: Those whose lives are marked by integrity. They keep their word even if it costs them something. They are characterized by righteous deeds. They act honorably to those they contact, and they view life and people through God's eyes. Their lifestyle is marked by truth. They don't slander others, and they treat their friends and neighbors with respect. This is the kind of person who will always be welcome in God's presence.

Who is welcome in God's presence to worship Him? A Christian, the man or woman of God, to be sure. And beyond that, those whose lives are marked by integrity, righteousness, and truth. Such people will never lose their secure foundation.

—*Mark S. Wheeler*

Celebrating His Birth

It's late. Everyone else is asleep. The lights on the tree blink on and off, like little eyes that can't stay shut. They open, and see hungry stockings hanging by the hearth. They open, and Christmas shadows crowd the room. Memories lie scattered here and there like old, heavy tinsel—the kind you can't buy anymore—the kind that counted for something. It's the quiet job of Christmas, and it wears well, like your favorite sweater that only seems to improve with the years. You've been here before, but every year, somehow it's better. Maybe because you've learned how to love a little better, a little deeper. Maybe because finally, giving has become better than getting.

And you find that the more deeply you love, the more you want to fill those stockings with the best. We all have someone special. Someone for whom the best is only half as good as we would like to give. That's the way it is when you love; and especially when you love Jesus.

If you love Jesus Christ, then it is only natural that you should want to give Him your best. Usually we express our best for Him in terms of our service to Him. We want that service to be state of the art—the best we have to offer. You may serve Him best by raising your children in a Christ-centered home. You may be discipling your spouse, or a friend, or serving as a Sunday school teacher in your local church. The desire to give Jesus your best is both natural and good; but there is danger here.

There is a twisted selfishness sitting, waiting in the shadows of your desire to serve Him with your best. It wears a servant's towel, and carries a basin to wash the feet of the world. It will seduce you slowly, painlessly, by making your service to Christ so fulfilling that it becomes an end in itself. Eventually, you find yourself falling in love with service and out of love with the One you serve. And Satan laughs. Who would have guessed he would sow selfishness alongside our desire to serve Christ, so that our motives for service emerge mixed like wheat and tares?

RITUAL OR REALITY?

Matthew 15:1-28 is like a field where wheat and tares, good and worthless, grow up side by side. The Canaanite woman of verses 21-28 is like good wheat. As we will see, she could teach the Pharisees a thing or two about the real meaning of Christmas. The Pharisees in verses 1-20 are like the tares. They have been seduced by state-of-the-art service—a self-propagating religious system that provided a number of perks for the ruling religious party. As a result, their motives for serving God were impure. The long-term effects on the rest of the nation were devastating. Not only had the religious leaders fallen out of love with God; they didn't even recognize Him when He walked among them. The tares were taking over the field; but they were about to be rooted up. State-of-the-art service does not guarantee a right relationship with God.

In verses 1 and 2, the Pharisees accused Jesus' disciples of breaking Jewish tradition by not washing their hands before eating. It seems to us a picky little point, but the Jews were concerned about "ceremonial defilement." God had warned Moses about being defiled (made unclean) by the false gods of the Gentiles. Jewish tradition had expanded on God's original commandment to prohibit contact with any Gentile (ancient rabbinical schools actually elevated the authority of this oral tradition above the authority of the written Law of Moses). Ritual hand washing were required before eating to remove the external defilement that resulted from coming in contact with a Gentile (or anything else considered unclean).

Jesus took the Pharisees' accusation and turned it against them. Verse 3 reads: "And why do you break the command of

God for the sake of your tradition?" He held up the mirror of truth, and made the Pharisees take a long hard look at themselves. What they saw was not pretty. The mirror of God's truth does not allow the unsaved man to see himself as he pretends to be or as he wished he were. Rather, it unmasks him for what he is. The Pharisees, so concerned with external purity, were rotting from the inside out. Jesus revealed to them that they were nothing but walking corpses, bound in the graveclothes of tradition. He condemned them for using that tradition to drain the lifeblood from the commandment of God (v. 6).

Specifically, they were guilty of weaseling out of their responsibility to care for their aged parents. The fifth commandment (Exod. 20:12) made it clear that children had an obligation to honor their parents. 1 Timothy 5:8 suggests that the obligation to "honor" extended beyond simple respect to include responsibility for financial support and other practical care for parents in their old age. The Pharisees had created a loophole in that requirement by applying a traditional teaching that restricted the use of any property which had been dedicated to God. They simply dedicated all their assets to God. That way, when their parents needed help, they could only mumble piously, "Sorry, I dedicated all my possessions to God."

A desire to serve God had degenerated into a desire to serve self. The privilege of serving God had turned into a business that could be strategically manipulated to exalt and insulate the spiritual power brokers of the nation.

WHAT IS THE OBJECT OF YOUR AFFECTION?

You would think we would have learned something from the mistakes of Israel. But, standing on the edge of the 21st century, we review almost 2,000 years of Christian service and notice a common thread stretching back, linking the church to the hem of the Pharisees' robes. The thread that connects us is our message, God's Word.

The Pharisees had the only true God and the only true message about that God. And they had that message for a long time. Long enough for their service to become an end in itself—a duty to be performed for its own sake and for its own reward.

We have held our New Testament message for almost as long as the Pharisees had held their Old Testament message before Jesus came. Long enough to develop some self-serving traditions. Long enough to lose sight of the One we serve.

Whatever your ministry is, it was never intended to be an end in itself. It was never intended to be the object of your affection.

As a Christian, you are bombarded with so many options, so many good things to do, that you can become a Martha and forget that it was Mary who had chosen the better part. It is not only a case of being distracted by too many options, but of letting any service divert your attention from Christ. That diversion, however good it may be in and of itself, can be the beginning of a long descent into Pharisaism. When it comes to worshipping Jesus, all our state-of-the-art service becomes a hindrance if it replaces Him as the object of our affection.

Not only will such misplaced priorities drain you spiritually, they can mangle you emotionally and physically. J. Hudson Taylor, the famous medical missionary to China in the 19th century, found his obsession with ministry to be crippling. Taylor loved his work among the Chinese and he gave himself to Christian service. But he was running the race of the Christian life so hard that, for a time, he lost the joy of running. Often, he put in 20-hour workdays and would see up to 150 patients a day. There were new workers to train, sermons to preach, lessons to teach, and the endless task of administration, not to mention the constant barrage of negative criticism from inside and outside the mission.

Taylor came to realize he was running (serving) in his own strength. In his quest for holiness, he got so wrapped up in serving that his service became a shroud. He had to stop and renew his focus on Jesus. Then, resting in Christ, drawing on His strength, Taylor's service became what it was always intended to be—a means to a much greater end—a deep knowledge of and dependence on his Lord. He was, in the words of one of his fellow missionaries, "a joyous man now." The ministry itself took on a new freshness as Taylor gave himself over to his Lord instead of to his Lord's work.

J. Hudson Taylor's ministry was a gift from God. Taylor, like us, wanted to take that gift of ministry and use it; he wanted to serve God by giving Him his best. And his ministry was vital, but it was eating him alive. Almost too late, he came to see that God doesn't give destructive gifts—He doesn't want you to use your ministry gift to destroy yourself. For the Pharisees who possessed so much, it was too late. But for those whom the Pharisees despised, for the unclean of the world, the door of heaven was swinging open.

THE STATE OF THE HEART

Jesus turned His back on the Pharisees and walked out of Palestine (the only departure from Palestine recorded in the Gospels) to go to the district of Tyre and Sidon (15:21). There he met a Canaanite woman. This lady could appeal to no state-of-the art qualifications to recommend her to Jesus. She had no social connections, no religious affiliations, no family ties. Her sex, her heritage, and her problem all worked against her. Her sex: she was a woman (women were property). Her heritage: she was a Gentile (Sidon was the hometown of wicked Queen Jezebel and a center of idolatrous worship).Her problem: she had a demon-possessed daughter (children were even beneath women on the social ladder). The only thing lower was the pet dog that licked crumbs off the floor. Unlike the Pharisees, she had nothing she could even pretend would earn her acceptance with God. Basically, this lady came looking for someone like Santa Claus.

Our Canaanite friend does not start out that well. She has something to learn herself. Keenly aware of her low social status in the eyes of the Jews perhaps she thought, "Maybe just a touch of flattery will work," so she appeals to Jesus by His Davidic title, "Son of David" (v. 22). She addressed Him as the Jewish Messiah. Jesus does not even acknowledge her petition. Rather, He says to His disciples: "I was sent only to the lost sheep of the house of Israel."

Then something must have clicked in her Canaanite mind. She bows down to worship Him in verse 25, saying, "LORD, help me!" And Jesus speaks to her for the first time, saying, "It is not good to take the children's bread and throw it to the dogs." She answers in verse 27, "Yes, LORD; but even the dogs feed on the crumbs which fall from their masters' table."

No more flattery—just an honest recognition of who Jesus is and who she is. Then a call for help. The Jewish leaders didn't need any help; they didn't need a Savior. Their ministry was all they wanted. They were self-sufficient, she was insufficient. They had a state-of-the-art ministry, she had next to nothing—only a humble heart that acknowledged Jesus as her master.

The Pharisees standing proudly contrast with this Canaanite on her knees to teach us that our state-of-the-art service for Christ doesn't guarantee friendship with Christ. In fact, our service can become a hindrance to worship if we make it an end in itself as the Pharisees did. On the other hand, when we seek Him first we will find joy in all our service because He is all our joy. Are you caught up in the pursuit of state-of-the-art ministry? Pursue Christ instead. Jesus does not love you for what you can do for Him. He just loves you...period.

He wants to give you His best, and He can. He can give you Himself. That's why this year can be better than all the years that have gone before. Because this year we do not come to worship the service of our Lord; we come to worship the Lord of our service. Because when it comes to worshipping Jesus, the issue isn't state of the art, but state of the heart.

—Reg Grant

Communicating With God

If God is sovereign and has our lives planned out and nothing happens to us that is beyond His control, need we ask God for anything? Do we really "change" anything by praying? And how long should a Christian pray for something important?

These and other questions about prayer require clear answers from God's Word if we hope to pursue a meaningful, effective prayer life. Let's examine four of the most frequently asked questions more closely.

WHY SHOULD WE ASK GOD FOR ANYTHING?

Requests, of course, are one of four reasons for praying Other reasons are praise, confession of sin, and thanksgiving. The Bible repeatedly encourages believers to bring their requests to God. "Call to Me and I will answer you and tell you great and unsearchable things you do not know" (Jer. 33:3).

"Ask and it will be given to you; seek and you will find; knock and the door will be opened to you. For everyone who asks receives; he who seeks finds; and to him who knocks, the door will be opened... If you, then, though you are evil, know how to give good gifts to your children, how much more will your Father in heaven give good gifts to those who ask Him" (Matt. 7:7-8, 11).

"If you believe, you will receive whatever you ask for in prayer" (Matt. 21:22). "Then Jesus told His disciples a parable to show them that they should always pray and not give up" (Luke 12:1). "Ask and you will receive" (John 16:24).

"Do not be anxious about anything but in everything, by prayer and petition, with thanksgiving, present your requests to God" (Phil. 4:6). "Pray continually" (1 Thess. 5:17). "If any of you lacks wisdom, he should ask God" (James 1:5). "Is any one of you in trouble? He should pray" (James 5:13). "Pray for each other...The prayer of a righteous man is powerful and effective" (James 5:16).

"If we ask anything according to His will, He hears us. And if we know that He hears us—whatever we ask—we know that we have what we asked of Him" (1 John 5:14-15). "Pray in the Holy Spirit" (Jude 20).

These verses make it clear that God wants us to bring our requests to Him. However, why is this necessary if God is in control of everything? Will not things happen anyway even if we do not pray? Since God knows our needs—"Your Father knows what you need before you ask Him" (Matt. 6:8)—why bother to tell Him?

This may be answered in three ways. First, we should voice our requests to God because He wants our submission. Prayer is not so much for the purpose of getting our will done in heaven as it is getting His will done on earth. Prayer is not a battle in which we fight with God to persuade Him to do what we want. Prayer is not pressuring, nagging, pleading, or cajoling God to give us our way. As Richard Halverson wrote, "By prayer man consents to the rule of God in his life. By prayer man seeks God's will and yields to it." Chuck Swindoll explains it this way: "Faith does not mean we give God deadlines....Faith says, 'I plug into heaven, and wait for His timing.'"

By praying we acknowledge our receptivity to God's will, our willingness to receive His answers. Years ago a writer affirmed, "The higher gifts of grace are never forced upon a reluctant or indifferent soul." When we face problems our normal reaction should be to pray. This is as God intends it. He wants us to keep on our knees.

A second reason for taking our requests to God is that He wants our communication. "Prayer is a communication between persons," wrote Gordon Lewis. When you talk with someone, you express your opinions, wishes, desires. You ask questions, you share information, you sometimes complain. By talking you know each other better. Similarly in talking with God we express our longings, wishes, complaints, concerns. When someone asked George Mueller how much time he spent in prayer, he responded, "Hours every day." He then explained, "But I live in the spirit of prayer. I pray as I walk and when I lie down and when I arise." Prayer then is communication with God, a Person, not just going through a ritual or routine.

A third reason God wants us to voice our requests is because of His foreordination. He has planned or ordained that He will do certain things in response to prayer. This is similar to His plan with regard to missions. He sends people to serve Him on mission fields, but He asks us to pray that workers will be sent into the spiritual harvests of the world (Matt. 9:38). Also in His grace God has elected some to be saved, but He chooses to bring about their salvation through the prayers of Christians. Some people reason that if God has chosen a person to be saved no one need witness to him, for he will be saved anyway. This, however, is not biblical. People will not be saved "anyway." They are saved by God's grace, but it is through the witnessing of God's believers. This is part of God's plan.

Praying is similar. God has chosen to do certain things and He has also chosen to do them in response to prayer. For example, God delivered Lot and his family in response to Abraham's prayers (Gen. 18). God spared the nation Israel in response to Moses' praying (Num. 14:11-12, 19-20). And God spared the Israelites when they were under attack by the Philistines, in response to Samuel's prayerful intercession (1 Sam. 7:5-9).

Requests in our praying, then, are part of God's plan for us. By taking our needs to Him we indicate our submission to His will, we enjoy communication with Him, and we take part in one of the means He has planned to accomplish His purposes.

Does Prayer Change Things?

The answer is "yes" in one sense, and "no" in another sense. From our finite vantage point it appears as if our prayers change circumstances. On the other hand we should not think of prayer as manipulation of God. If anything has changed, we are the ones who are changed as we are submissive to His will and as we communicate with Him.

Why Are Some Requests Not Answered?

One may ponder, "Okay, I am in touch with God—I am submissive, I communicate with Him, and I sense my part in praying so that He may accomplish His will. However, sometimes my praying seems to make no difference. Verses suggest that if I ask, the request will be fulfilled (e.g., Matt. 7:7, 11; John 15:7, 16:23), but sometimes the answers do not come."

Does this mean God is not true to His Word? Why is He seemingly silent, refusing to answer our prayers? Perhaps you have prayed for years for your unsaved husband, and he is still not saved. Perhaps you are praying for health, and you still must undergo medical treatments to sustain your health. You pray for some other need in your life and matters may not seem to improve.

Why Does God Do This?

Rather than being bitter with God we should examine the biblical conditions for answered prayer. They are four:

(a) Praying is to be in Jesus' name (John 14:13; 16:23). This means that we should pray as if Jesus were praying. Our prayers should conform to His requests and concerns.
(b) Trust or belief (Matt. 21:22). We should have confidence in His ability to met our needs. (c) Abiding in Him (John 15:7). This means we should confess sin and be right before God if our prayers are to be answered. Unconfessed sin blocks the way to answered prayer (Ps. 66:18; Prov. 28:9; Isa. 59:2). (d) Right motives (James 4:2-3). We must pray not only for the right things but also from the right motives. Our concerns ought not be selfish. Our ultimate motive should be to bring glory to the Father.

Several years ago Ralph Keiper, a well-known Bible teacher, wrote about learning to pray with reference to God's glory. Mr. Keiper is nearly blind and for years he prayed that God would remove that problem. But the Lord did not grant his request. One day he sensed that the Holy Spirit was reminding him that the chief end of man is to glorify God and to enjoy Him forever. It was as if the Holy Spirit had asked him, "If you had the choice, what would you do, glorify God or have perfect vision?" He paused for a long time because, of course, he wanted his sight restored but in the struggle of his heart he had to recognize that only one proper answer could be given to the question.

At last he responded to the Lord, "My vision, or lack of it, is not worthy to be compared to the glory of God!" Then he sensed God saying to him, "If you really wish to glorify God, why worry about the method which God chooses for doing it?" He wrote, "Suddenly a peace came to my soul which has been mine for the past 25 years. The goal of prayer is not the fulfilling of our requests; it is the glorification of God."

Prayer, then, is not a means of our getting what we want from God; we should think of it as a means of God getting from us what He wants, namely glory to Himself.

HOW PERSISTENT SHOULD WE BE IN PRAYING?

The Bible affirms that we should continue to pray for whatever we know in God's Word is His will. We know that God longs for people to be saved (1 Tim. 2:3-4; 2 Pet. 3:9), so we should continue to pray for the salvation of others. Also we should pray for daily provision of food (Matt. 6:11). Other matters for which we should continue to pray, without giving up, include: strength to resist temptation (Matt. 6:13), sanctification (1 Thess. 4:3), needs of other Christians (Eph. 6:18), our leaders (1 Tim. 2:2), our enemies (Luke 6:28), and missionaries (Luke 10:2).

God is willing to give (Matt. 7:11). He is not like the unjust judge in Luke 18:1-8 who had to be persuaded to give. And yet God wants us to persist in prayer, recognizing that He has His timing for answering. For example, His delay in answering the request of the Syro-Phoenician woman suggests that He was testing her faith (Mark 7:24-30).

Other times we need not persist in prayer for something when God indicates the answer is not forthcoming. Paul, for example, prayed three times that his "thorn in the flesh" would be removed; but when he sensed that God would not remove it, he stopped praying (2 Cor. 12:7-9).

Sometimes we must accept the Lord's "no" answer or "not-now" answer and simply go on. We should thank Him for that answer and not be anxious (Phil. 4:6).

A group of amateur climbers were scaling part of the Matterhorn mountain near Zermatt, Switzerland. As they came to a narrow, hazardous passage, about to make a turn, a gust of wind swept down on them. The experienced guide, knowing the danger this posed for the group, quickly shouted, "Get down on your knees! You are safe only on your knees!"

How true this is in the Christian life as well. We are safe only as we are continually in fellowship with our Lord in prayer. As Paul wrote, "Pray continually" (1 Thess. 5:17).

—Roy B. Zuck

Talking to God at the Table

Most or us did not learn to pray in church. And we weren't taught it in school, or even in pajamas beside our bed at night. If the truth were known, we've done more praying around the kitchen table than anywhere else on earth. From our earliest years we've been programmed: if you don't pray, you don't eat. It started with Pablum in the high chair, and it continues through porterhouse at the restaurant. Right? Like passing the salt or doing the dishes, a meal is incomplete without it.

THE "STAGES OF GRACE"

Our first impressions of communication with the Almighty were formed in the high chair with cereal and pudding smeared all over our faces. We peeked and gurgled while everybody else sat silent and still. We then learned to fold our hands and close our eyes. Soon we picked up the cue to add our own "Amen" (which usually followed "in Jesus name"). Then came the day we soloed. We mumbled, looked around, got mixed up, then quickly closed with a relieved "Amen!" as we searched mom and dad's faces for approval.

Then we went through three very definite stages over the next eight to ten years of grace—stages that are common in most Christian families. Stage one: snickering. For some strange reason, prayer before the meal became the "comedy hour" when I was growing up. In spite of parental frowns and glares, threats and thrashings, my sister and I could not keep from laughing. I remember one time we giggled so long and so loud that our mother finally joined in. My older brother was praying (he usually remembered every missionary from Alaska to Zurich) and purposely refused to quit. He finished by praying for the three of us.

Stage two: doubting. This is a cynical cycle, a tough one to endure. We start questioning the habit, the custom. With an air of pseudo-sophistication we think: "What does it matter if I don't say grace? This is a ritual. It serves no purpose. God knows I'm grateful." Junior high years abound with these maverick thoughts. The whole scene of bowing heads and closing eyes and saying "religious words" suddenly seems childish—and needless.

Stage three: preaching. This one is difficult to handle because it usually comes from well-meaning lips. Out of sincerity and a desire to prompt obedience, we use the time in prayer as an avenue to rebuke a family member or (very subtly) reinforce our own piety. Parents can easily fall into this manipulative technique, since it's impossible to be interrupted in prayer. The temptation of taking to the platform before our captive audience seems irresistible.

After passing through these stages, however, we begin to realize how good it is to cultivate this healthy habit. "Asking the blessing" is a sweet, much-needed, refreshing pause during hectic days. But since it occurs so often, the easiest trap to fall into is sameness: the perfunctory uttering of meaningless, repetitious clichés that become boring even to God! Our Lord Jesus thundered warning after warning against the empty verbosity which characterized the Pharisees.

Without claiming to have all the answers, I offer several suggestions a family can build on together.

Think before your pray. What's on the table? Call the food and drink by name. "Thank you, Lord, for the hot chicken-and-rice casserole in front of us. Thank you for the cold lemonade...." What kind of day are you facing—or have you faced? Pray with those things in mind. Draw your prayer out of real life. Don't lapse into mechanical mutterings or convenient religious jargon. You're not just "saying a blessing," you're talking to God!

Involve others in your prayer. Try some sentence prayers around the table. Ask the family for requests.

Sing your table blessing. Try it a few times. After the family has recovered from the shock of shattering the norm, it might catch on. The doxology, a familiar hymn, or a chorus of worship works great—and offers a change of pace. Holding hands can also be meaningful.

Keep it brief, please. There's nothing like watching a thick film form over the gravy while you plow through all five stanzas of Wesley's "And Can It Be?" Remember what the blessing is about—a pause to praise our faithful Provider, a moment of focus on the Giver of every good gift. You don't have to pray around the world three times or highlight every relative between the poles and all the ships at sea. God's watching the heart, not totaling up the verbiage.

Occasionally pray after the meal. When the mood is loose or the meal is served in shifts or picnic-style settings, be flexible. An attitude of worship is occasionally much easier when the hunger pangs have eased up.

Is your prayer time at the table losing its punch? Here's a way to find out. When the meal is over and you get up to do the dishes, ask if anyone remembers what was prayed for. If they do, great. If they don't, sit back down at the table and ask why. You've got a lot more to be concerned about than a stack of dishes.

—Charles R.. Swindoll

Discovering the Importance of Prayer

Why don't we pray more? There are many reasons. We forget to pray. We think we are too busy. Sometimes we quit praying too soon. But I believe a more fundamental reason is that we don't feel we need to pray. We don't forget to eat or sleep because we know we can't get along without food or rest. Yet we think we can survive without prayer so we don't pray.

This is a serious mistake and a grave delusion. If we realized just how desperately we need God's help, we would pray more and our lives would become more powerful spiritually. Instead, we are comfortable, peaceful, and full—and we don't pray.

In an essay published by Time magazine, Alexander Solzhenitsyn wrote of "…the spiritual impotence that comes from living a life of ease; people are unwilling to risk their comforts." Christians have a tendency to say, "I am rich; I have acquired wealth and do not need a thing." But we do not realize that we are "wretched, pitiful, poor, blind, and naked" (Rev. 3:17).

How can we realize just how essential prayer is to our daily lives? Let me suggest three truths that illustrate our daily dependence on God.

DEPENDENT ON GOD FOR SALVATION

First, God's Word reveals that we are absolutely dependent on Him for eternal salvation. Isaiah wrote, "All of us have become like one who is unclean, and all our righteous acts are like filthy rags; we all shrivel up like a leaf, and like the wind our sins sweep us away" (Isa. 64:6).

As we study the lives of God's great servants in the Bible we notice that when these men recognized their dependence on God, they were transformed. Job said, "My ears had heard of you but now my eyes have seen you. Therefore I despise myself and repent in dust and ashes" (Job 42:5-6). Moses pleaded with God: "If your Presence does not go with us, do not send us up from here" (Ex. 33:15). Having seen a vision of God's sovereign power at work in future world events, Daniel said, "I am overcome with anguish because of the vision, my lord, and I am helpless" (Dan. 10;16). When the Apostle John saw the Lord as He really is he said, "I fell at his feet as though dead" (Rev. 1:17).

DEPENDENT ON GOD FOR DELIVERANCE

Second, along with salvation we are completely dependent on God for deliverance from temptation. Paul testified, "I know that nothing good lives in me, that is, in my sinful nature. For I have the desire to do what is good, but I cannot carry it out. ...What a wretched man I am! Who will rescue me from this body of death?" (Rom. 7:18, 24).

Actually Jesus Christ stated as forcefully as possible that His disciples are completely dependent on God for any success. "I am the vine; you are the branches. If a man remains in me and I in him, he will bear much fruit; apart from me you can do nothing" (John 15:5). He did not say that until we have been a Christian for so many years we can do nothing. Neither did He say that until we have become a leader in our church or have memorized so many verses of Scripture we can do nothing. On the contrary, He said, "Apart from me you can do nothing."

How we need to learn who God really is! When we come to know Him as the holy, sovereign and all-powerful God, then we will understand who we are: unclean, helpless, and pitifully weak instruments. I believe that we should seek God for greater perception of who He is and who we are, even as Moses and Paul did (Ex. 33:18; Phil. 3:10).

Since God's Word so clearly tells us that without Him we can do nothing, prayerlessness indicates unbelief of what God says regarding our deep and ever-present need of Him. Little prayer reflects disbelief of God.

DEPENDENT ON GOD FOR ALL THINGS

Third, experience teaches us that we are completely dependent on God. David Brainerd was a man of great spiritual power. The work which he accomplished by prayer is amazing.

His biographer, A.J. Gordon, wrote that in the depths of the New England forests where Brainerd lived and worked, unable to speak the language of the Indians whom he sought to win to Christ, Brainerd spent entire days in prayer. He knew he could not communicate with those Indians because he did not understand their language. If he wanted to speak at all he had to find someone who could at least interpret his thoughts. Therefore, he knew that anything he might do must be absolutely dependent on the power of God. He spent whole days in prayer, asking that the power of God might come upon him so unmistakably that these people should not be able to stand before him. And what happened? During one of his initial sermons scores of Indians were converted despite the fact the interpreter was so intoxicated that he could barely stand up! It was the tremendous power of God behind David Brainerd.

We might be tempted to say, "Well, if I had nothing else to do but wander through the woods and pray, God might use me that way too. But I just don't have that much time."

Martin Luther was a busy man, too. He wrote scores of books, translated the Scriptures into the German language, and led the Protestant Reformation. Yet Luther is reported to have said, "I have so many things to do that I cannot get along without three hours a day in prayer."

George Washington's secretary, Robert Lewis, wrote that it was the president's custom to go to his library at 4:00 in the morning for his devotions. And he concluded each day with Bible reading and prayer.

Stonewall Jackson was a man of prayer. According to E.M. Bounds in *Purpose in Prayer*, Jackson said, "I have so fixed the habit of prayer in my mind that I never raise a glass of water to my lips without asking God's blessing, never seal a letter from the post without a brief sending of my thoughts heavenward."

We pray little, not because we have little time, but because we think of ourselves as self-sufficient. It's a matter of priorities, not time. Our spiritual impact is directly proportionate to our conscious dependence on God. God's Word tells us we are completely dependent on Him, and experience confirms this. The challenges we face in the world prove our desperate need for God's power, too.

Our world needs a spiritual revival. Turmoil in the Middle East, anarchy abroad, lawlessness at home—all these conditions underline our great need. Not only are the experts in biblical prophecy saying that the end is near, but perceptive unbelievers are shouting the same thing. A recent best seller, The Third World War: August, 1985, by General John Hackett and other high ranking NATO officers, is just one example of the fact that people everywhere sense that our world is in serious danger.

In view of the urgency of our times, we who know the Lord need to take on whole countries for God. William Carey was once reproached for spending so much time in prayer that he neglected his business as a shoe repairman. He replied that supplication, thanksgiving, and intercession were much more important in his life than laying up treasurers on earth. "Prayer is my real business," he said. "Repairing shoes is a sideline; it just helps me pay expenses." The Lord honored this cobbler's vigorous faith. He became a renowned missionary and was mightily used by God in India, Burma, and the East Indies. Kneeling in prayer before a map of the world Carey asked God for whole countries to be brought to faith in Christ through his prayers and witness.

People all around us are going to hell! What do you think of when you walk down a sidewalk in a rough part of town? Is that man going to attack me? Is that boy getting ready to stick a knife in my ribs? How can I get away from these people?

I have read that during the Welsh revival at the beginning of this century Christians were so filled with the Spirit that as they walked silently down the public sidewalks in Wales, unbelievers would fall on their knees and cry out to God to have mercy on them as the Christians passed.

This is not the time to retreat but to advance! The challenges we face in our world today prove our desperate need for God's power. We cannot hope to be of much help to others without it. The task is too great.

We desperately need God's help. His Word says so, our experience say so, and the challenges we face say so. May God impress each of us with how desperately we need Him so that we feel driven to pray. Only as we realize this will we pray as we must.

In my study at home, I have hung a prayer of John Wesley. I have made it my own: "Lord, give me one hundred men who fear nothing but sin, and desire nothing but God, and I will shake the world."

—Thomas L. Constable

Praying From the Heart

God's plan for Elijah was on schedule. When Elijah feared for his life, God told him where to hide. When there was no food, God used the ravens to feed him. When the brook dried up, God sent him to a widow in Sidon. And when Elijah discovered she had no food left to share, God provided enough oil and meal each day so the widow, her son, and Elijah could survive. As this man of God faced what appeared to be one insurmountable problem after another, God faithfully cared for His servant.

We read that "some time later the son of the woman who owned the house became ill" (1 Kings 17:17). Again we do not know what specific time period is involved. However, from the overall time references in Elijah's story we can conclude it must have been several months. Although the widow's oil jug and her meal jar never ran empty, enabling them to make bread each day, it did not keep sickness away from her home. Her son "became ill."

It was not a sudden attack that left him near death. Rather, the boy's health deteriorated over a period of time. He grew "worse and worse, and finally stopped breathing" (17:17).

Though the biblical text reports this tragic event very succinctly, it allows room for a lot of realistic speculation as to what happened. When the boy finally "stopped breathing," the widow openly expressed her deep feelings of anxiety and distress to Elijah. "What do you have against me, man of God? Did you come to remind me of my sin and kill my son?" (17:18).

Imagine what must have happened. For days, or perhaps weeks, the boy's illness worsened. The first day or two the widow no doubt showed little concern—nor did Elijah. After all, the oil and meal were always there! And all of us have faced periods of illness that come and go.

But as the days passed, it became evident this was no ordinary illness. The boy was not recovering. His mother's casual concern turned to intense fear—and penetrating introspection. In times like these, it is natural to begin to ask the question, "Why?" Human tragedy is always sobering—especially when it involves death.

PRAYING WITH EMOTION

The widow's reactions were predictable. As her son lay dying, this woman's introspection focused on her former lifestyle. Was it her sin that was causing her son's illness? Was it God's judgment? Had Elijah come to reveal her sinful ways and then to bring God's judgment upon her? Was this why her son lay dying?

On the one hand, the widow was tempted to do what many people do when tragedy strikes. Their view of God often leads them to wonder if God is punishing them for some sin either in their past life or in the present. Lingering guilt has ways of causing this paranoia. She had not yet learned that God does not hold grudges. Though on rare occasions God had punished sin in this way—as He did with David for his terrible sin of adultery and murder—it is not the normal way God works. That is especially true when it comes to our past sins. And even when we are committing sins in the present, He is very long-suffering. Even in David's case, when God's law specifically declared that he should die for taking life, God let him live.

On the other hand, this widow knew that it did not seem logical for Elijah to save both her and her son from starvation, only to turn round and take his life once he became aware of her sins. From this vantage point we can certainly understand her questions, her fears, and her confusion.

Death of a loved one brings sadness and heartache. It's

very real! There standing before Elijah was a woman with a broken heart. In her arms was a little boy who was no longer breathing. And even more painful to Elijah were the questions she was asking. In her emotional pain she was actually rejecting the man who had saved her life—accusing him of making her aware of her own sin and then taking the life of her son to punish her.

PRAYING WITH YOUR HEART

But there was another factor involved in Elijah's emotional response. He had come to this family in the name of God. He had shared his mission and how God had cared for him in the ravine of Kerith. The woman and her son had responded to his message and to his God. They had put their trust in Elijah and in the Lord. And now, her son had died and Elijah was feeling deeply her distrust of both him and the God he represented. There was no human explanation. God's very name and reputation were at stake. What would people say once they found out what happened? Elijah, too, was confused, distraught, and fearful!

"Give me your son," Elijah replied, no doubt with intense emotion. He then took the boy in his arms, climbed to the upper room where he had been staying, laid him on his own bed, and began to pray earnestly for the boy. In fact, we read that "he cried out to the LORD." Elijah's own emotional distress and frustration are obvious. "O LORD my God," he cried, "have you brought tragedy also upon this widow I am staying with, by causing her son to die?" (1 Kings 17:19-20).

Elijah then "stretched himself out on the boy three times and cried out to the Lord, 'O LORD my God, let this boy's life return to him!'" (17:21). Like Elisha, the man who was eventually to succeed him as a prophet of God in Israel, Elijah probably "laid upon the boy, mouth to mouth, eyes to eyes, hands to hands" (2 Kings 4:34) as he cried to God for mercy.

As so often happens when God's people pray in earnest,

the Lord heard and answered Elijah's prayer. Life returned to the boy and "he lived." You can imagine the joy that gripped Elijah's soul as he descended the stairs with the boy in his arms and presented him to his mother. "Look," he said, "your son is alive!" (1 Kings 17:23).

The woman's response must have been just as rewarding to Elijah. "Now I know," she said, "that you are a man of God and that the word of the Lord from your mouth is the truth" (17:24). In these words we discover even more of what had happened as the boy lay dying. As his condition worsened, the widow began to point an accusing finger at Elijah. In reality, she had begun to doubt if Elijah was indeed God's representative. As long as things were going well because of his presence with her, she responded to his message of truth. But when things began to sour, she began to doubt and to point a finger of accusation.

Elijah, at this moment, also experienced that kind of pain. And we see that pain expressed in his prayer for the boy. He, too, did not understand what was happening. Was he the cause of the boy's death? Had the Lord brought tragedy into this family because of his presence in the home?

PRAYING WITH PERSISTENCE

At this point, Elijah also began to question God's ways. It was confusing enough not to understand what was happening, but to be rejected in the process by the one he had saved from starvation was indeed frustrating.

But God honored Elijah's persistence and prayer. In the process, God also honored his honesty and forthrightness regarding his doubts, his fears, his disillusionment, and his disappointment. He gave the boy new life. And in doing so, the widow's faith was restored and Elijah experienced the joy of seeing his new friends reunited and responding positively to the will of God.

But more important to Elijah and his relationships with

this little family was the fact that she no longer rejected the God he served. The Lord's reputation was once again preserved. To Elijah, this was particularly important since his own people had turned to false gods. In essence, this concern was why Elijah was there in the first place—because he had taken this stand for the one true God. It is not surprising that he wanted God's name vindicated and honored.

PRAYING IN DIFFICULT CIRCUMSTANCES

What can we learn from this Old Testament experience? The most important lesson revolves around Elijah and what God was doing to continue to prepare him for even greater struggles against the forces of evil. All along God had been getting Elijah ready for an encounter, first with King Ahab and then the prophets of Baal. What Elijah asked God to do for the widow's son would seem minor compared with what he was eventually going to ask God to do on Mount Carmel. The Lord was continuing to prepare Elijah for the task ahead!

The point for us to understand and remember is that God is preparing us for the big challenges in life when we face the smaller challenges victoriously. But the most important lesson we can learn in the process is that God wants us to understand our motives and why we are asking Him for help.

Let's look at some of the more specific points the Lord want to call to our attention.

First, it is in the midst of situations that are beyond our control that we really learn to pray. How true in Elijah's experience! How true in our own!

In some respects it is unfortunate that we have to be in a position where our backs are against the wall before we take the privilege of prayer seriously. But this has always been true in the history of God's people. And God understands our human tendencies. In these situations He does not turn a deaf ear. Though the outcome is not always what we might choose, He responds with what is best.

So we should not hesitate to pray when we are facing serious problems, even though we've been neglecting this important spiritual exercise. It is only natural that we pray more during this kind of trial and that we pray more intently.

Second, God understands our anxieties, our fears, our disappointments, and our disillusionments. We should not be fearful of expressing these thoughts and feelings to Him in prayer.

Some people see God as an angry father figure who is ready to punish when they share how they really feel. Not so! If that were true, God would act before we speak, for He clearly knows what we think and feel. Consequently, we might as well tell Him. We must also remember that He is God. He cannot be manipulated. But there are times that He responds in unusual ways, especially when His reputation and name are at stake.

Third, God is particularly responsive to our prayers when we are able to get beyond our own interests and concerns and focus on other people's needs, and especially on His reputation. Though he felt personal rejection, Elijah's prayers were based on his concern for the widow and, most of all, his concern about God's reputation. After all, he was identified as a "man of God"—a man who represented the one true God. For tragedy to strike in this instance would cause unbelievers to question even more the message Elijah was proclaiming. How obvious this was from the widow's response!

And remember, too, that God can bring honor to Himself in all situations, no matter what the outcome. In this instance, God answered Elijah's prayer and restored the boy because it would bring the most honor to His name, but there are times when He can bring more honor to His name in the midst of human tragedy.

One final question: How do we respond if God does not answer our specific prayers for physical healing? First, we must realize that God has never promised to heal all physical infirmities, even though we pray in faith. He has promised, however, to provide grace and strength for every situation, but not always to provide deliverance from death.

The Apostle Paul illustrates this in his own life. Though Paul often healed people with God's power, there came a time in his life when God did not answer his own prayers for personal healing. Writing to the Corinthians, he informed them he had asked the Lord three times to heal him. In fact, he said, "I pleaded with the LORD to take it away from me." However, the Lord's response to Paul was that His grace was sufficient for him (2 Cor. 12:8-9).

It is important to understand this point, for an inaccurate view of God's sovereignty in healing can lead people to false guilt, feeling they are to blame for illness that is not cured through prayer. Remember that God's will is more important than ours in these matters, and when it comes to physical healing He has chosen not to reveal His particular will.

On the other hand, God does choose to respond to our prayers for healing when it is His will. Furthermore, if we do not pray, He may not respond. Prayer, then, does make a difference, whether He responds with healing or with grace to enable us to bear the burden.

—*Gene A. Getz*

Our Model for Prayer

One of the more difficult truths for us to understand is also one of the most important in Scripture—the Trinity. But beyond the challenge of understanding our three-in-one God is the need to personalize our relationships with all three Persons.

We seem to relate with apparent ease to Christ because He died for us. We relate to the Spirit because He indwells and comforts us through life. But the Father is different. To many of us He is the unseen, unheard, unfelt, sometimes unjust, and always remote Stranger whom we acknowledge for purposes of orthodoxy. This is a tragic error because the Bible teaches with irrefutable emphasis that "our Father" is the believer's loving, holy, and powerful prayer partner. He is the caring One who can meet our daily and deepest needs when we pray.

THE EXAMPLE OF THE LORD'S PRAYER

The Lord's prayer in Matthew 6:5-15 teaches this important truth. This prayer is a part of the Sermon on the Mount (Matt. 5-7) in which Christ teaches His assembled followers about righteous living (5:1-2) as opposed to the mistaken notions of righteousness in their society.

Christ places His teaching on prayer at the midpoint of the Sermon. This emphasizes that righteous living is central to communication with the Father. In other words, the quality of our life can be measured and will be affected by our practice of proper prayer. That's significant!

Our Lord stresses that righteousness must be practiced for the praises of God rather than for ourselves. This is the governing principle of the Sermon and it should be the ever present motive in our lives. In 5:13-16 we see that biblical righteousness on earth glorifies our Father in heaven because it radiates His standards, values, and interests. The point of the salt and light metaphors in that passage is that we should care so much about pleasing God that we should dare to be distinctive in a self-promoting world. One cannot serve our righteous Father in this sinful world for self-praise. That is professing God-centeredness and practicing self-concern—which is hypocrisy.

In 5:20 the Lord contrasts godly doctrines and living with the traditions and hypocrisy of the scribes and Pharisees. In 6:1-18 He compares God-centeredness and self-promotion through giving, prayer, and fasting. Proper prayer is the second and central illustration. It is the key to maintaining proper perspectives and priorities because all of us are prone to wander during the pressures and routines of each day. If we examine the Lord's prayer, we see several sides for our prayer relationship with our heavenly Father.

COUNTERFEIT PRAYERS

Preceding the model prayer (6:9-15) are two examples of hypocritical counterfeits. First, the Pharisees practiced public showiness. They wanted to be seen praying. When public impression replaces the Father's glory, then the image is all that counts. Genuineness becomes irrelevant. "Hypocrite" is a dramatic word. Actors would "mask" themselves as characters when performing for audiences. The Pharisee's public prayers actually masked the deeper motive of public applause. The emphasis was not upon a worshipful relationship with the Father but rather on hype for audience response. The key here is the motive, and the father cannot be mocked. When prayer is done only for people, it will be seen only by people. The full reward is a moment of applause instead of our Father's eternal blessings.

A lesson to be learned here is that sincerity is not a criterion of truth. Many people have followed apparently "sincere" charlatans only to discover that they have been led astray. Is Jonestown too remote for us to remember that this can be a disaster?

True sincerity is best demonstrated by unostentatious practices (6:6). Prayer with the Father should be in your "inner room with the door closed." Apparently this was the storeroom, which was without windows and could be locked. It would have been a private place of personal fellowship with the Father. The emphasis of being "in secret" is undistracted, intimate communication with Him. The motive and atmosphere of proper prayer should be praise rather than being praised (6:4, 16, 18). In turn, the Father rewards. This is the dynamic of the prayer relationship: reciprocal giving with incomparable fulfillment.

Second, the gentiles counterfeited prayer with meaningless repetitions (6:7). The visual impact of the pharisaical hypocrites parallels the verbal babblings of Gentile paganism with its elaborate incantations. The idea was, "If God did not hear me the first time, then perhaps He will listen to me on the fiftieth repetition." This practice gave prominence to repetitions, beads and prayer wheels instead of communication with the one and only living God.

TRUE PRAYER PRAISES GOD

The difference between these false practices and true prayer is our perception of God (6:8). Verse eight contains an astonishing truth: Our Father knows our needs before we ask!

Here is a subtle point. If our prayers focus on our needs, then what are we wanting them to accomplish? Are we trying to "remind" our Father of something? Are we trying to force a "yes" answer? Are we trying to appease Him? If we answer yes to those questions, then we are not worshipfully praising our Father. And this is what the model prayer is all about.

True prayer praises the Father. His rewards involve meeting our needs. The need for wrong requests is removed, because the loving father delights in giving good gifts to His children to an immeasurably greater degree than loving fathers (7:11). He knows our real needs, even when we don't.

The personalness and love of the Father are emphasized in the address "Our Father in heaven" (6:9). The balance of prayer is here. Perhaps it is fair to say that the problem with many prayers is that they lack this balance. On the one hand, He is our loving Father. He is a caring, concerned Parent who is involved in the lives of His beloved children. He supremely demonstrated His love in history by the sending of our Savior. On the other hand, He is the only one who can meet our deepest needs. He is powerfully sovereign over any conceivable need. He is our Father in heaven.

The association of the Father and His abode is common in the Sermon. However, the point is that His character —more than His dwelling place—seems to be in view. As exalted Creator and Ruler of all, He is worthy of reverence, devotion, and confidence. True prayer with the Father is an intimacy that promotes worship.

HE IS HOLY

Let's further apply the Lord's prayer to our lives by noting three "your petitions" that precede three "our petitions" (6:11-13). "Hallowed be your name" means "let your name be treated with holiness and reverence." "Name" in the biblical context is the identify of a person indicated by his character. Here again is our familiar theme of righteousness and prayer.

One who loves the Father will express concern through prayer that He in heaven will be treated as the Holy One on earth. And through prayer the disparity between our holy Father and His fallen creation will create a desire in a worshipping believer for the new creation of biblical prophecy. In that context profession and practice in heaven and on earth will be one (Rev. 21-22).

The second and third "your petitions" quickly follow:

"your kingdom come, your will be done." In the Bible the believer's concern for God's holiness and His will on earth are important motivations for personal righteousness. The two are made analogous in Leviticus 11:44-45: "Consecrate yourselves, and be holy, because I am holy..." (also 19:2). The analogy appears in the Sermon (5:48). And in 1 Peter 1:13-16 the Leviticus principle is applied to the church's purifying hope. Our hope is that we will be changed at any moment into glorious perfection. This is presented as one of our primary motivations for righteous living (1 John 3:2-3). It fosters our greater and growing desire for God's holy will and glory on earth, which will be realized in Christ's Kingdom to come (Rev. 22:20; 1 Cor. 16:22). Thus, those who "hunger and thirst for righteousness" (5:6) will be satisfied as a foretaste of unending, unhindered, glorious prayer with the Father in the future.

These three "thou" petitions control the three "our" petitions of verses 11-13 because they concern our righteousness rather than our usual "Christmas lists": give us, forgive us, and deliver us.

SEEING THE SACREDNESS OF ORDINARY LIVING

"Our daily bread" stresses the Father's provision. We need not worry because He knows our needs. His sufficiency follows our concern for holiness. The inference from this is that our daily prayer with the Father and His faithful provision for our needs are assurances of our unending fellowship with Him. Eternal fellowship with the Father is best lived one day at a time (6:34).

One of today's most formidable enemies is a "secular" outlook on life, which ignores or removes the Father from daily matters. Too easily we can profess great truths like God's love, holiness, and power and then "place them on the shelf" in decisions, schedules, and relationships. True prayer, as much as anything else, will help us to see progressively the sacredness of every facet of life. In this perspective, profound talk can hypocritically "mask" profound activity in subtle ways.

For example, the request for daily provision is followed by a second request for forgiveness (6:12). The concern for material needs is now focused on personal relationships. This request and its explanation in verses 14-15 may sound strange to those who are accustomed to hearing that our sins have been fully and finally forgiven in Christ. Here the Father may not forgive (6:14-15)! How can we bring these seemingly contradictory teachings about forgiveness into harmony? The answer is that two distinct dimensions of forgiveness are in view. The eternally secure, saving forgiveness in Christ is absolutely true. But that is not what Christ is talking about here. He is teaching about how our relationship with our Holy Father should influence our relationships in an unholy world. Our growth and relative maturity in daily relationships is the key.

Related matters of reconciliation (5:23-26), nonvengeance (5:38-42), and nonjudgment (7:1-5) are taught in the Sermon. But the best illustration is in 18:21-35, the "seventy times seven" passage. In compassion a king forgives a heavily obligated slave for his debts (18:29-30). The king then taught the unforgiving slave an important lesson. The connection of 6:14 with 18:35 is obvious.

The problem is that an unforgiving believer has forgotten his own need for forgiveness before his holy Father. We allow self-centeredness in temporal obligations to obscure love and mercy of the heavenly Father at an incomparably higher level. We need to forgive so we in turn can reflect the Father to a needy world. This will revitalize our appreciation for the Father's love.

CONCERN FOR THE FATHER'S WILL

The final petition is for the Father to "deliver us from the evil one" (6:13). Concern for the Father's will on earth and our role in it will make us sensitive during life's trials to our need for the Father's strength. Satan is very strong. But He is also very weak before the believer-Father combination. The Father does not lead us into temptation (James 1:13). But the trials of life are so numerous and debilitating that we will fall if we do not depend on Him. If we know the Father, then we will be sensitive to potential compromise. If we pray like this, then we can realize that the words of our mouths and the meditations of our hearts will be acceptable to Him who is our Rock and Redeemer (Ps. 19:14).

We can see that the Father is not remote, impersonal or unjust. He is holy, but He cares for us and can provide for every need. He is exalted, but He is as close as prayer. Prayer life indicates the quality for the Christian's relationship with the Father. In the future we will be with Him "as He is" forever. In the meantime He wants us to know Him as He is every day in prayer.

—J. Lanier Burns

When God Doesn't Answer

While president of Dallas Seminary I saw many dramatic answers to prayer, but I also saw many of my prayers go unanswered. The answered prayers have built my faith, strengthened my walk with God, and given me hope in the midst of perplexing problems. But the silence of God creates tension for me. I find God's silence difficult or sometimes impossible to explain.

Because of this tension, I have done a great deal of thinking and a great deal of Scripture-searching. I want to know why the same God who miraculously supplies a faculty member to our school allows the family of another faculty member to experience grief and tragedy in the midst of our prayers to the contrary. I want to know why some of our needs are met so miraculously while other needs are seemingly ignored.

In the midst of these questions I remain firmly convinced that God answers prayer. This is my testimony and yours. But all of us have also experienced the silence of God. We have echoed the experience of , "How long, O LORD, will I call for help, And Thou wilt not hear?" (Hab. 1:2). We share David's prophetic anticipation of the experience of Christ, "O my God, I cry by day, but Thou dost not answer; And by night, but I have no rest" (Ps. 22:2).

What is the secret of answered prayer? Why are some prayers unanswered? I find my answers to those perplexing questions in the Bible. The same Scriptures that assure us God will answer prayer also explain why some of our prayers are seemingly unanswered. These passages have taught me to ask four basic questions about my prayers.

HAVE YOU PRAYED?

The first and fundamental principle of answered prayer is faithfulness in prayer itself. Paul urged the Thessalonians, "pray continually; give thanks in all circumstances, for this is God's will for you in Christ Jesus" (1 Thess. 5:17-18). Paul exhorted the Ephesians, "And pray in the Spirit on all occasions with all kinds of prayers and requests" (Eph. 6:18a). Christ assured His disciples, "Ask and it will be given you; seek and you will find; knock and the door will be opened to you. For everyone who asks receives; he who seeks finds; and to him who knocks, the door will be opened" (Matt. 7:7-8).

Faithful continued prayer is one key to answered prayer. As James expresses it, "You do not have, because you do not ask God" (James 4:2b). In the words of "What a Friend We Have in Jesus": O what peace we often forfeit, O what needless pain we bear, All because we do not carry Everything to God in prayer.

If we expect God to answer, we must be faithful in prayer. Yet there is also the wonderful principle of grace that enables God to give us more than we ask. Countless blessings are showered on the Christian every day. Paul expressed this, "Now to him who is able to do immeasurably more than all we ask or imagine, according to his power that is at work within us" (Eph. 3:20). But it all begins with faithful prayer.

HAVE YOU PRAYED ACCORDING TO THE WILL OF GOD?

Again and again in the Bible the truth is emphasized that prayer must be according to God's will. Prayer is not a means for us to persuade a reluctant God to do something which is against His better judgment. Prayer, rather is coming to God for the fulfillment of His will, coming to a God who delights to answer prayer.

Praying in the will of God means that the prayer must be in harmony with what God has revealed to be His plan for the world. Our petitions must be in harmony with God's holy and righteous character. What we desire from God must be to the best interest of ourselves and others, even though we may not always know what is ultimately best.

But if we pray in the will of God, we can be sure that God will answer. The Apostle John wrote, "We have this assurance in approaching God, that if we ask anything according to his will, he hears us. And if we know that he hears us—whatever we ask—we know that we have what we asked of him" (1 John 5:14-15). These are great promises. In prayer we can approach God with complete assurance of His ability to answer us. There is no limit to what we can ask, if it is according to His will.

John goes on to say that there are prayer requests that God cannot answer because they're not according to His will and not for our best interest (1 John 5:16). James expressed it,

"When you ask, you do not receive, because you ask with wrong motives, that you may spend what you get on your pleasures" (James 4:3). Selfish prayers will not be honored by God. Prayer is God's appointed means to receive what is best for us and others and to realize what Paul called "what God's will is—his good, pleasing and perfect will" (Rom. 12:2b). But what infinite power and possibilities there are in prayer that is according to the will of God!

IS IT GOD'S TIME TO ANSWER OUR PRAYERS?

Many times in the experience of those who pray faithfully, God does not say, "No," but, "Wait." There is a proper timing for answered prayer. Sometimes God needs to wait until we are ready for the answer, or perhaps others need to be made ready. Sometimes a delay is necessary to fit into God's overall program. Daniel learned that lesson.

For sixty years Daniel prayed for the return of Israel to Jerusalem, for the rebuilding of the city of God which lay in ruins. It seemed that there was no answer from God. Then Daniel discovered the word of the Lord to Jeremiah, which had said that there would be a wait of seventy years before the captives of Israel could return to their city (Jer. 29:10). With this information, Daniel went to the Lord in fervent prayer. His prayer is one of the great prayers of Scripture (Dan. 9:3-19). When Daniel began to pray, about sixty-eight of the seventy years had already passed. In answer to Daniel's prayer—and in keeping with God's timetable—the Book of Ezra records the return of Israel to its ancient land and capital city. So delay in answering prayer does not mean that God has not heard.

I know a godly Christian family that had a wayward son. For many years they prayed for that boy, but there was no answer. Long after the parents had gone to glory, God wonderfully touched that son and restored him to Himself. The prayers were answered, but in God's time. God is never late and never early in answering prayer.

IS YOUR PRAYER TO THE GLORY OF GOD?

The most searching question we face in prayer is whether our petition is for our own selfish interest, pride, or attainment, or whether it is really to the glory of God. Answers to prayer must always honor God and bring glory to Him. This is one reason prayer must be offered in the name of Christ. Christ assured His disciples, "If you remain in me and my words remain in you, ask whatever you wish, and it will be given you...the Father will give you whatever you ask in my name" (John 15:7, 16b; cf. John 14:13-14).

God delights in honoring His Son. He loves to recognize what His Son has done on the cross to open the flood tides of grace for the believer. Prayer that is offered in the name of Christ and to the glory of Christ is prayer that God can answer. Praying in the name of Christ is a recognition of His infinite person, His deity and majesty. It is recognition of His power to do anything He wills to do. It is recognition of His grace that makes it possible for Him to answer the prayers of imperfect believers. Answered prayer also honors God's promised word, for God cannot lie.

But prayer which glorifies God requires that the person who prays be one whom God delights to honor. We must do some heart searching to be sure that there is no hindering sin in our lives. As the Psalmist prayed, "Search me, O God, and know my heart; Try me and know my anxious thoughts; And see if there be any hurtful way in me, And lead me in the everlasting way" (Ps. 139:23-24). As the Psalmist expressed it elsewhere, "If I regard wickedness in my heart, The LORD will not hear" (Ps. 66:18). The Psalmist goes on, however, with the reassuring word, "But certainly God has heard; He has given heed to the voice of my prayer" (Ps. 66:19).

Prayer is not a reward for perfection, but rather is God honoring His servants who earnestly seek to please Him. James writes, "The prayer of a righteous man is powerful and effective" (James 5:16b). John expressed it, "Dear friends, if our hearts do not condemn us, we have confidence before God and receive from him anything we ask, because we obey his commands and do what pleases him" (1 John 3:21-22).

GOD HAS PROMISED TO ANSWER PRAYER

God answers prayer according to His marvelous grace, according to His infinite power, and in keeping with His infinite love and faithfulness. When prayers seem to be unanswered, we must first ask ourselves if we have met the four conditions of answered prayer. Then we can continue to be faithful in prayer. Our attitude can be one of implicit confidence that He "is able to do immeasurably more than all we ask or imagine, according to his power that is at work within us" (Eph. 3:20). As we praise Him for His faithfulness, seek His will and glory, pray faithfully, and wait patiently until God's time, He will answer us.

—*John F. Walvoord*

Esteeming God's People

How good and pleasant it is
When brothers lives together in unity!
It is like precious oil poured on the head,
Running down on the beard,
Running down on Aaron's beard,
Down upon the collar of his robes.
(PSALM 133:1-2)

❧

As members of the body of Christ, we have a responsibility to care for one another. But I have discovered that many people in the church don't have time or inclination to involve themselves in the lives of others. How sad, that in a world of no-commitment, low-value relationships the Ambassadors of the King will not set the example of caring for one another. I have specially selected the choicest writings to assist those Christians who need to improve their "caring quotient." Here you will find wisdom on building friendships, comforting in times of crisis, and restoring the wounded. May this book help you in esteeming your brothers and sisters in Christ.

What Marks Your Friendships?

How many friends do you have? I suspect that most of you would respond by saying, "Quite a few." However, I think what you are really saying is that you have quite a few acquaintances but very few friends.

I've been doing some interesting study in the life of Christ recently and I've discovered that first of all He was known for having very special friends. He chose twelve that they might be with Him and go forth to preach. From these He chose three who occasionally shared special experiences with Him such as the Transfiguration and the night of prayer in Gethsemane. And then there was one individual who unashamedly and consistently referred to himself as the beloved disciple, a title that was never challenged.

In the second place it was known that certain homes gave Jesus a special welcome. We automatically think of the home of Mary and Martha where He must have been incredibly comfortable because He sought it as a retreat on so many occasions.

Third, we are aware that women supported Christ and the apostles as seen in the Gospel of Luke.

Finally, it was also known to whose garden Jesus went when He desired quiet.

What does biblical friendship involve? If you had a biblical friendship, what would it look like? I'd like to suggest two marks, each embraces a balancing element.

FRIENDSHIP REQUIRES UNCONDITIONAL LOVE

The first mark of a biblical friendship is unconditional love. That demands two things that must be kept in proper tension or you won't have the genuine item.

First, unconditional love demands commitment. "A friend loves at all times, and a brother is born for adversity" (Prov. 17:17). The most remarkable thing about that verse is to see it in the context of the book. Proverbs repeatedly points out the danger in false friendships.

I was in the Dallas Cowboys' locker room sometime ago after a practice session. Most of the guys had gone but one was sitting by himself. I sat down next to him and he said, "Doc, I can't tell my friends from my enemies." He then related how he had just been swindled out of $75,000. "It would be wonderful," continued the player, "if I had a friend whose primary concern was not my number or my name but just me." Do you hear the scream of the human heart in those words?

Proverbs 17:17 is talking about the fact that true love gives more than it receives. To be sure, the relationship is reciprocal; but it must begin with the person who is willing to take the initiative, particularly in the early stages of a friendship. It's the result of spontaneous combustion, which takes time. I have a friend whom I've known for over thirty-five years. If I called him right now it would be just like continuing the conversation I ended about two weeks ago. We go to each other's home, we eat in restaurants, and we travel together. The interesting thing is he never says, "Now let's see, in whose home were we last? Were we at your place? Oh, yes, well then it's my turn." We don't keep score; we do have wrestling matches over restaurant tabs that nearly cost us our testimonies! I care for him and he cares for me. Who cares who pays the bill? Who cares which home we visit?

Did you ever ask yourself, "Why is it that I don't have more friends like that?" It's because of the fear of rejection: "I don't want to be open with you because I fear if you really knew what I was like, you'd never want to be my friend, and I can't afford that risk."

That fear, by the way, is one reason why a husband doesn't have a closer relationship with his wife. Why does it take us so long to become open and transparent in a marriage? Sooner or later reality will break through, and everyone of us who has experienced it thanked God that when we dropped the whole ball of wax, that lovely woman looked us straight in the face and said, "That's okay. I love you." The front disappeared.

John's comment of Jesus Christ continues to fascinate me: "Having loved His own which were in the world, He loved them to the end." Why did He love them? It was not because He had no basis for repudiating them. They had dropped the ball on many occasions. In fact, in the most critical hours they were out to lunch. They let Him down. He loved them because His friendship with them was not resident in them, it was resident in Him. That's where biblical friendships begin.

COMMITMENT AND CONFRONTATION

Unconditional love involves not only commitment but also confrontation. "Better is open rebuke than hidden love. The kisses of an enemy may be profuse, but faithful are the wounds of a friend" (Prov. 27:5-6). Please note "faithful" is not "enjoyable." In our generation there is a softness that is a weakness but this passage teaches me that my commitment has got to be so great that it cares enough to confront.

I remember one such occasion at Wheaton College where I was not living up to my image as a student leader. There was a man on the administration staff who saw through my facade. Just before graduation he called me into his office and said, "Son, I want to tell you something. Sit down." Talk about a communicator—I got the message. Every time I opened my mouth he told me to keep it shut. I stormed out of that office hotter than a hornet, only to discover with some reflection that I finally found the first individual in twenty-two years who loved me enough to confront me with a great problem that would have wiped out my ministry.

I'm not advocating arbitrary confrontation; I'm stressing a friendship that has already been developed. In the New Testament rebuke is always on the basis of relationship. The moment I begin to build a friendship, I am compelled to develop a relationship of confrontation. If I love the individual without a string attached, then I may have to confront him with whatever spiritual deficiency he may experience. That's why I'm convinced that true friendships are forged, not formed.

FRIENDSHIP REQUIRES UNCOMPROMISING LOYALTY

A second characteristic of biblical friendship is uncompromising loyalty. Because loyalty always involves a sustaining relationship, the wisdom writer said, "Perfume and incense bring joy to the heart, and the pleasantness of one's friend springs from his earnest counsel" (Prov. 27:9).

A good biblical example of a sustaining friendship is the relationship between Jonathan and David. Most of us are running scared from this illustration because we live in such a homosexually-sensitive society. We're afraid to build that kind of relationship with the same sex.

But let me ask you this: How many individuals do you know who would die for you? For the first time in my life I've finally found two or three people who would do that. Over a number of years our friendships have ripened and matured to that kind of commitment. That was the relationship of Jonathan and David.

A STIMULATING RELATIONSHIP

Along with a sustaining relationship we need a stimulating relationship. "As iron sharpens iron, so one man sharpens another" (Prov. 27:17). There are some people that I cannot be around without coming away a better person.

My wife and I recently spent some time in Colorado with two of our closest friends. The most beautiful experience of my life is to be around that man and his wife. Jeanne and I have never had five minutes with that couple that didn't create in us a greater hunger for Jesus Christ.

In John 15:15 our Lord said, "I no longer call you servants, because a servant does not know his master's business. Instead, I have called you friends, for everything that I learned from my Father I have made known to you." In a true friendship there are no secrets. Transparency is total.

A real biblical friendship must have both elements in balance: unconditional love and uncompromising loyalty. Are you looking for that kind of a friend? Then stop looking and start praying that God will make you that kind of a friend.

—Howard G. Hendricks

You Can Count On Me

John Donne, a 17th century English poet, wisely warns us that "no man is an island." I believe he is saying that we need some other significant person in our lives, someone other than a husband or a wife. We need a friend, a true friend.

In essence, the problem is that there are a lot of lonely people in the body of Jesus Christ. When Chuck Swindoll spoke at the Founders Banquet in Dallas, he related the following event which took place during his student years: "I want to tell you something that I have never told anyone before this banquet. I remember between my semesters in my fourth year I had one of the best kept secrets on campus. Cynthia and I were at a low ebb, we had a little boy, Kurt, he's now a big man. But after Kurt we lost a baby. Five and a half months of pregnancy and we lost that little baby. It was a little girl. That broke our hearts. And on top of that we got news that Cynthia's dear godly mother had terminal breast cancer. Cynthia was now pregnant again and we drove down to Houston to see her mother and father. There on Sunday afternoon while driving home from church our car was hit by a drunk. It totalled our car, threw our son into the window and broke his jaw, and it threw Cynthia into the gearshift and steering wheel and she began to hemorrhage. And she hemorrhaged throughout the pregnancy. I borrowed a car to go back to Dallas, I missed the seating of the seniors, but more importantly, I began to be seized with panic. I needed a friend, I needed somebody to love me, but I didn't know how to ask for one."

Not only are lonely Christians found in seminaries or sitting in the pew, they can be found standing behind the pulpit as well. As one pastor recently lamented, "On the surface it looks like I have dozens of friends, but the truth is that I'm the loneliest man in town." Vocational Christian ministry provides no insulation from the chill of loneliness.

What Is A Friend?

By the way, how many friends do you have? Would it take a while to count them all? Would you need a calculator? Or would it take about two or three seconds, if that long?

I suppose that the answer depends on how you define a friend. Some would define a friend very broadly. They would include what you and I might call an acquaintance, a next-door neighbor, or someone with whom you carpool. Others would narrow that definition. For them an acquaintance would not suffice. The difference is the depth of the relationship.

The following anonymous definition illustrates this distinction: "What is a friend? I'll tell you. A friend is a person with whom you dare to be yourself. Your soul can go naked with him. He seems to ask you to put on nothing, to be what you really are. When you are with him, you do not have to be on your guard. You can say what you think, so long as it is genuinely you. He understands those contradictions in your nature that cause others to misjudge you. With him you breathe freely…He understands. You may weep with him, laugh with him, pray with him, and through and underneath it all, he sees, knows, and loves you. A friend, I repeat, is one with whom you dare to be yourself!" To sum it up, he is one who sees your warts as well as your beauty marks, and accepts you anyway. Again, I wonder how many friends do you have?

What are the characteristics of a true friend? How would you know one if you found him? Is unconditional acceptance the only criterion? In the Book of Proverbs we discover that a true friend displays a number of character qualities. We will briefly examine three.

A TRUE FRIEND IS CONSTANT

First, a true friend is constant, dependable in times of adversity. Far too often those who appear to be friends are in reality only "fair-weather friends" who desert the ship when dark clouds appear on our horizon. They are not constant, nor are they dependable. Their chief characteristic is that they tend to evaporate under the heat of our adversity. Things begin to go wrong and you look around and ask, "Where are they? Where have they all gone? They have disappeared!" We soon learn that adversity is the acid test of a relationship. Recently, I read an interview with Tony Dorsett in a local newspaper. In the article he says, "The best advice given me was from my dad who told me you can have all the friends in the world, but you will have only one or two buddies. I used to drive old cars, and he told me I would find out real quick who my buddies were…when the car broke down. There are a lot of people who like to jump on the bandwagon that are not true friends."

By way of contrast, Proverbs teaches that a true friend is constant in times of adversity. In Proverbs 18:24 Solomon writes, "A man of many companions may come to ruin, but there is a friend who sticks closer than a brother." A loyal friend, unlike "many companions," does not desert in difficulty. With a true friend there is a depth of relationship which may exceed that of one's own family. In Proverbs 17:17 Solomon wisely instructs, "A friend loves at all times, and a brother is born for adversity." A close friend loves during the bad times as well as the good. He is not absent in adversity, but alert to adversity.

Our youngest son at age three endured four operations to correct a muscle problem with his eyes. He may still lose the vision in one of those eyes. During each of those operations, a special couple, whom I consider our closest friends, were right there in the waiting room with us. They knew how important the operations were and took time out of both their busy schedules to "stick closer than a brother" for comfort and encouragement. Why? Because true friends are constant in times of adversity.

A True Friend is Candid

Second, a true friend is candid. Our "fickle friends" tend only to flatter us. Instead of being honest with us they often tell us what they think we want to hear. I recall occasions in my professional career when I have either taught a Sunday school class or preached a sermon and have been told by friends that it was the best sermon or lesson they had ever heard. They were convinced that I was destined to be the Spurgeon of the 21st century! However, in my heart I knew it was a "lead balloon" sermon—one that grudgingly rolls off the tip of your tongue and if it manages to clear the edge of the pulpit it promptly dies somewhere between the pulpit and the first row.

By way of contrast, Proverbs tells us that true friends are candid. They are honest and trustworthy. They "tell it like it is," and are to be trusted for their candor even though it may hurt our pride. Proverbs 27:6 says, "The kisses [flattery] of an enemy may be profuse, but faithful are the wounds [correction] of a friend." And Proverbs 28:23 also says, "He who rebukes a man will in the end gain more favor than he who has a flattering tongue." Friends do not condone sin in our lives, they confront sin in our lives. While they accept the warts, they do not overlook the warts, they lovingly call our attention to them even though it may temporarily strain the relationship.

A TRUE FRIEND IS CONSIDERATE

Not only is a true friend constant and candid, but finally, a true friend is considerate. True friends are considerate or caring in that they do not take advantage of the relationship. For example, they do not take advantage of your hospitality. Solomon writes in Proverbs 25:16-17, "If you find honey, eat just enough—too much of it, and you will vomit. Seldom set foot in your neighbor's house—too much of you, and he will hate you." Too much familiarity, even among Christian friends, breeds contempt. Too many Christians have experienced the pain of asking friends to leave because they have taken advantage of their hospitality. For example, one family visited another while vacationing and asked to stay in their home. It became evident after several days that they planned to stay "as long as you'll have us." In these situations, the immortal words of Samuel Johnson prove most insightful, "Fish and friends smell after three days."

We have discovered that true friends display no less than three character qualities: they are constant in that they do not desert in times of adversity; they are candid, they lovingly "tell it like it is" and; they are considerate, they do not take advantage of the relationship. But there is a question that begs to be answered, "How?" "How do we develop that kind of relationship?"

DEVELOPING FRIENDSHIPS

To develop a close friendship we must be friendly. There is an old adage, which is a mistranslation of Proverbs 18:24, that says, "A man that has friends must show himself friendly." Now on the surface that seems rather easy. But far too many Christians are not very friendly. What do I mean? Sometimes at church when you catch someone's eye, you are greeted by utter silence or even contempt. And far too often visitors are completely ignored by a cold congregation! To develop close relationships we must be friendly.

Second, we must communicate acceptance. We must allow people to be themselves. When they are around us they need to feel that they can relax and "peel off the mask." In short, we must learn to tolerate warts. We must stop trying to impress one another and begin accepting one another.

Third, in order to develop close friends, and this is the hard one, we must risk vulnerability. This means we may have to pay a price, we may have to bleed a little. That is, we will have to risk rejection, which is not easy on our feelings of self-worth. But we are not the first to experience this rejection, and when we read the Scriptures, we find that we are in good company.

Finally, to develop a close friendship, we must demonstrate availability. I overheard a conversation between two seminary students as one was looking at his calendar trying to determine when he had some free time to get together with the other. Finally, he said, "I think I'll be able to work you into my schedule in about two months!" Obviously, availability was not very high on his priority list. On the other hand, the Southern Methodist Bulletin relates the following account: "Our riding lawnmower had broken down and I had been working fruitlessly trying to get it back together. Suddenly, my new neighbor appeared with a handful of tools. 'Can I give you a hand?' he asked. In 20 minutes he had the mower functioning beautifully. 'Say, what do you make with such a fine kit of tools?' I asked. He smiled broadly. 'Mostly friends. I'm available anytime.'"

It is my prayer that we will discover that people do not care how much we know until they know how much we care. It does not take a theological education to learn to care about people, just a little bit of love. As Chuck Swindoll said, "I needed a friend, I needed somebody to love me." I suspect, you do too.

In an article in Moody Monthly, James Corley writes in the caption, "Few American men have a friend who is so close that they would be willing to say publicly, 'I love him.'" In the article he relates the following. "When Chicago Bear running backs Gale Sayers and Brian Piccolo began rooming together, it marked a first for pro football. A white and a black sharing a room was news in 1967. During the 1969 season, doctors diagnosed Piccolo as having cancer. By the end of the season he lay bedridden. Meanwhile, the Professional Football Writers honored Sayers at their annual dinner as the league's most courageous player. With tears Sayers said, "You flatter me by giving me this award, but I tell you here and now that I accept it for Brian Piccolo. Brian Piccolo is the man of courage...I love Brian Piccolo, and I'd like you to love him. Tonight, when you hit your knees, please ask God to love him, too."

How about you? Do you care about anyone that way? Have you ever experienced the kind of love for a friend that these men had for one another?

—*Aubrey Malphurs*

We're In This Together

Several years ago I became keenly interested in an idea that flows through the New Testament, particularly in the letters that were written to various churches located throughout the first century world. The idea focuses on two little words—one another—which are used in our English text approximately sixty times. The Apostle Paul leads the list for frequency, penning this concept nearly forty times.

As I personally traced this concept through the New Testament and looked at how it was used by various biblical writers, I found that most of the injunctions and exhortations that use the words "one another" can be organized and categorized around twelve unique statements. And to my surprise, I discovered that Paul used seven of these twelve statements in the practical section of his Roman epistle. In fact, these seven "one another" injunctions in Romans 12-16 provide unique points around which Paul's major concerns in this section of his letter can be organized. Let's look at these "one another" injunctions one by one.

MEMBERS ONE OF ANOTHER

First, we are "members one of another" (Rom. 12:5b). In Romans 12:4 Paul used an analogy, that of a human body, to illustrate the nature of the church and how it should function. "For just as we have many members in one body," he wrote, "and all the members do not have the same function, so we," and then Paul applied the analogy, "so we who are many, are one body in Christ, and individually members one of another" (Rom. 12:4, 5).

This is the most basic "one another" concept in the New Testament. All others build on the fact that we belong to each other. And before the other injunctions become relevant and meaningful, we must accept the basic truth outlined for us here. The fact is that we cannot grow in Christ as we should unless we believe in this concept and participate in a body of believers where, as Paul stated in his classic Ephesians passage, "every joint supplies, according to the proper working of each individual part" (Eph. 4:16). Then, and only then, the body grows and builds itself up in love.

DEVOTED TO ONE ANOTHER

Second, we are to "be devoted to one another" (Rom. 12:10a). Paul was not a theorist, and he demonstrated this forcibly by immediately instructing these New Testament Christians as to how they could become functioning "members one of another." They were to "be devoted to one another in brotherly love."

Actually this is Paul's second analogy. He first used the illustration of the human body, but here he refers to the family. In essence he is saying that just as family units are made up of brothers and sisters, so we are members of God's family and brothers and sisters in Christ. This is the basic meaning of the term "brotherly love."

In many respects I like the analogy of the family better than the body, though both are very beautiful illustrations. However the "body" concept is more physiological, whereas the concept of the "family" adds dimensions of warmth, of emotion, and of reality.

One of the great tragedies throughout human history is that many people grow up in families where they are not taught by example and experience to love at the feeling level. Consequently, they eventually have difficulty emotionally loving their "brothers and sisters in Christ."

But there is good news! God designed His family to be a "re-parenting organism" for Christians who have not learned to love at the feeling level. God desires that Christians relate to one another, not only at the cognitive and behavioral level, but also at the level of deep devotedness. The Body of Christ, when it functions properly, helps Christians develop these internal desires and abilities which were not nurtured in their early years.

HONOR ONE ANOTHER

Third, we are to "give preference to one another in honor" (Rom. 12: 10b). I have a friend in Dallas. His name is Brent and he plays the piano. Brent is a musician par excellence, a soloist in his own right. But one of his most unique abilities is to accompany vocalists and to make them sound great. He understands the support role and never overshadows or competes with their performance. The facts are that Brent really enjoys making other musicians "look and sound good."

I believe Brent's attitude illustrates in a specific way what all Christians are to do in general. We are all to make other Christians "look and sound good." This is what Paul meant when he wrote to the Roman Christians, "honor one another above yourselves."

Think of what would happen in many local churches all around the world if every Christian honored other Christians in this way. There would be unity in the body and spiritual and emotional healing would be constant. The church would experience renewal as never before and our impact on the world would be unparalleled in history.

UNIFIED WITH ONE ANOTHER

Fourth, we are "to be of the same mind with one another" (Rom. 15:5b). All that Paul has written to this point culminates in this fourth "one another" injunction. Unity and oneness result when Christians really believe and understand they are "members of one another", when they are really "devoted to one another", and when they truly "honor one another." But Romans 15:5 is also a pivotal verse, for it recapitulates Paul's concern for body function at this point, and then serves as a launching point for three more "one another" injunctions which further this dynamic process.

ACCEPT ONE ANOTHER

We are to "accept one another" (Rom. 15:7a). As a young Christian growing up I became a part of a religious group where acceptance was based on a set of predetermined standards. If you measured up to those standards you were accepted; if you did not you felt rejected. Later, after leaving this legalistic system, I discovered that most, if not all, of these predetermined standards were not in the Bible.

Imagine what would have happened to you if Christ had accepted you into His family conditionally; that is, what if He had said, "I will accept you...If you are a certain color...If you wear a certain kind of clothes...If your hair is a certain length...If you speak a certain language or with a certain accent!" Very few of us would be members of the family of God. The fact is, He accepted us just as we were. Paul said, "Accept one another, just as Christ also accepted us" (Rom. 15:7).

But, someone responds, "What about sin? Are we to accept sin?" The Bible is a marvelous book of balances. Paul answers those questions immediately, with his next one another injunction.

ADMONISH ONE ANOTHER

Sixth, we are to "admonish one another" (Rom. 15:14). This is the most difficult injunction to do properly. And yet it can be the most rewarding and is absolutely essential as a parallel injunction to unconditional acceptance.

I remember a young man who called me one Sunday afternoon. He was mad at everyone: me, the elders at the church, and a few other people in Dallas. I immediately detected he had a serious problem with himself, which was verified the next day when we got together to talk. His family was falling apart, he was losing his job, and he was really very angry at God. Down deep he was basically angry with himself.

As lovingly, but as directly as possible, I pointed out his problem. That is always a very difficult thing for me, for I always fear rejection in these situations. But somehow he sensed my vulnerability and love. I will never forget his parting words to me, as he smiled through his tears and said, "You are the first one who has ever loved me enough to tell me what is wrong with me." That was indeed rewarding!

Note too that Paul carefully outlines in this verse what qualifies a Christian to admonish another Christian. We must have our own spiritual "act" together before we have the right to tell others how to "get theirs together." This is why Paul said, "I myself also am convinced that you yourselves are full of goodness, filled with all knowledge..." which, concluded Paul, makes us able also "to admonish one another" (Rom. 15:14).

GREET ONE ANOTHER

Believers, Paul says finally, are to "greet one another" (Rom. 16: 16a). Paul ends his Roman letter with a seventh "one another" injunction that often causes pause for those of us who live in the twentieth-century American culture. "Greet one another," Paul wrote, "with a holy kiss."

It is very easy to dismiss this "one another" injunction as purely cultural. We must acknowledge that part of it is cultural, for the exact form of the greeting is never fully described in the New Testament. We can however reconstruct the form generally from the Middle Eastern culture today. We have all seen heads of state get off airplanes and greet one another with a kiss on either side of the cheek. Unfortunately, this greeting is neither holy nor meaningful, but rather, pure protocol, about as meaningful as when some Christians greet one another and say, "Hello, how are you?" and others respond, "I'm fine, how are you?"

Whatever Paul means, one thing is clear. Christians should greet one another not perfunctorily or mechanically, but in a holy, righteous, meaningful fashion.

This point came home to me forcefully one evening when I met a young high school student at church and said, "Hi, Bruce. How are you?"

About three minutes later one of the elders approached me having overheard the conversation and admonished me in love saying, "Gene, when you asked Bruce how he was, you didn't stay around to hear his answer." He went on to tell me this young man had answered my question stating that he wasn't very well since his brother was in a motorcycle accident that day.

I was, of course, mortified, but so thankful the elder was sensitive, and bold enough, to tell me what I had done. I immediately apologized to the young man, but also learned a great lesson. When we greet other Christians and ask them how they are, we should really be concerned about their welfare. This I believe is at least one application of what it means to "greet one another with a holy kiss."

To sum up, there are at least five more unique "one another" injunctions used by Paul in additional letters which we could add to these seven. In Galatians he wrote that Christians are to "serve one another" and "bear one another's burdens." In Ephesians he said, "bearing with one another" (NIV), and "be subject to one another." And twice in 1 Thessalonians he admonished, "encourage one another." But when all is said and done, the seven in his letter to the Romans actually include these additional five and give us all we really need to know and do to "attain to the unity of the faith, and of the knowledge of the Son of God, to a mature man, to the measure of the stature which belongs to the fullness of Christ" (Eph. 4: 13). When we practice these "one another" injunctions, it "causes the growth of the body for the building up of itself in love" (Eph. 4:16b).

—*Gene A. Getz*

Serving Each Other

The idea of becoming a servant seemed either wrong or weird to me. I realize now I rejected it because my concept of a servant was somewhere between an African slave named Kunta Kinte straight out of Roots and those thousands of nameless migrant workers who, at harvest time, populate the farmlands and orchards across America. Both represented ignorance, objects of mistreatment, a gross absence of human dignity, and the epitome of many of the things Christianity opposes.

The mental image turned me off completely. Walking around in my head was a caricature of a pathetic creature virtually without will or purpose in life…bent over, crushed in spirit, lacking self-esteem, soiled, wrinkled, and weary. You know, sort of a human mule who, with a sigh, shuffles and trudges down the long rows of life. Don't ask me why, but that was my perception every time I heard the word servant. Candidly, the idea disgusted me.

And confusion was added to my disgust when I heard people (especially preachers) link the two terms servant and leader. They seemed as opposite as light and dark or like the classic example of the round peg in a square hole. I distinctly remember saying, "Who, me a servant? You gotta be kidding!"

That was my initial reaction. But I was in for a pleasant surprise. God changed my mind and introduced me to the truth concerning authentic servanthood. How desperately I needed to improve my serve!

THE IMAGE OF CHRIST

I had never stopped to consider that God was committed to one major objective in the lives of His people: to conform us to the image of His Son. What is this image? I believe the answer is found in Christ's own words: "For even the Son of Man did not come to be served, but to serve, and to give his life as a ransom for many" (Mk. 10:45).

No mumbo jumbo. Just a straight-from-the-shoulder admission. He came to serve and to give. It makes sense, then, to say that God desires the same for us. After bringing us into His family through faith in His Son, the Lord God sets His sights on building into us the same quality that made Jesus distinct from all others in His day. He is engaged in building into His people the same serving and giving qualities that characterized His Son.

Nothing is more refreshing than a servant's heart and a giving spirit, especially when we see them displayed in a person many would tag as a celebrity. A couple of years ago my wife and I attended the National Religious Broadcasters convention in Washington, D.C., where one of the main speakers was Colonel James B. Irwin, former astronaut who was a part of the crew that had made the successful moon walk. He spoke of the thrill connected with leaving this planet and seeing it shrink in size. He mentioned watching earthrise one day…and thinking how privileged he was to be a member of that unique crew. And then he began to realize en route back home that many would consider him a "superstar," for sure an international celebrity.

Humbled by the awesome goodness of God, Colonel Irwin shared his true feelings, which went something like this:

"As I was returning to earth, I realized that I was a servant—not a celebrity. So I am here as God's servant on planet Earth to share what I have experienced that others might know the glory of God."

God allowed this man to break loose from the small cage we call "Earth," during which time He revealed to him a basic motto all of us would do well to learn: "A servant, not a celebrity." Caught up in the fast-lane treadmill of Century

Twenty—making mad dashes through airports, meeting deadlines, being responsible for big-time decisions, and coping with the stress of people's demands mixed with our own high expectations—it's easy to lose sight of our primary calling as Christians, isn't it? Even the busy mother of small children struggles with this. Mounds of ironing and the endless needs of her husband and kids block out the big picture.

SERVANT, OR CELEBRITY?

If you're like me, you sometimes think, "I would give anything to be able to step back into the time when Jesus cast His shadow on earth. How great it must have been to sit back as one of the Twelve and soak up all those truths He taught. I mean, they must have really learned how to serve, to give of themselves." Right? Wrong!

Allow me to journey back with you to one of the many scenes that demonstrated just how typical those guys really were. I'm referring to an occasion when our Lord's popularity was on the rise...the knowledge of His kingdom was spreading...and the disciples began to be anxious about being recognized as members of His chosen band.

What makes this account a bit more interesting is the presence of a mother of two of the disciples. She's Mrs. Zebedee, wife of the Galilean fisherman and mother of James and John. Let's consider her request:

"Then the mother of Zebedee's sons came to Jesus with her sons and, kneeling down, asked a favor of him. 'What is it you want?' he asked. She said, 'Grant that one of these two sons of mine may sit at your right and the other at your left in your kingdom'" (Matt. 20:20-21).

Now don't be too tough on this dear Jewish mother. She's proud of her sons! She had thought about that request for quite some time. Her motive was probably pure and her idea was in proper perspective. She didn't ask that her sons occupy the center throne, of course not—that belonged to Jesus. But like any good mother who watches out for "breaks in life" that could lead to a nice promotion, she pushed for James and John as candidates for thrones number two and number three. She wanted to enhance their image before the public. She wanted people to think highly of her boys who had left their nets and entered this up-and-coming ministry. They were among "the Twelve." And that needed recognition!

Just in case you're wondering how the other ten felt about this, check out verse 24. It says the other ten disciples became indignant. Guess why. Hey, no way were they going to give up those top spots without a fight. They got downright upset that maybe James and John might get the glory they wanted. Sound familiar?

With biting conviction Jesus answers the mother with this penetrating comment: "You don't know what you are asking …" (Matt. 20:22). That must have stung. She really thought she did. Enamored of her world of soldiers with medals, emperors with jeweled crowns, governors with slaves awaiting their every need, and even merchants with their employees…it seemed only fitting for those two sons of hers to have thrones, especially if they were charter members of the God movement, soon to be a "kingdom." Rulers need thrones!

No. This movement is different. Jesus pulls His disciples aside and spells out the sharp contrast between His philosophy and the world system in which they lived. Read His words slowly and carefully:

"Jesus called them together and said, 'You know that the rulers of the Gentiles lord it over them, and their high officials exercise authority over them. Not so with you. Instead, whoever wants to become great among you must be your servant, and whoever wants to be first must be your slave—just as the Son of Man did not come to be served, but to serve, and to give his life as a ransom for many'" (Matt. 20:25-28).

Notice some important words in that passage: "…whoever wants to become great among you must be your servant." Not only are they important, but they also appear to be forgotten. There doesn't seem to be much of either a servant mentality or a servant-hearted leadership in today's world. If only people today would follow a great biblical example.

To me, the finest model, except Christ Himself, was that young Jew from Tarsus who was radically transformed from a strong-willed official in Judaism to a bond servant of Jesus Christ. The Apostle Paul was a remarkable man.

It's possible you have the notion that the Apostle Paul rammed his way through life like a fully-loaded battleship at sea. Blasting and pounding toward objectives, he was just too important to worry about the little people or those who got in his way. After all, he was Paul! I must confess that is not too far removed from my original impression of the man in my earlier years as a Christian. He was, in my mind, the blend of a Christian John Wayne, Clint Eastwood, and the Hulk.

But that false impression began to fade when I made an in-depth study of Paul—his style, his own self-description, even his comments to various churches and people as he wrote to each. I discovered that the man I had thought was the prima donna par excellence considered himself quite the contrary. Almost without exception he begins every piece of correspondence with words to this effect: "Paul, a servant …" or "Paul, a bond-slave …. "

The more I pondered those words, the deeper they penetrated. This man, the one who certainly could have expected preferential treatment or demanded a high-and-mighty role of authority over others, referred to himself most often as a "servant" of God. He was indeed an apostle, but he conducted and carried himself as a servant. I found this extremely appealing.

The longer I thought about this concept, the more evidence emerged from the Scripture to support it. In fact, most of the discoveries fell into one of three categories of characteristics related to this servant image: transparent humanity, genuine humility, and absolute honesty.

THE EXAMPLE OF PAUL

Listen to Paul's words to the Corinthians. "When I came to you, brothers, I did not come with eloquence or superior wisdom as I proclaimed to you the testimony about God. For I resolved to know nothing while I was with you except Jesus Christ and him crucified. I came to you in weakness and fear, and with much trembling" (1 Cor. 2:1-3).

Now compare those words with a popular opinion of him: "...His letters are weighty and forceful, but in person he is unimpressive and his speaking amounts to nothing" (2 Cor. 10:10).

That's quite a shock. The man didn't have it all together—he wasn't perfect—and (best of all) he didn't attempt to hide it! He admitted to his friends in Corinth he was weak, fearful, and even trembling when he stood before them. I admire such transparency. Everybody does if it's the truth.

I forget where I found the following statement, but it's been in my possession for years. It vividly describes Paul as being "...a man of moderate stature with curly hair and scanty, crooked legs, protruding eyeballs, large knit eyebrows, a long nose, and thick lips."

That certainly doesn't sound like any one of the many smooth public idols of our day. And we know for a fact he suffered terribly from poor eyesight (Gal. 6:11), plus some are convinced the man had a hunchback.

Without hiding a bit of his humanity (see Romans 7 if you still struggle believing he was a cut above human), Paul openly declares his true condition. He had needs and admitted them. Servants do that. He didn't have everything in life wired perfectly. Servants are like that. Immediately you can begin to see some of the comforting aspects of having a servant's heart. Paul admitted his humanity.

That brings us to the second characteristic of servants: genuine humility. In that first Corinthian letter Paul also admits:

"My message and my preaching were not with wise and persuasive words, but with a demonstration of the Spirit's power, so that your faith might not rest on men's wisdom, but on God's power" (1 Cor. 2:4-5).

Now for a preacher, that's quite a comment. The man comes up front and declares not only his lack of persuasiveness, but his reason why—that they might not be impressed with his ability, but rather with God's power. There's something very authentic in Paul's humility. Over and over we read similar words in his writings. I'm convinced that those who were instructed, face to face, by the man became increasingly more impressed with the living Christ and less impressed with him.

Paul's was a revealing case of humility. He had a nondefensive spirit when he was confronted. This reveals a willingness to be accountable. Paul also had an authentic desire to help others. A true servant stays in touch with the struggles of others and continually looks for ways to serve and to give.

This leads us to our final principle: absolute honesty. Remember what Paul wrote to the Thessalonians? "For the appeal we make does not spring from error or impure motives, nor are we trying to trick you. On the contrary, we speak as men approved by God to be entrusted with the gospel. We are not trying to please men but God, who tests our hearts" (1 Thess. 2:3-4).

Honesty has a beautiful and refreshing simplicity, as do servants of God. There are no ulterior motives or hidden meanings. As honesty and real integrity characterize our lives, there will be no need to manipulate others. We'll come to the place where all the substitutes will turn us off once we cultivate a taste for the genuine.

Take time to give some thought to your own life. Think about becoming more of a servant. Be real. Be who you really are and then allow God to develop within you a style of serving that fits you.

—Charles R. Swindoll

Practicing Hospitality

For weeks she had talked of nothing but the upcoming trip to the zoo. The day had finally arrived! Her small hand in mine, we walked through the entrance gates. "Please, Jeanette, can we see the lion first?"

As we neared the lion's cage I sensed her disappointment. "He's sleeping," she exclaimed. "I wanted to see him do something!" Although we didn't know it, it was almost feeding time. Aroused by the scent of raw meat, the lion began to stir. Nostrils quivering, he began to pace. Looking most intent, he seemed captivated by his pursuit of the origin of the smell. Instinctively, Carrie tightened her grip on my hand. "I wouldn't want to get in his way" she whispered and suddenly shivered.

I was reminded of my trip to the zoo recently as I studied Romans 12:13. In this verse Paul urges believers to practice hospitality. The implication is that we should pursue hospitality with the same intensity that a hungry lion demonstrates when stalking his prey. Never before had I thought of hospitality in that light!

First Timothy 3:2 teaches that a man cannot qualify as an overseer of the church unless he is marked by hospitality. First Peter 4:9 reminds us to offer hospitality to each other without grumbling. Hospitality, then, is one sign of Christian maturity and obedience. But believing that hospitality is crucial is not enough. Acting upon this belief is the true test of our obedience. We must put hospitality into action.

PLANNING FOR HOSPITALITY

First comes planning. Generally speaking, good intentions remain exactly that unless we formulate a blueprint for implementing action. For that reason, we must plan to be hospitable! Who do you want to invite into your home? A lonely widow, a new neighbor, a struggling student, or perhaps the newcomers at church? Don't limit yourself to those whom you already know. Use hospitality as a way to open new avenues of friendship, to encourage the despondent, to minister to the lonely.

Also consider selecting guests who can minister to you and your family. When he was still a single medical student, my husband Bill received a dinner invitation from a Christian physician and his family. With his three impressionable children looking on, Dr. Cooper asked Bill to tell how he became a Christian. What a great exposure for those kids! What an opportunity for Bill to articulate his faith in Christ.

What do you want to do with your guests? Historically, sharing a meal together has been a means of showing honor and affection to the invited guest. We need not limit ourselves to dinner invitations though. Be creative! What about Sunday brunch, Saturday breakfast, or coffee and dessert one evening? We recently participated in a "build your own pizza" party. I made the dough. Everyone else brought the toppings. The group concurred that it could have competed with our neighborhood pizza parlor!

Being hospitable means more than meeting the physical and material needs of your guests. Plan specific ways to minister to your guests' spiritual needs too. Ask them questions. Stimulate their thinking. Share what you are gleaning from God's Word. Learn from one another. Share your struggles. Urge each other on to a greater commitment to Christ.

PREPARING FOR HOSPITALITY

The second step is preparation. Adequate preparatory measures all but eliminate most disasters. Since your goal is to entertain with a view to serve and encourage others, I think it's important to have most things ready before your guests arrive. I recall my friend Janet recounting one of her experiences as a visitor. Invited for dinner at seven o'clock, she and her husband arrived, on time and hungry, only to have their hostess say, "Oh, I'm so glad you are finally here. Now I can start cooking dinner!" They did not begin to eat until nine o'clock. It was hard for my friends to enjoy the company of their hostess while she was busy over the hot stove.

Preparation does require two treasured commodities: time and money. Because most of us are limited in these areas, use your ingenuity. Consider a potluck dinner. Enlist the help of a friend. Don't be shy. Most people are just waiting to be asked.

Many of us are reluctant to invite others into our homes because we think that it's just not good enough. Over and over I have heard people say, "We'll start entertaining in our home when...we are settled in...the living room is finally redecorated...we can afford to serve filet mignon...the new couch finally arrives." God calls us to serve Him with our best, whether it be hot dogs on paper plates or crab-stuffed lobster served on fine china. People come to visit you, not to take an inventory of your furnishings. All God requires is a willingness to receive guests into your home, no matter how small or large it may be.

PRAYING FOR HOSPITALITY

Meeting spiritual needs requires preparation, too. This leads us to the third step which is prayer. Pray that God will give you the sensitivity and wisdom to minister to the spiritual needs of your guests. It is amazing how a good, relaxing dinner will cause people to open up about their feelings. Some of the most exciting times we've had around our dinner table have been after dinner! I can remember times when we've sat at the table until late at night answering questions for searching friends God has brought into our home.

Ask God to show you whom to invite. My husband and I find it helpful to block off time each week to pray for our friends and acquaintances. We ask God to show us who has needs and whom we could encourage by inviting into our home. Pray too that God will continue to equip you to meet the needs of others. Pray that the time you spend being hospitable will bring glory to Him. Pray for pure motivation in opening your home to others. "Whatever you do, work at it with all your heart, as working for the Lord, not for men" (Col. 3:23). If your intentions are not genuine, discouragement is imminent. You may never receive a compliment, a thank you, or a reciprocal invitation. Remember that it is the Lord who rewards our efforts.

PERSISTENCE IN HOSPITALITY

The last step is persistence. Persist in being hospitable. Paul encouraged the Galatians, "Let us not become weary in doing good" (Gal. 6:9). This exhortation still applies. Occasionally you will feel that you've failed. I can remember an evening that was (from a human perspective) an absolute flop! One couple arrived late, another had to leave early, and in the middle of dinner a sick friend dropped by seeking medical advice from my husband. No one had much in common and try as I did, the evening never really got off the ground. Although I was discouraged, I had to remember that we invited these guests in obedience to God's command to be hospitable. God only requires obedience. It's up to Him to take care of the results.

The essence of hospitality is practical Christianity. As I grew up, this was exemplified for me by my family's Christmas celebrations. As the festive season drew near we searched for people who would be alone on Christmas day. College students, couples, or widows all received an invitation for the 25th. We would crowd around our small dining room table to enjoy food and fun. We shared our lives with our guests for that one day, and many lasting friendships developed. I learned early that hospitality is a way of life.

Who says you can't be hospitable? Plan, prepare, pray, and persist. Leave the rest to God. You'll be surprised at the results!

—Jeanette A. Stewart

Words That Heal

Words can be tremendously healing or brutally destructive. They can foster despair and anxiety or encourage confidence and hope. One of my professors in Seminary made it a daily habit to encourage at least one person. Maybe it was the janitor for his good job of keeping the classroom clean. Or perhaps the secretary for the efficiency of her work. I wonder what would happen in our homes and in our churches if we kept such an assignment every day?

An examination of the Scriptures gives us potent prescriptions for words that heal. Let's focus our attention on three therapeutic uses: words which relieve anxiety, words which bring healing, and words that persuade with eternally redeeming value.

RELIEVING ANXIETY

In an age crippled by anxiety, some see little hope of healing. But the Bible says there is a basic way in which we all can help others with their worries: "Anxiety in the heart of a man weighs it down, but a kind word makes it glad" (Proverbs 12:25).

All of us have suffered from worry and the heaviness of heart that it brings. Like a cancer that tears at our souls, so persistent anxiety begins to take its toll. However, a word of comfort or encouragement from a friend or loved one helps to relieve the pressure.

Many of our brothers and sisters in Christ are suffering from feelings of inadequacy and inferiority. Perhaps others have criticized them and reminded them, "You can't do anything right!" A genuine word of encouragement which emphasizes their strengths can bring gladness to their hearts.

In Samuel we find David running for his life from Saul. In spite of his father's jealous rage, Jonathan went to David in the wilderness of Ziph and lifted his spirits. According to 1 Samuel 23:16, 17 "Jonathan, Saul's son, arose and went to David at Horesh and encouraged him in God. Thus he said to him, 'Do not be afraid, because the hand of Saul my father shall not find you, and you will be king over Israel and I will be next to you; and Saul my father knows that also.'" Surely the anxiety that David was experiencing was greatly relieved through the kind words of his friend Jonathan.

When others appear to be weighted down by particular burdens it isn't necessary to pry and hunt for every detail. A kind expression like "I'm not sure what's causing the pressure in your life but I want you to know that I'm praying for you" often brings renewed confidence and strength.

HEALING WORDS

Just as a kind word gives help to the anxious, so words spoken in godly wisdom bring healing. "The tongue of the wise brings healing" says Solomon in Proverbs 12:18b. He says the same thing in Proverbs 15:4: "A soothing [the marginal reading has the word healing] tongue is a tree of life."

Today there is much interest in healing and faith healers. Many are desperately seeking for dramatic cures for their physical needs. I am personally convinced that there is a greater need for spiritual healing in our relationships and attitudes. And one practical way to bring about this healing is through our speech.

Many broken marriages have been restored through the healing power of words. The difficult but essential words, "Honey, I'm sorry," have been used by God to bring emotional and spiritual health to a strained marriage. Sure, it is possible to mouth an apology without meaning it; but if the words are genuine, then sweet reconciliation can follow.

Tension between parents and teenagers can be mended by saying the right thing at the right time. Again, an honest apology may be just the spark to unity and openness. Or a sincere word of praise to a discouraged youngster might be the beginning of new hope and confidence.

Frayed relationships are also common in our churches. Resentment and bitterness frequently replace patience and understanding. But the healing balm of kindness and forgiveness can flow when we confront one another with words of love.

The division that Paul and Barnabas experienced over John Mark in Acts 15 could have left permanent scars on the rejected Mark. But the words of Paul to Timothy a few years later were full of healing and forgiveness. In 2 Timothy 4:11 Paul told Timothy, "Pick up Mark and bring him with you, for he is useful to me for service." Those words "useful to me" were probably music in the ears of Mark. There were no longer personal barriers between him and the Apostle. The wounds of an earlier tear in their relationship had been healed.

Solomon's statement that the "tongue of the wise brings healing" is also reinforced by James in the third chapter of his epistle. This chapter is one of the most graphic in describing the destruction of an uncontrolled tongue. But in 3:17 James says that the tongue of the wise Christian "is first pure, then peaceable, gentle, reasonable, full of mercy and good fruits, unwavering, without hypocrisy."

PERSUASIVE WORDS

Not only do the words of the wise bring relief to anxiety and healing to the wounded in spirit, but so also do pleasant words have a power to persuade which can be healing for eternity. Proverbs 16:21 says that "The wise in heart will be called discerning, and sweetness of speech increases persuasiveness." That word sweetness is used in Proverbs 24:13 with reference to honey that is sweet to the taste. Solomon is thus describing speech that is tasteful and attractive to the listener. Harshness in our language usually alienates and creates immediate barriers. But kindness in what we say and how we say it makes others more open to listening.

Even the words of rebuke and correction, when coated with pleasantness, are received more readily than stinging words of sarcasm. In 2 Timothy 2 Paul exhorts Timothy to correct those who are in opposition to his ministry. But Timothy was to preface his words of admonition with gentleness. "And the Lord's bond-servant must not be quarrelsome, but be kind to all, able to teach, patient when wronged, with gentleness correcting those who are in opposition, if perhaps God may grant them repentance leading to the knowledge of the truth" (2:24,25).

Teaching that is geared to correcting the false views of others must be conveyed in kindness and patience. Too often in our attempt to uphold the truth we rob its message by attacking in harshness and impatience. This does not mean we are passively to compromise our conviction. But it does mean that others will be more receptive to instruction if it is marked with pleasantness and sweetness.

The persuasiveness of kind words is true in evangelism as

well as in our relationships with believers. I wonder how many non-Christians have tuned out the gospel due to dogmatic and argumentative assertions by believers? On the other hand, how many have been compelled to listen further because of pleasant kindness in our speech?

Paul knew the magnetic power of our language and the impact it can have on the unsaved. In Colossians 4:5, he exhorts us, "Conduct yourselves with wisdom toward outsiders, making the most of the opportunity." Then he suggests in verse 6 a practical way to walk in wisdom: "Let your speech always be with grace, seasoned, as it were, with salt, so that you may know how you should respond to each person." The connection between these two verses is not accidental. It is crucial to our success in evangelism.

In Proverbs 16:24 Solomon indicates how deeply the tongue can effect others: "Pleasant words are a honeycomb, Sweet to the soul and healing to the bones." The terms soul and bones refer to internal parts of our being. The thought is simply that pleasant words leave deep and lasting impressions. They penetrate to the inner resources of our nature. Physical surgery temporarily heals and mends diseased or broken bodies, but pleasant words to others can have a permanent, even eternal, impact for good.

A speech pathologist at Ithaca College in New York has recently invented a machine that studies the tongue. The machine is able to examine a patient's tongue and detect areas that are insensitive. Since such areas can produce speech abnormalities, such as slurring, the patient is able to compensate for it and speak more clearly.

As believers we do not have a machine to test the sensitive and insensitive areas of our speech. But we have something far greater. We possess supernatural power through the ministry of the Holy Spirit. He longs to control our tongues so that others may be helped and strengthened. When we submit to

Him we can minister to others with welcome words that heal. As Solomon said:

> "A word fitly spoken
> is like apples of gold
> in a setting of silver."

—Ken Parlin

Comforting in a Crisis

Several years ago a serious auto accident left my daughter Barb unconscious with severe head injuries. Anxiety gripped my wife, Dottie, and me during Barb's two lengthy brain surgeries. We felt utterly helpless as we faced her possible death or permanent brain damage.

Our frustration intensified as our then seventeen-year-old daughter continued unconscious for ten weeks—and underwent sixteen surgeries during her half-year stay in the hospital. And yet Barb improved—though ever so gradually—to the amazement of her many doctors, nurses, and therapists. In the long hours of waiting and of desperation, we also experienced God's peace. As we placed her in God's hands to do as He sovereignly desired, we were reassured that "His way is best" (Ps. 18:30), regardless of the outcome.

Barb, now fully recovered, is happily married, and is deeply grateful to the Lord for His marvelous working in her life. Barb, our son Ken, and my wife and I are also intensely grateful to the many friends who rallied to our needs, giving lovingly and unsparingly of their time and energy. Through this agonizingly prolonged process of one unexpected surgery after another, of continued therapy, and of snail-paced rehabilitation and recovery, our family came to appreciate the immeasurable emotional support needed by the family of a critically injured or seriously ill patient.

Have you ever faced the difficulty of knowing what to say to a parent or spouse of a hospitalized person? Have you perhaps realized later that you said the wrong thing, that you sensed your words were empty or misdirected? Have you pondered, "How can I possibly do any good in such a seemingly hopeless situation?" Have you wondered how you can minister meaningfully to someone facing major surgery when you've never been under the knife yourself?

Perhaps you have wanted to help someone in distress but have hesitated—and hence done nothing—because you have not known what would be most suitable and appreciated? May I suggest, from our experiences, some things that helped us—and mention some things that hurt? These observations may differ from the reactions of others undergoing similar crises, but some of these suggestions will help at least some of the people whom you will have opportunity to comfort, and may help you "encourage the fainthearted, [and] help the weak" (1 Thess. 5:14).

STATE YOUR CONCERN

Though you may not know how the person in the bed feels, you can assure him of your concern. The words, "I'm so sorry," or "I've been thinking about you and praying for you," spoken tenderly, can convey your empathy. Assuring the patient or his relatives by saying, "We love you and we're with you," can bring great comfort.

Also decide beforehand what you will not say. If you have not experienced what the patient and his family are undergoing, then avoid saying, "I understand" or "I know how you feel." Also don't pretend you know more than the doctors by predicting, "I'm sure he'll be all right."

Another statement to avoid in hospital calls is "God has a purpose in this tragedy." While that is certainly true, those words seldom relieve the grief of the moment. It is better to let the Lord point out His purpose(s) to the patient in His time and way. Instead, point him to the fact that the Lord is with him and won't forsake him.

To us, the presence, not the sage counsel, of visitors was the most meaningful. They chatted with us about various subjects, helping to pass the time. We sensed little value in attempts to "theologize" about the purpose for this trial. We needed encouragement for the immediate moment more than speculation about the past or future.

One well-intentioned person caused grief rather than encouragement by mentioning a relative who had died at about Barb's age. His words alerted me to avoid mentioning the death of someone else in such a situation.

Another comment that sliced like a knife into my wife's heart was a question by people who did not know our family well: "Do you have other children?" Though they sincerely wanted to know about the rest of the family, to Dottie it implied: "You are losing your daughter; do you have other children to compensate for this loss?" The question would be better if it were pointed clearly to the other children: "Tell me about the rest of your family."

SHOW YOUR CONCERN

Comforting involves more than words. One action that speaks loudly is your presence. Any surgery is suspenseful because of the unknown outcome, but surgery with a higher-than-normal degree of risk is troubling. Thus your presence in the surgery waiting area can be especially supportive and meaningful.

I'll never forget the immense comfort my wife and I experienced when friends stayed with us at the hospital during several of Barb's surgeries. Their presence vividly communicated the message, "We care, and we want to carry the burden with you."

Visit the patient at the hospital. Of course, if a patient is in an intensive care unit and only close relatives are permitted to enter, do not expect to go in unless the relative invites you and the hospital regulations allow it. If a relative asks you to see the patient (and the hospital permits it), do not hesitate to do so. Try not to stay long, and comment on your concern rather than the patient's appearance. Though the patient appears unconscious, he may be able to hear and remember what is said.

In addition to visiting at the hospital, you can telephone the family at home or at the hospital room. Though some people might not care to be answering the phone frequently, I found that inquiries by telephone were encouraging. The absence of phone calls seemed to say that people had forgotten our desperate situation.

Sometimes it was easier to talk with them over the phone than in person. Phone calls, particularly during Barb's critical times, were more personal than cards or notes. Some people with a critically ill loved one want to talk because voicing the burden helps ease the load. Immeasurable support came to Dottie when a friend occasionally called her simply to say, "I love you."

Be ready to listen. Let the grieving person or the patient talk if he so desires. But be sensitive to the situation. If he does not want to talk, then make your call brief.

Another tangible way to show your concern is to send cards with notes to the patient and/or his loved ones. I used to think sending a card with my signature and a Scripture verse was a sufficient expression of my concern, but receiving cards from friends during Barb's hospitalization showed me that a card which included a handwritten note of comfort and encouragement was much more uplifting.

Notice I wrote "cards," plural. Receiving a second or third card from the same friend was a guarantee of his sharing the burden. We sensed they were saying, "We are still here and concerned," and that was especially encouraging.

One person continued to send cards to Barb for several months beyond the accident. They did not arrive according to any discernible pattern of time; their unexpectedness added to our and Barb's appreciation of them. An elderly woman who heard of Barb's accident and introduced herself to us at the hospital wrote to Barb for several months, though she had never met Barb. These notes of love are a unique ministry carried on quietly by many of God's saints.

Don't say—as so many people wrongly do —"If I can help, let me know." It's hard to respond to such a generalized, though well-intended, offer. Of greater help is the offer of specific assistance. One example: "We want to bring you your supper. Would tomorrow night or the next night be better?" Preparing a meal for the family of a hospital patient may not seem to be much help, but it is a highly appreciated load carrier. For months Dottie found it difficult because of her tired physical condition to prepare meals for Ken, herself, and me. You can render a wonderful, loving service by preparing a meal for a family in such need; we know what this means! And, by the way, take the food in disposable aluminum pans so that the family doesn't need to be bothered with the additional chore of getting dishes back to you.

Some gave us money, knowing we would have additional financial needs at that time. Still others made known their loving support by thoughtful gifts—a planter, a book, a basket of fruit, a plaque.

MOBILIZE YOUR CONCERN

There is no need for you to try bringing all the comfort yourself. Get others to share in that ministry. For an ill person, there's comfort in knowing that many others care. Church officers, women's fellowship members, Sunday school class officers, small-group members—ask these and others to help. Encourage others to pray, visit, write, take meals, or sit with the patient if necessary. Numerous people sat with Barb at the hospital both before and after she regained consciousness. They insisted on coming each week for two or three hours at a time, thus relieving us of an endless vigil. When Barb was fully conscious, she enjoyed people coming to talk with her and to play Scrabble with her.

Some patients, released from the hospital, may need transportation several times a week to the hospital for therapy. In adult Sunday school classes you could enlist volunteers for this important ministry.

You might ask the patient or his relatives directly, "What can we do for you?" or "What needs can we help you with?" This gives the person in need the opportunity to voice some problem he may not otherwise feel free to mention.

PRAY YOUR CONCERN

One of our evangelical mistakes is promising to pray for someone but then failing to keep that promise. If you say to a patient, "I'll be praying," then pray! And pray earnestly and regularly. Pray for God's healing in His time and way; pray for His will to be done; pray that spiritual benefits will accrue from the medical problem regardless of the outcome physically.

Ask what specific needs you can pray for. Knowing that people were interceding for Barb's particular needs was more encouraging to us than general prayer support. And God answered in response to specific prayer burdens. For example, not long after several people prayed for Barb's left eye, it began to open. Others, after praying for her left arm, were thrilled to see her move it.

Prayers by God's people recorded in the Bible were specific. Ours should be too. Therefore you can help by asking a patient or the relatives what needs you can pray for. Indeed, "The prayer of a righteous man is powerful and effective" (James 5:16).

Also pray in their presence. For the believer, your praying with him in his hospital room brings spiritual comfort. Most unsaved people, when helplessly facing a serious medical dilemma, appreciate prayer. These occasions sometimes soften their hearts, thus opening the way for you to explain God's plan of salvation. Helping tangibly in times of crisis is part of what is involved in being a true friend in Christ.

—*Roy B. Zuck*

Restoring the Wounded

A black, threadlike "V" moves slowly across the leaden autumn sky. United in their customary alphabetical formation, flocks of geese instinctively seek refuge from the icy harshness of the coming winter. Suddenly, the formation appears erratic and disjointed. A stricken goose plummets earthward, like a heavy stone, leaving behind a gaping hole in the ranks. Responding instantly, two flanking geese track their fallen comrade and, with agility, drop to his aid. As the main flock continues its southward migration, the two loyal birds remain at the side of their wounded brother until he is fully restored to health...or dies.

Restore means "to renew, return or reestablish; to bring into the former or original state." Restoration as described by this definition has become a lost art in our current age of easily disposable items. Mass production of goods has prompted mass reduction of intrinsic value; things are cheap. It's easier to replace something than fix it. Sadly, this throw-away mentality has even infiltrated our relationships.

In a world where people seem eager to end things, Jesus seeks to mend things. Christ's supreme investment on Calvary gives an important clue to the Father's estimation of the value of one soul. Jesus counted the cost and paid it in full with His own lifeblood. Christ's climactic victory on the cross—redemption—eloquently expresses His heart of love for the world.

Considering the depths of His love, God's heart must break to watch His redeemed people limp along in life, impotent from spiritual injuries. God longs to heal His wounded bride with the eternal remedy provided by the same Cross—restoration.

Geese cannot articulate their reasons or motives for breaking ranks at their own peril to station themselves beside a crippled fellow. Driven by an invisible urgency, geese simply respond to a companion's desperate situation.

In contrast to the loyal geese, wolves viciously turn on their wounded den-mates and devour them so as not to endanger the pack or impede its progress. Wolves address the need for restoration not with gracious renewal, but with systematic removal.

In order to perpetrate an effective rescue operation in the hearts and lives of men, God seeks volunteers who, like courageous geese, will interrupt their "flight plans" long enough to assist a broken brother. However, many who have received spiritual comfort from the Great Physician seem ill-prepared to pass on that relief to someone else, sometimes appearing strangely unmoved by the pain around them. Why do Christians pass by needy, broken believers? What can be done to alter the lack of compassion? Perhaps we can discover some answers by considering the provision, portrayal, and priority of restoration.

PROVISION FOR ALL

From the peaceful lyrics of the shepherd's song comes the familiar line, "He restores my soul." God's offer of restoration to the sheep of His pasture stands recorded in just four simple words. His gracious initiative to the broken entreats a response, but the recognition of need must precede a response. How can we identify people who would benefit from God's unique promise of restoration?

In his book, A Shepherd Looks at Psalm 23, W. Phillip Keller writes of helpless "cast" sheep. A cast sheep is one which has turned over on its back and cannot right itself. As the sheep thrashes around, gases begin to build up in its stomach restricting blood circulation to the extremities. Unless set upright again, the suffering sheep will die within hours.

Keller describes three reasons why sheep become cast: they seek out the soft comfort of hollows in the grass and roll over on their backs; they collect debris in their long, matted fleece, and the sheer weight of the wool pulls them down; or they amass such great body weight that they are unstable on their feet and fall easily.

There are parallels between cast sheep and broken believers. Christians become "cast" when they seek out worldly pleasures, succumb to sinful desires or habits, or settle for lives of complacency and ease. Despite a self-sufficient veneer, human beings can be as cast and helpless as any defenseless lamb. Recognizing this helplessness becomes the very qualification for God to begin His work of restoration.

The Savior's heart pulsates with love for hurting people. He sees men and women as they truly are, and He is moved with compassion. As the Good Shepherd, Jesus vigilantly watches with concern for those who are cast and tenderly sets them on their feet once more through the restoring power of the Cross. Like the watchful Savior, we must be sensitive, able to discern a brother or sister in dire straits, and be prepared to come to their rescue in patience and gentleness.

PORTRAYAL OF GRACE

Restoration demonstrates the gracious character of God. It has been said that surgeons can rebuild, but only God's grace can fully restore. And the utter brilliance of God's restoring grace is best reflected in the dreary valley experiences of life. Broken by guilt, David cried out to God in Psalm 51, "Restore to me the joy of Thy salvation." In fact, the entire text of the psalm reflects a plaintive plea for God to accomplish His restoring work in David's aching heart. God faithfully provided renewal for Israel's king. David fully appreciated God's work of restoration in his heart.

Allowing ourselves to be pierced by the pain around us—depression, apathy, failure—reminds us that, at best, we are simply "wounded healers." Only God possesses sufficient grace and wisdom to sort through the wreckage of shattered lives. And when God restores, He does it in style!

The Presbyterian pastor, A.B. Simpson, was broken in body and spirit and happened to hear an old spiritual, "Nothing is too hard for Jesus; No man can work like Him."

The song's message penetrated his heart and renewed hope and life within him. After spending a time alone with God, Simpson returned to the ministry fully restored and established the Christian and Missionary Alliance organization. Simpson labored joyfully in the service of Christ for another 35 years after his restoration. He received all the strength he needed from the God of limitless power.

Brokenness need not disqualify anyone from active service for Christ. Rather it serves as a vital catalyst in the recognition of our utter helplessness apart from God. Returning to the precious message of Calvary accords Christ His rightful place in our lives and compels us to come to the Cross finding sufficient grace in our time of need.

PRIORITY IN MINISTRY

It is true that the church is full of broken yet valuable people and that God can effect His transforming miracle of restoration in their lives by the power of His Spirit. What, then should be our approach in reaching out to help?

Galatians 6:1 sets out a very definite emphasis in ministering to hurting people. Mature believers must seek to restore those who have been overtaken in a fault—a lapse or deviation from truth or uprightness. This careful encouragement and rebuilding in a spirit of gentleness is the hallmark of the community of faith.

As fellow members of one body we must join God's ongoing rescue mission for battle-scarred saints. Like the Good Samaritan, we ought to be willing to take all necessary steps and pay any cost involved to ensure the complete restoration of a fallen brother. Of course, this may mean relinquishing such things as coveted leisure time and the dispensing of resources at our own discretion. In the ministry of restoration, inconvenience is the rule rather than the exception.

By God's grace we can be instrumental in stemming the tidal wave of destruction and defeat which Satan has unleashed on the church. If the world is ever to know the glorious victory Jesus accomplished on the Cross, we cannot afford to let another wounded soldier die unattended. We cannot, like a horde of ravenous wolves, turn on our brothers and sisters broken by discouragement, defeat, or depression. Instead, we must allow the Holy Spirit to exhibit through us the disposition of the parakletos (helper), as we come alongside hurting people offering help as yielded vessels of God's grace and comfort.

With the violent fluttering of wings a silent squadron of geese swiftly mounts into the pre-dawn light, gaining their bearings in the open sky. The restoration process complete, the close-knit band heads south in pursuit of the main formation. Eventually reunited, the entire flock will reach its final destination…together.

—*JoAnn M.Hummel*

You've Been Chosen to Clap and Cheer

After dinner, Mrs. Roberson and her husband edged me towards the living room. Suddenly, Jenny, their freckled, seven-year-old daughter, protested. "Mom, are you going to tell him or not?" Apparently, something very important was about to be revealed, or so I thought. Mrs. Roberson, red-faced and embarrassed, said, "Mark, Jenny wants me to tell you that she thinks you're cute."

For a twenty-three-year-old youth pastor, that can be real salve for the wounds received on the ministerial battlefield.

Jenny persisted, "Tell him the whole story, Mom?"

By now Mrs. Roberson was scarlet, but at this point there was no turning back. She continued, "Well, one night about a month after you arrived, we were discussing church at the table. Jim asked Jenny what she thought of the new youth pastor. She replied, 'You mean the little shrimpy guy with the crinkly hair?' Then without even pausing, she added, 'I like him. I think he's cute.'"

It's nice to know that, even though you are a little shrimpy guy with crinkly hair, someone on earth still thinks you're cute. That was encouraging. A bit roundabout and humbling, perhaps, but still an encouragement.

The famed actress Celeste Holm said it well, "We live by encouragement and die without it—slowly, sadly, and angrily." People are marked forever by the presence or absence of encouragement. One good word can lift a load of anxiety (Prov. 12:25): a compliment can warm the heart with new vitality. As Mark Twain observed, "I can live off one good compliment for a week!"

Unfortunately, too often our infrequent encouragements focus merely on looks or small gestures. The Scriptures reveal, however, that encouragement goes far beyond nice compliments and jovial slaps on the back. Paul commands us to encourage each other on numerous occasions. But what do we do or say to encourage others? There are at least four Scriptural approaches we can take to encouraging one another. Each is designed for a specific need or circumstance.

URGE ONE ANOTHER TO PRACTICE GOD'S TRUTH

From both Jesus and Paul emerges a first principle: Encouragement is urging one another to practice God's truth. I have always marveled at the fervency and exuberance of Paul's letters. Paul was an encourager. He continually built up believers in the truth of the gospel. Jesus was the same way; He must have been an incredible encourager to keep twelve men motivated when they blundered so often and felt like failures. How else can we account for the determined followers of the Savior?

Paul was especially fond of using the Greek word for "encourage" in his letters. You can see it in such passages as Romans 12:1: "I urge you therefore, brethren, by the mercies of God ..." and Ephesians 4: 1: "I, therefore, the prisoner of the Lord, entreat you to walk...." In both cases Paul encourages his readers by urging them to practice God's Word. But how do we carry this out?

I see at least two applications. First, we can encourage by showing one another how God's Word applies in a situation. This means we must know and understand Scripture, if only a small part of it.

On one occasion, my grandfather had suffered a stroke and was in the hospital. My grandmother was anxious and fearful. I stayed with her to help out and supply what comfort I could. About three o'clock one morning I awoke and heard muffled coughing and crying in her room. I got out of bed and walked over nervously, tapping on her door. As I entered, I asked her what was wrong.

"Oh, I'm just so worried about Grandpop. What are we going to do?"

At first I just sat down and took her hand silently, groping for a word from God. Suddenly Proverbs 3:5-6 rang into my consciousness and I knew what to say. I explained the verses and attempted to show how they applied to her situation.

The next morning she was talking to a friend in my presence and said, "Boy, that grandson of mine really helped me last night. He said it all better than I've ever heard in a sermon."

This brand of encouragement is also key when we speak the truth in love (Eph. 4: 15). This practice is essential to our spiritual healing, for only by receiving the objective reproof and correction of others— tempered with love—will we be cured of certain sins. Often this rockets our spirits with encouragement. I had always found criticism to be stifling and/or depressing, but "speaking the truth in love" encourages like nothing else.

COMFORT ONE ANOTHER IN TIME OF NEED

However, not only is biblical encouragement geared to helping us make God's truth functional in our daily lives, but it also operates in the realm of specific circumstances. Thus we encounter the principle that we encourage by comforting one another in a time of need. This concept is central in passages such as 2 Corinthians 1:4-6 and 2:7. There Paul exhorts us to comfort the distressed, to accept those who have sinned, to love others who have failed. When we demonstrate love and acceptance to the needy we are actually encouraging them as Scripture directs us.

However, not only do those waylaid by pain need comfort, but also those blown about by the storm of their own sin and failure. A person who has failed and fallen is a favorite target of Satan. That's where our job comes in. We must encourage by demonstrating love and acceptance to those who have sinned or failed, just as Paul advised the Corinthians (2 Cor. 2:7).

REMIND EACH OTHER OF OUR FUTURE HOPE

The kind of encouragement which releases people from the chains of the past reveals a beautiful balance when we discover that we are also to encourage by reminding one another of our future hope. Have you ever noticed how Christians jolt out of listlessness when they start talking about heaven, or the rapture, or what it will be like to be forever with Jesus? We need timely doses of dialogue about heaven, our sure hope for the future.

Paul was always writing about this future hope. He tells us in 1 Thessalonians 4: 18, after a flurry of expositional details about the rapture, "Therefore comfort (or encourage) one another with these words." The writer to the Hebrews urges us in Hebrews 10:25: "...encouraging one another...as you see the day drawing near." This is an event bigger than the Super Bowl, the Academy Awards, or a landing on Mars! Christians should encourage one another by talking about their glorious future with the Lord.

The Bible doesn't tell us much about heaven except in Revelation 21 and 22, but get a pair or more of heavenly-minded Christians talking about it and you've got a conversation that has much earthly good. Suddenly we are excited, encouraged. We pulsate with spiritual ardor. And that's the point! Whatever else we may imagine heaven to be like, we know for sure that we will be with Jesus, forever. He will be right there, in our midst, to receive our worship and to fellowship with us. Anticipating such a glorious future should charge us with renewed encouragement and determination to go on.

PRAISE OTHERS FOR THEIR SPIRITUAL GROWTH

The encouragement we thus derive from the invigorating experience of thinking about heaven can be further strengthened by focusing on what God is also doing with us here on earth. That brings us to our final principle: we encourage by praising God and one another for our spiritual growth. Notice how lavish Paul is in his praise to the Thessalonians: "We give thanks to God always for all of you…constantly bearing in mind your work of faith and labor of love and steadfastness of hope in our Lord Jesus Christ" (1 Thess. 1:2-3).

To have someone open a letter like that about me would certainly inflame my faith! Take a moment to look over Paul's opening remarks in each of his letters. He soaks his readers with praise—refreshing, revitalizing praise. Paul never held back a rebuke, but neither did he hold back a well-deserved compliment.

A Japanese proverb says, "One kind word can warm three winter months." Unfortunately, many Christians suffer long winters of worthlessness because no one acknowledges their progress. Be on the lookout for responsible, growing Christians. Whenever you see a glimmer of growth, stoke it with the spiritual fires of encouragement. It will warm many chilly hearts.

But how exactly do we encourage in this manner? Won't it produce spiritual pride? Not at all, for by thanking God for a person's growth we are putting the praise where it belongs— on the Lord. He gave the growth! There are, in fact, a number of things we can scripturally praise men for with God's approval.

For Christians, however, it is both simple and sinister to overlook a person's good deeds and ravage him for the bad ones. Don't be the coach always yelling about the strikeouts. Be a coach who lavishes praise for the singles and walks. Your fellow players in the Christian life will love you for it.

Our lives can be characterized by the attitude of little Jamie Scott. A second-grader, he was trying out for a part in the school play. His mother was fearful that he wouldn't make it.

On the great and terrible day, Jamie's mother and a friend came to school after the tryouts. When Jamie spotted them he rushed up brimming with joy and pride. "Mom, guess what? I've been chosen to clap and to cheer!"

That's our job as encouragers. We have been chosen to clap and cheer for those unheralded masses of Christian people all around us. How? By urging them to follow God's word. By comforting them in a time of need. By reminding them of our future hope. By praising them for their spiritual growth.

Encouragement will enrich our friends and make us far richer. So encourage one another! It will make you a great and favored Christian—in the sight of God and men.

—*Mark R. Littleton*

Mark L. Bailey is assistant professor of Bible Exposition at Dallas Seminary.

Jerry Benjamin is an itinerant Bible teacher from St. Paul, Minnesota.

Dr. James A. Borror is executive director of Golden Minutes Ministries in Long Beach, California, and a Bible conference teacher and pastor.

Dr. J. Lanier Burns is chairman and professor of the Systematic Theology Department at Dallas Seminary.

Steven A. Breedlove is the pastor of Bethany Chapel in Calgary, Alberta, Canada, and a D. Min. student at Dallas Seminary.

Dr. Donald K. Campbell is president emeritus of Dallas Seminary, and served as the seminary's third president.

Dr. Lewis Sperry Chafer was the first president of Dallas Theological Seminary.

Dr. Thomas L. Constable is director of the D.Min. studies and professor of Bible Exposition at Dallas Seminary.

Dr. Anthony Evans is president of The Urban Alternative, and senior pastor of Oak Cliff Bible Fellowship in Dallas.

Dr. Kenneth O. Gangel is Vice President for Academic Affairs and Academic Dean, as well as senior professor of Christian Education at Dallas Seminary.

Dr. Gene A. Getz is a longtime adjunct faculty member at Dallas seminary, and author.

Dr. Reg Grant is professor of Pastoral Ministries at Dallas Seminary, and author.

Dr. Gary L. Hauck is the pastor of Berean Baptist Church in Grand Rapids, Michigan.

Dr. Howard G. Hendricks is Distinguished Professor and chairman of the Center for Christian Leadership at Dallas Seminary.

William D. Hendricks is a graduate of Dallas seminary and president of The Hendricks Group in Dallas.

JoAnn M. Hummel is associate pastor for Christian Education at Bent Tree Bible Fellowship in Dallas.

Alan J. Johnson is pastor of Berean Evangelical Free Church in Brooklyn Center, Minnesota.

Ronald L. Jones is pastor of adult ministries at the First Baptist Church of Atlanta, Georgia.

Jim Killion, senior partner in a Dallas consulting firm, was the first editor of Kindred Spirit.

Mark R. Littleton, author of several books, is customer service manager for MHI Corrugating Machinery in Maryland.

Dr. Aubrey Malphurs is chairman of Field Education at Dallas Seminary.

Dorothy Martin is a writer and Bible study leader in Dallas.

Carole Mayhall is an author and Bible study leader in Colorado Springs, Colorado.

Dr. Gary L. Nebeker is a Ph.D. candidate at Dallas Seminary.

Dr. Menaja Obinali is newsletter editor for Oak Cliff Bible Fellowship in Dallas.

Ken Parlin is the pastor of Living Hope Church in Fort Worth.

W. Ross Rainey is an itinerant Bible teacher.

Paula Rinehart is a wife, mother and author in Raleigh, North Carolina.

Donald G. Shoff is the pastor of Cornerstone Bible Church in Glendora, California.

Jeanette A. Stewart is associated with the Dept. of Opthalmology at the Medical University of South Carolina.

Dr. Joseph M. Stowell III is president of Moody Bible Institute in Chicago.

Dr. Richard L. Strauss was a pastor and longtime board member of Dallas Seminary.

Dr. Charles R. Swindoll, international Bible teacher and author, is the fourth president of Dallas Theological Seminary and president of Insight for Living.

Maxine Toussaint is a women's conference and retreat speaker from Flint, Texas.

Ed Underwood, Jr. is the pastor of North Umpqua Bible Fellowship in Oregon.

Dr. John F. Walvoord, chancellor of Dallas Theological Seminary, served as the seminary's second president.

Dr. Waylon O. Ward leads a Christian counseling center in Dallas.

Peggy Wehmeyer is religion correspondent for ABC news.

Mark S. Wheeler is minister of adults at Crossroads Baptist Church in Bellevue, Washington.

Dr. Bruce Wilkinson is president of Walk Thru the Bible Ministries in Atlanta, Georgia.

Dr. Roy B. Zuck is chairman and senior professor of Bible Exposition at Dallas Seminary and editor of *Bibliotheca Sacra*.

"Talking to God at the Table" from "Grace Revisited" - Taken from the book, *Home: Where Life Makes Up Its Mind* by Chuck Swindoll. Copyright © 1979,1983 by Charles R. Swindoll, Inc. Used by permission of Zondervan Publishing House.

"The Perfect Mouth" - Reprinted from *Tongue In Check* by Joseph Stowell, published by Victor Books, © 1983 Scripture Press Publications, Inc., Wheaton IL 60187.

"Your Bible Can Help You Grow" from "For Growth That's Real"—Taken from the book *Living by the Book* by Howard G. Hendricks and William D. Hendricks. Copyright © 1991. Moody Press. Used by permission.

"Serving Each Other" from *Improving Your Serve* by Charles R. Swindoll, copyright ©1981, Word Publishing, Dallas, Texas. All rights reserved.

"Is the Holy Spirit Transforming You?" from *Flying Closer to the Flame*, by Charles R. Swindoll. Copyright © 1993, Word, Inc., Dallas, Texas. All rights reserved.